Conceptions of God
in Ancient Egypt

ℵ ERIK HORNUNG

Conceptions of God
in Ancient Egypt

THE ONE AND THE MANY

TRANSLATED BY

JOHN BAINES

Cornell University Press

ITHACA, NEW YORK

International Standard Book Number 0-8014-1223-4
Library of Congress Catalog Card Number 82-71602
Printed in the United States of America

*Librarians: Library of Congress cataloging information
appears on the last page of the book.*

♾ The paper used in this book meets the minimum requirements of the American National Standard for Information Sciences—Permanence of Paper for Printed Library Materials, ANSI Z39.48-1984.

∿ Contents

Contents

6

↘ Preface to the English Edition

Ten years ago *Der Eine und die Vielen* was published in German. The book was intended to stimulate renewed reflection on the nature and meaning of the gods both within and beyond the confines of egyptology, and to help overcome the bewilderment that is felt by many people in the face of the "abstruse" figures of gods "invented" by priestly schools. These aims seem to have been achieved, but the book's influence and critical analysis of it have been confined mostly to German-speaking countries.

It has therefore been a pleasure for me that Cornell University Press have proposed an English edition on their own initiative and have kept to their plan despite many difficulties. It was particularly fortunate to find a translator, John Baines, who has already produced a magisterial rendering of the difficult German of Heinrich Schäfer's *Von ägyptischer Kunst* (*Principles of Egyptian Art*)—I hope my German has caused him fewer problems—and who is also very familiar with the subject of the Egyptian gods. I am extremely grateful to him not just for translating my book but also for working through it critically and in many places correcting it, making it more precise and more complete. In the process some errors and wrong references have been removed, and references to recent publications have been added where necessary. So the English edition is an improved version of the original German.

The debate about the foundations of Egyptian thought and Egyptian ontology, which has been taken up by Jan Assmann in particular,[1] is still in progress. I therefore thought it best to leave my text on these questions as it was, so that it can serve as a starting point for further discussion; any modification or extension of it would have been much too provisional. I hope that the debate will be continued and clarified further in the English-speaking world. There is no end to the question of the gods and their meaning.

ERIK HORNUNG

Basel, March 1981

[1] J. Assmann, *Zeit und Ewigkeit im alten Ägypten* (AHAW 1975, 1) esp. pp. 18–28, and "Ewigkeit," in W. Helck et al., eds., *Lexikon der Ägyptologie* II (Wiesbaden 1977) 47–54; for a partial response see E. Hornung, "Zeitliches Jenseits im alten Ägypten," *Eranos-Jahrbuch* 47 (1978, Frankfurt a.M. 1981) 269–307, esp. pp. 291–307.

ॽ Translator's Note

In this edition references to material in English have been added where possible in the footnotes. The list of abbreviations also gives details of easily available English translations of Egyptian texts cited.

The translations of ancient texts quoted in the German edition are new versions from the originals; they were made with an eye to the German renderings, but may differ occasionally from them. All quotations from modern writers have been translated into English. Where the German cites German editions of works first published in other languages, either the original (for English) or a translation from the original language is given here.

The text of the English edition has been amplified in a few places to make it more accessible to the general reader.

I am greatly indebted to Erik Hornung, who has read the complete draft translation, and to John Tait, who for the second time has read the text of an entire book, suggested hundreds of improvements, and checked classical material. Elizabeth Mansour typed the manuscript. For further advice I am grateful to Sebastian Brock, David Constantine, John Eland, Brian McGuinness, Nigel Palmer, Peter Parsons, S. S. Prawer, John Rea, and T. J. Reed.

The cost of preparing the translation was borne by Inter Nationes of Bonn.

JOHN BAINES

Oxford, April 1981

◌ Preface to the German Edition

For various reasons it was necessary to complete this book to a fixed deadline. My colleagues in the Ägyptologisches Seminar in Basel helped me to meet the deadline. I am grateful to all of them, and especially to Elisabeth Staehelin and Andreas Brodbeck, for their contribution and for relieving me of other work. I should also like to thank Wissenschaftliche Buchgesellschaft for their growing interest in egyptology.

In the course of work it became increasingly clear that a study of this sort is never "finished." A god is generally considered to be something without end in space or time. Even if one questions this familiar assumption, one cannot deny that the problem of the gods tends toward the infinite and has no final solution.

The main focus of my inquiry is the notion of "the one and the many," and my immediate aim is to provide a critical review of existing opinions in the field and to open up new approaches. But an examination of this particular issue should be related to the totality of Egyptian thought and life.

The reader is free to emphasize other aspects of the abundant material and to choose a different approach or different criteria of analysis. Anyone who takes history seriously will not accept a single method as definitive; the same should be true of anyone who studies belief seriously. Modesty is appropriate to these age-old problems of mankind. Every "final" insight is only a signpost on a road that leads farther and may be trodden in the company of others who think differently.

This book, which often takes issue with Siegfried Morenz

11

and his rich and stimulating presentation of Egyptian religion, was meant to be a further exchange in my dialogue with my friend and colleague in Leipzig. He would certainly have disagreed fiercely with many sections of it. But he died before the copy of the typescript which was intended for him could reach him. I shall miss his replies and his criticism.

ERIK HORNUNG

Basel, October 1970

Conceptions of God
in Ancient Egypt

1 ✎ Historical Introduction

In classical antiquity the seemingly abstruse deities of Egypt already aroused reactions of antipathy and scornful rejection. For some people the bewildering array of strange forms and the unfamiliar mixtures of human body and animal head were the symbolic garb of deep mysteries, but others found them an offensive contradiction of their ideas of what a god or a pantheon should be. In the second century A.D. Lucian placed the two attitudes on opposing sides in a dialogue;[1] Momos, "Blame," is the spokesman for rejection:

> MOMOS: But you, you dog-faced Egyptian, dressed-up in linen, who do you think you are, my friend? How do you expect to pass for a god, when you howl as you do? And what does that bull from Memphis with the fancy markings mean with his worshipers prostrating themselves before him, and his oracular pronouncements and his attendant priests? I am ashamed to mention the ibises and the apes, or the goats and the other far more ridiculous creatures from Egypt who have been crammed into heaven, goodness knows how. How, gods, can you tolerate seeing them worshiped on equal terms with yourselves or even honored above you? And you, Zeus, how can you bear it when they transplant a ram's horns onto you?
>
> ZEUS: These things you observe about the Egyptians are truly shocking. All the same, Momos, the greater part of them has a mystic significance, and it is not at all right to laugh at them, just because you are not one of the initiated.

[1]*Deorum concilium* 10–11. [I am grateful to John Tait for the English translation. —tr.]

15

> Momos: We certainly need the enlightenment of the Mysteries, Zeus, to let us recognize the Gods as gods, and dogs' heads as dogs' heads!

Transmitted by the early Christian fathers,[2] Momos' rejection lasted into modern times, but it has been complemented repeatedly by those who believed that there were deep mysteries beneath the surface of Egyptian religion. The appearance of Egyptian deities continued to seem a confusing "patchwork of animal heads and human bodies" (Jean Paul[3]), and who can forget the resonance of Goethe's sharp rejection:

> Now I must take my pleasure by the Nile
> in extolling dog-headed gods;
> oh if my halls were only rid
> of Isis and Osiris!

In fact these lines in the series of poems *Zahme Xenien* (1820) were not directed specifically against the Egyptian gods, but rather against a journal of the times called *Isis*,[4] while they also attacked modern egyptomania and its offshoots, which disguised their own, often absurd, ideas in the forms of Egyptian gods. But these lines on the "dog-headed gods" and an earlier passage concerning the Indian "ape Hanuman" betray a deeper rejection of both Indian and Egyptian forms of divinity which goes beyond the immediate occasion of the piece. Goethe's contemporaries themselves interpreted the poem in this way. His condemnation of Indian gods was objected to by F. W. von Schelling in his lectures published as *Introduction to the Philosophy of Myth*, which I shall cite often in the following pages: "they cannot be dismissed with a simple pronounce-

---

[2]F. Zimmermann, *Die ägyptische Religion nach der Darstellung der Kirchenschriftsteller* (Paderborn 1912) e.g. 81, 87ff; even among the Church fathers the symbolic interpretation propounded by Lucian's Zeus occurs alongside mockery (p. 89). On ancient polemics against animal forms for gods see also G. Michaelides, *BIFAO* 49 (1950) 23–43.

[3]Preface to his early novel *Die unsichtbare Loge* (1792).

[4]S. Morenz, *Die Begegnung Europas mit Ägypten* (SBSAW 113, 5, 1968) 163 with n. 6 = (2d ed., Zurich and Stuttgart 1969) 141 with n. 32.

ment of distaste; detestable or not, they exist, and since they exist they must be explained."[5]

That is a most pertinent observation, and one equally valid for Egyptian gods. Of course, we no longer attempt to "explain" gods—the farther we penetrate into the world of these ancient images the less we can explain what a god is. Even in Egypt the choice of forms for the gods was influenced by aesthetic considerations, as will become clear in Chapter 4. But the crucial point is that Schelling perceived clearly the *existence*, as against the changing forms, of the gods.

Egyptology has often been less able to tackle the existence of Egyptian gods, as it is encountered in the texts and representations of the ancient culture of the Nile valley, than have people outside the subject. For long stretches of its history, egyptology has suffered from the chasm that appears to divide the cultural and ethical achievements of ancient Egypt, on the one hand, and Egyptian conceptions of god, which have widely been considered to be "unworthy," on the other.

At a time when there was beginning to be a more profound encounter with Egypt and its gods, as we find in the works of Rilke and Thomas Mann; when the poet sensed "the might of these lands that were / once permeated by gods" and wished to appeal to his own time:

> Let none of the gods vanish. We need each and every one,
> every one should matter to us, every perfected image.[6]

at that time Adolf Erman published his standard work *Die ägyptische Religion*, in which, at the end of a description of the chief Egyptian deities, he could provide no more commentary for his readers than an embarrassed confession that "many readers may have had more than enough of the deities mentioned, but they are only a small proportion of the total number worshiped in Egypt" (1st ed. [1905] p. 24).

---

[5]*Einleitung in die Philosophie der Mythologie* (Sämmtliche Werke, Zweite Abtheilung I, Stuttgart and Augsburg 1856, reprinted Darmstadt 1957) 24.

[6]Rainer Maria Rilke, posthumously published poem related to the *Sonette an Orpheus*. See *Sämtliche Werke* II (Wiesbaden: Insel Verlag 1956) 468; for the other phrase see p. 79.

We can be certain that Erman was not alone in his opinion and that most readers approved of phrases like these. His position was itself the result of quite a long period of development and controversy in the subject, and was reached in response to early attempts to prove that this multiplicity of deities was "superficial" and inessential, whereas the core of Egyptian religion was "monotheistic."

But I have taken a leap forward in tracing the history of our question, and must now consider the nineteenth-century attempts to cleanse the Egyptians of the taint of primitive idolatry and to show that they were early representatives of the higher religions, or even of monotheistic belief.

In the middle of the last century, after a period of stagnation following the premature death of Champollion, Emmanuel de Rougé initiated a new and lasting period of achievement in French egyptology. He was probably the first explicit exponent of the conviction that Egyptian religion was originally and fundamentally monotheistic.[7] For de Rougé its "enduring and sublime foundation" was the unity of the Supreme Being, his eternity and omnipotence,[8] which were never "smothered" by polytheism.[9] In a lecture of 1869 de Rougé declared:

> I said God, not the gods. The first characteristic of [Egyptian] religion is the Unity [of God] most energetically expressed: God, One, Sole and Only; no others with Him.—He is the Only Being —living in truth.—Thou art One, and millions of beings proceed from thee.—He has made everything, and he alone has not been made. . . .
>
> . . . One idea predominates, that of a single and primeval God; everywhere and always it is One Substance, self-existent and an unapproachable God.[10]

[7]According to E. A. W. Budge, *The Gods of the Egyptians or Studies in Egyptian Mythology* I (London 1904) 142, Champollion-Figeac, the brother of the decipherer of the hieroglyphic script, had already proposed a "monotheistic" interpretation of Egyptian religion.
[8]*Revue archéologique* n.s. 1, 1 (1860) 72–73.
[9]*Ibid.* 357.
[10]"Conférence sur la religion des anciens Egyptiens," *Annales de philosophie chrétienne* 5th ser. 20 (1869) 330; English translation quoted from le Page Renouf, *Lectures* 89–90.

Here de Rougé based himself on the precise wording of Egyptian texts, which undoubtedly have a monotheistic "ring," seeming to anticipate the teachings of the later founders of world religions. Both his arguments and the authority of his opinion provided welcome confirmation of the view, which was widespread among cultured people of the nineteenth century, that monotheism preceded polytheism;[11] as early as 1845 Edgar Allan Poe provided an ironical gloss on it in his story "Some Words with a Mummy."[12] As so often happens, egyptology was dependent on the questions and solutions of its time; its history mirrors the general history of ideas in the West.

A decade later the English egyptologist and historian of religion Sir Peter le Page Renouf published his *Lectures on the Origin and Growth of Religion* (London 1880), in which he took over with few reservations the views of his French colleague. He believed that although some of the passages in ancient texts cited by de Rougé had "a somewhat different meaning . . . , the facts upon which he relies are in the main unassailable. It is incontestably true that the sublimer portions of the Egyptian religion are not the comparatively late result of a process of development or elimination from the grosser. The sublimer portions are demonstrably ancient. . . ."[13]

The element le Page Renouf called "sublime" was monotheism; to him it was obvious that this was the highest form of religion. The gods who were "unworthy" in their characteristics and their forms—the "dog-heads" of Lucian—were for le Page Renouf a later degeneration, of lesser importance than the sublime, primeval grandeur of the belief in the One and Only.[14] His primary concern, however, was not to study what Egyptian texts have to say about god and gods, but to evaluate

[11]E.g. Schelling, *Einleitung in die Philosophie der Mythologie* (n. 5 above) esp. p. 83, where he states: "It has been considered virtually impossible that polytheism could arise except through the corruption of a purer religion . . ."; cf. also the summary, p. 119.

[12]*The Works of Edgar Allan Poe in Ten Volumes* II (Chicago 1894) 298.

[13]*Lectures* (4th ed., 1897 [1st ed. 1880]) 91.

[14]Note, however, that in the preface to the second edition of his *Lectures* (p. xv, reprinted in the 4th ed.) le Page Renouf denied explicitly that he had stated that "the Egyptians commenced with monotheism," or that he was a "partizan of 'primitive henotheism'" (see Chapter 7).

19

Egyptian beliefs and to provide an apologia directed against previous denigrations of them. In this evaluation all monotheistic features and tendencies are judged favorably and polytheistic ones unfavorably, and the critic starts with preconceived, very definite ideas of what a god should be.

Fixed values of this sort can provide the safe, positive points of reference which are lacking in many disciplines today. They allow the data to be ordered, but do not provide the means for describing and elucidating them correctly. And since it seems inevitable—especially in the humanities—that our own values should influence whatever is evaluated, they must be reassessed from time to time and their fitness must be tested. We must therefore guard against two kinds of reaction: first, against concluding that the interpretations of le Page Renouf and his contemporaries are wrong because of the criteria they used; second, against taking over the criteria without testing their validity.

Le Page Renouf formulated his interpretation of Egyptian religion as a primeval monotheism with emphatic clarity and well-considered method. He was the most important, but by no means the only, successor of de Rougé. In the 1870s French egyptologists unanimously propounded the "monotheistic" interpretation of Egyptian religion, with only the slightest of variations. In 1870 Eugène Grébaut wrote that the monotheism was "incontestable,"[15] and in 1879 Paul Pierret gave to the first chapter of his *Essai sur la mythologie égyptienne* (Paris) the title "Le monothéisme égyptien." For Pierret Egyptian religion appeared polytheistic, but was "essentially" monotheistic, and it could not be otherwise, for "God is one, or he does not exist" ("Dieu est un ou il n'est pas," p. 6)—polytheism would therefore be a denial of God, unless it were viewed as "purely symbolic" and the gods as different roles or functions of the supreme, single, hidden God (p. 7), for whom Egyptian religious texts contain many apparently "monotheistic" epithets (pp. 8–16). For François Joseph Chabas, too, the many gods are only

[15]*Rec. trav.* 1 (1870) 120, in an article "Des deux yeux du disque solaire," in which he maintains at other points too that there was a solar monotheism in Egypt.

aspects of the One,[16] while the great excavator Auguste Mariette assumed that there was a single, immortal, uncreated, invisible, and hidden God "reserved for those initiated into the sanctuary."[17]

In their early works the great scholars of the generation that followed de Rougé, Pierret, and Mariette were still completely under the influence of this interpretation, which had been self-evident to their teachers. Thus, in an early lecture on ancient Egyptian religious literature, Gaston Maspero, Mariette's successor as director of the Egyptian Antiquities Service, speaks of an "immaterial God," who only secondarily "became flesh" in the multiplicity of deities.[18] Eugène Lefébure held for many years to the belief in Egyptian monotheism, but in his case it acquired a more pantheistic hue.[19]

A passage in le Page Renouf's *Lectures* shows how widespread this view of the Egyptian pantheon was around 1880:

> There are many very eminent scholars who, with full knowledge of all that can be said to the contrary, maintain that the Egyptian religion is essentially monotheistic, and that the multiplicity of gods is only due to the personification of "the attributes, characters and offices of the supreme God." (p. 89)

Among these "eminent scholars" was Heinrich Brugsch, who was, next to Carl Richard Lepsius, the leading German egyptologist of the day. In 1885 there appeared the first volume of his standard work, *Religion und Mythologie der alten Ägypter*, in

[16]*Le calendrier des jours fastes et néfastes de l'année égyptienne* (Châlons-sur-Sâone and Paris 1870) 110. This "unique, uncreated god" is, however, the god only of the "initiates."

[17]*Notice des principaux monuments exposés dans les galeries provisoires du Musée des antiquités égyptiennes* (2d ed., Alexandria 1868) 20 = (5th ed., Cairo 1874) 21.

[18]"Sur la littérature religieuse des anciens égyptiens," *Revue politique et littéraire* 2d ser. 2 (1872) 460–66; reprinted in *Etudes de mythologie et d'archéologie égyptiennes* II (Bibliothèque égyptologique 2, Paris 1893) 445–62; passage cited on pp. 446–47 of the latter. For the later development of Maspero's views see below.

[19]E.g. *RHR* 14 (1886) 35; compare also pp. 44–45 for Lefébure's version of the views of de Rougé and Chabas, which he saw as continuing those of Friedrich Creuzer.

21

which he professed his conviction that "already in the earliest times" the Egyptians adored "the one, nameless, incomprehensible, eternal God in his highest purity."[20] In 1889 Victor von Strauss und Torney still depicted, under the influence of Schelling's ideas about the derivation of the gods, a "mythological monotheism" with the god Nun at the beginning of Egyptian religious history.[21]

The view that the Egyptians were at first purely monotheistic could not be maintained for long in this exaggerated form. Shortly before the appearance of Brugsch's great work, which was for long the standard presentation of Egyptian religion, J. Lieblein had made the first criticism of the received opinion,[22] while as early as 1880 Maspero had been sharply critical of Pierret and his monotheistic "preconception,"[23] stating that monotheism was a secondary phenomenon, "deriving from an earlier polytheism." From 1888 on Maspero admitted that independent study of Egyptian religious texts had led him to abandon his earlier views about Egyptian monotheism—to which Brugsch continued to adhere. In his detailed reviews of his German colleague's work[24] Maspero rejected the earlier interpretation quite explicitly:

> I believe, in contrast to what [Brugsch] says, that the Egyptians were first of all polytheists, and that if they arrived at the conception of a single deity, that deity was not exclusive or jealous. (p. 185)
>
> I take [the Egyptian religion] to be what it says it is, a polytheism with all its contradictions, repetitions, doctrines that are to modern eyes sometimes indecent, sometimes cruel, sometimes ridiculous. . . . (p. 278)

[20]Vol. II appeared in 1888, and the new edition in one volume in 1891. Quotation from p. 90.

[21]*Götterglaube* I (1889) *passim*, esp. pp. 47–48; in the second volume of the work (1891) von Strauss und Torney still placed a single god at the beginning of religion (p. 72).

[22]*Egyptian Religion* (Christiania and Leipzig 1884).

[23]*RHR* 1 (1880) 119–29, reprinted in *Etudes de mythologie* I (n. 18 above) 115–27; phrase quoted on p. 124 of the latter.

[24]*Revue critique d'histoire et de littérature* n.s. 26 (1888, 2) 445–48; *RHR* 18 (1888) 253–79; 19 (1889) 1–45; reprinted in *Etudes de mythologie* II (n. 18 above) 183–278.

In Germany Alfred Wiedemann wrote in *Die Religion der alten Ägypter* (Münster 1890):[25]

> It has often been deduced that passages where, for example, god or a god . . . is praised, or god knows the wicked, grants a field, loves the obedient, etc. refer to the true, eternal God. This cannot, however, be maintained without qualification; the same texts that make these statements also speak of individual deities and show that the writer meant by "god" his own particular god, the god of his nome, . . . who was for him an all-embracing power, but whose existence did not exclude that of others, which might for other men be more important or higher. . . . But although expressions of this sort cannot in themselves provide any proof of an original, pure monotheistic apprehension of god which returned to the Egyptians' consciousness from time to time, one cannot, on the other hand, prove from the inscriptions that such a belief did not exist.

Wiedemann explains his studied caution by saying that "so far, only a small part of the material preserved from ancient Egypt is available." He therefore guards against throwing out the baby with the bathwater; he is content to indicate the problematic character of the evidence for Egyptian monotheism cited since the time of de Rougé. His clear presentation of his argument could have saved some modern proponents of Egyptian monotheism from untenable conclusions, but his voice was scarcely heeded in the controversy.

In the next decade the early dynastic period in Egypt was discovered, principally through the excavations of Emile Amélineau and W. M. F. Petrie at Abydos,[26] while in 1893 Gaston Maspero completed the first edition of the Fifth and Sixth Dynasty Pyramid Texts.[27] Neither in this early collection of spells,

---

[25]Pp. 62–63; English edition, *Religion of the Ancient Egyptians* (London 1897) 109–10; retranslated here.

[26]The history of the discovery is described by W. Wolf, *Funde in Ägypten* (Göttingen 1966) 18–38.

[27]The texts were discovered in 1880–81 (cf. *ibid.* 107–8) and published by Maspero in *Rec. trav.* 3 (1882)–14 (1893). Brugsch, as well as Maspero, at once recognized the importance of these ritual texts (see *ZÄS* 19 [1881] 1–15, and his autobiography *Mein Leben und mein Wandern* [2d ed., Berlin 1894] 347–50), but was not able to evaluate them for the problem of conceptions of god; for

inscribed from 2350 B.C. on, nor in the inscriptions and representations of the pre- and early dynastic periods could the original and "pure" Egyptian monotheism, which had been assumed a priori, be found. Rather, what is especially striking in these archaic sources is the multiplicity of deities. Together with the earlier attack on the methods used to establish the hypothesis, this great increase in our sources had the result that the idea of an original monotheism, which had for so long been the received dogma, was quietly dropped.

Egyptological writings of the next few decades give the impression that interest in defining the Egyptian conception of god disappeared with the old dogma. The positivist concentration on the "concrete" (*das "Tatsächliche"*), on the immediate facts of Egyptian beliefs, was no longer sidetracked by arguments over monotheism or pantheism or polytheism. Adolf Erman's presentation of Egyptian religion, the first edition of which appeared in 1905, provided a new model that became the guiding light of the next generation. Hermann Kees's *Der Götterglaube im alten Ägypten,* first published in 1941, crowned almost a lifetime's research and remains the standard work on the outward forms and facts of these beliefs, but does not tackle the problem of defining the nature of the object of study; Jaroslav Černý's *Ancient Egyptian Religion* (Hutchinson's University Library, London 1952) also belongs in the same tradition. But in its own way, a half-century's abstinence from considering our problem has advanced it—we must acknowledge gratefully that the basic facts, on which new definitions of the nature of Egyptian beliefs can be based, have been assembled and established.

The few writers who took up the question of Egyptian conceptions of god early in this century (especially James Henry Breasted)[28] rejected explicitly the monotheistic interpretation and tended instead to see pantheistic features in Egyptian religion. The concept of henotheism also appears again and again (see also Chapter 7). Only E. A. Wallis Budge held to the view that

---

Wiedemann too this new source remained on the periphery. The latest translation of the texts is R. O. Faulkner, *The Ancient Egyptian Pyramid Texts* (Oxford 1969).

[28]*The Development of Religion and Thought in Ancient Egypt* (New York 1912).

"foolish priests" obscured the "pure" monotheistic belief that had existed in Egypt since the earliest times, and which he maintained he could find especially in wisdom texts.[29] Like Mariette, Budge assumed that Egyptian beliefs ran down two paths, a solution that still seems easy—far too easy—to many of his successors: the One for the wise, the many for the mass. Wiedemann soon attacked the idea of a "monotheism for initiates," as one might call it,[30] but this did not stop the "neo-monotheistic" school, which I discuss below, from taking up Budge's idea.

Wiedemann contributed the article "God (Egyptian)" to volume six of James Hastings's *Encyclopaedia of Religion and Ethics* (1913, 274–79)—a happy choice by the editor, for Wiedemann gave in a few pages a well-organized and considered survey of the basic issues concerning Egyptian conceptions of god. He devoted a separate section (pp. 275–77) to the question "Monotheism or Henotheism?"—the chief problem in the previous literature—and argued decisively both against the assumption of an original monotheism and against the idea of a monotheistic god for "initiates" in wisdom texts. The phraseology of Egyptian sources, on which de Rougé and his contemporaries had based their arguments, must be explained in a different way: "The apparently monotheistic expressions on Egyptian monuments rest in reality upon henotheistic modes of thought" (p. 276). In an article "The Egyptian Pantheon,"[31] which appeared at almost the same time, Günther Roeder expressed a similar view in rather different terms. He rejected the theory of an original monotheism as decisively as Wiedemann did, and assumed that there had been a process of "selection" among the mass of original deities, which he compared with the then popular "survival of the fittest" of living creatures.

The great deities become many-sided, acquire many names and qualities, and their adherents can end by thinking that their god

---

[29]*Gods* I, 138–45; passage quoted from p. 144. He maintained the same position in *Osiris and the Egyptian Resurrection* I (London and New York 1911) 348ff. Von Strauss und Torney had already taken issue with this idea and compared the use of *theos* in Homer (*Götterglaube* I, 340ff).

[30]P. 276 of the article cited in the next paragraph.

[31]*Archiv für Religionswissenschaft* 15 (1912) 59–98.

is the only one and omnipotent. Thus Egyptian theology acquires monotheistic features as a result of secondary identifications, but nowhere does it discard its polytheistic structure. (p. 95)

The new phrase "monotheistic feature" had ominous consequences, for it contributed to the imprecision of the concepts used by the neomonotheistic school and hence to their vagueness in treating the entire problem. But for the moment the question of Egyptian conceptions of god was thought to require no further discussion, if we except the thesis of Gerardus van der Leeuw (1916), which is concerned specifically with conceptions of god in the Pyramid Texts—that is, with the earliest group of sources which could then be examined.[32] This study by the great Dutch historian of religion supports and expands the new polytheistic/henotheistic interpretation which we have already seen in the works of Wiedemann and Roeder. Van der Leeuw was unable to discover any elements of monotheism or of a "high god" in the earliest known Egyptian conception of god; rather he compared it with the concept of god established by Konrad Theodor Preuss for the Cora Indians of the Mexican Sierra Madre. It is not possible to speak of a "transcendent" god in Old Kingdom Egypt, but rather of a "pantheistically tinged" confidence in the continuation of existence. In talking of a certain "vagueness" in the Egyptian conception of god van der Leeuw made an important point, to which I shall return at the end of Chapter 3; but the question of monism or dualism, to which he devoted much space, is now dated and less fruitful for the study of our problem.

Equally unfruitful was the 1916–20 controversy between Karl Beth and Hermann Grapow in *Zeitschrift für die alttestamentliche Wissenschaft*;[33] this is a classic example of how a historian of religion and a philologist can address each other without either

[32]*Godsvoorstellingen in de oudaegyptische Pyramidetexten* (Leiden 1916), esp. chap. 4 ("The Concept of God . . . ," pp. 117–49), from which the quotations below are taken.

[33]K. Beth, "El und Neter," *ZAW* 36 (1916) 129–86; H. Grapow, "Zu dem Aufsatz von Prof. Beth 'El und Neter,'" *ZAW* 37 (1917) 199–208; K. Beth, "Noch einiges zum ägyptischen Neter," *ZAW* 38 (1920) 87–104. Quotation from the first article.

having any real appreciation of the methods and approaches of the other. In his critique of Beth, Grapow missed the opportunity to illuminate the essential meaning of *ntr* "god" offered by his knowledge of the "thousands of examples of *ntr*" in the files of the Berlin Egyptian dictionary; instead he took inessential details for his target. But Beth's comparisons of *ntr* with *el* and *wakonda* are unsatisfactory for egyptologists, while his assumption of a special *ntr* in wisdom texts (pp. 180–83) or of a "great All-Neter" (pp. 182–83) follows familiar paths. The wider perspective of a historian of religion did, however, enable Beth to formulate one insight that had not been vouchsafed to specialists:

> Monotheism or polytheism? This has been the great issue in egyptology since the discovery of the first Egyptian texts. The survey I have given here shows that both answers have their justification; it also shows that the proponents of both use these concepts like slogans, yet neither concept can characterize the true individuality of Egyptian religion. (p. 183)

At that point the discussion had reached a dead end, and it must have seemed pointless to return to it without opening up new approaches to "the true individuality of religion." The first new stimulus to studying Egyptian conceptions of god came from Hermann Junker, who identified an alleged ancient high god, the "Great One" (*Wr*), about 1930, and thus came close to Father Wilhelm Schmidt's idea of a "primal monotheism" (*Urmonotheismus*). Since Junker treated a divine epithet in isolation, I shall leave his idea aside and return to it toward the end of Chapter 5 in the section on the divine quality of greatness.

The monotheistic interpretation of the Egyptian conception of god was reaffirmed by French egyptologists, just as the original theory had been put forward by a Frenchman. The initiative in forming a "neomonotheistic school" came from Abbé Etienne Drioton, who was then the influential director-general of the Egyptian Antiquities Service. The first two editions of the volume *L'Egypte* (Paris 1938, 1946), which Drioton and Jacques Vandier made into a fundamental treatment of Egyptian political and intellectual history, do not waste any words

27

on Egyptian monotheism, but from the third edition (1952) on, the topic is central to the section on Egyptian religion.[34]

Drioton had already developed his ideas in 1948 in his article "Le monothéisme de l'ancienne Egypte,"[35] where he maintained that there had been monotheism in Egypt long before the reforms of Akhenaten. For him the vital sources are the wisdom texts with their "god of the wise" ("dieu des sages"), whom he had discussed in an earlier article.[36] Although Drioton referred to Junker, he assumed that there was a very ancient, but not original, monotheism; the new doctrine is that Egyptian monotheism was a secondary growth on the soil of polytheism. The predominance of polytheism at all periods of Egyptian history could no longer be questioned, so that the monotheism that was proposed had to be one for "initiates," as Mariette and Budge had already assumed.

Although there was no lack of critical voices and reservations about Drioton's method of argument,[37] many more recent French egyptologists have succumbed to the attractions of his formulations, and the monotheistic interpretation has again become popular outside France, too. Thus in *A Dictionary of Egyptian Civilization* (edited by Georges Posener), Serge Sauneron spoke of "a very general belief . . . in the universality and singleness of a nameless divine being, without form, but able to take on any form."[38] Drioton's views were soon adopted by German

---

[34]Esp. pp. 63–64, 109–10; cf. J. Leclant, *RdE* 15 (1963) 137. Drioton expressed himself more cautiously in his contribution to the collection *Die Religionen des Alten Orients* (in the encyclopedia *Der Christ in der Welt*, Zurich 1958). Cf. also J. Vandier, *La religion égyptienne* (Paris 1944) 227–29, and the careful criticisms of R. Weill, *BIFAO* 47 (1948) 140.

[35]*CHE* 1 (1948) 149–68; resumé in *Or* 18 (1949) 503–4.

[36]"La religion égyptienne dans ses grandes lignes," *La revue du Caire* 84 (1945) 3–23; reprinted in *Pages d'égyptologie* (Cairo 1957) 77–110. Cf. his remarks already in *ASAE* 43 (1943) 43, on Ramessid monotheism as a consequence of the Amarna period.

[37]E.g. H. Stock, *Saeculum* 1 (1950) 631–35 (against Junker and Drioton). Cf. also R. Weill (n. 34 above) and S. A. B. Mercer, *The Religion of Ancient Egypt* (London 1949) 306–7, for whom Egyptian religion "was always polytheistic, without exception." F. Daumas, *Les dieux de l'Egypte* (Que sais-je 1194, Paris 1965) 115ff., follows Drioton in the main, but denies that there was an "exclusive monotheism" in Egypt.

[38]*Dictionnaire de la civilisation égyptienne* (Paris 1959) 87 = *A Dictionary of Egyptian Civilization* (London 1962) 110; retranslated here.

28

egyptologists; thus Eberhard Otto assumed in an article "The Concept of God in Egypt in the Late Period" that Egyptians of the late period "experienced the multiple manifestations of deities as possible realizations of an anonymous divine power that lay behind them."[39]

Siegfried Morenz was more explicit still in seeing in Egyptian theologians direct precursors of the modern theology of revealed religion:

> In the long run their principal ways of thinking about the relationships of deities with one another and with the One, and their ideas about the boundaries and the links between god and image favored all those who sought the great, single reality of God behind the profusion of his manifestations. A religion that has developed in history, but has never experienced the breakthrough of revelation, must inevitably carry with it the burden of a long past—a colorful world of different deities. The best that theologians could do in the face of this burden of tradition was to anchor every single deity firmly in the depths of the single divine essence. Egyptian religious thinkers were so successful in this that we may legitimately seek and observe the historical tendency to transcendence in all their deities, and with this in mind may tacitly substitute the singular where literal interpretation of texts and pictures would require us to read the plural.[40]

The "profusion of manifestations," the colorful abundance of polytheism, is again set aside as being superficial. But this time there is no distant perspective of an original monotheism that had been obscured in the course of history. Instead, the vanishing point is in the "depths of the single divine essence"; behind and intersecting with all the stage wings of history is the one and only God of revelation.

This is a grandiose, western-style perspective—but it has little in common with Egyptian ways of looking and thinking. Egyptians knew no stage wings and no depth of perspective. Behind a god may be his retinue; the foundations of the world may be divine, but they are not a god. It is fascinating to arrange the Egyptian pantheon in three dimensions and to make

[39]*FuF* 35 (1961) 278.
[40]*Gott und Mensch* 116. Schelling had already expressed similar ideas, *Einleitung in die Philosophie der Mythologie* (n. 5 above) 74.

the One the vanishing point—but does there not lie behind such an exercise the old apologist's endeavor to render the Egyptian gods more credible to us? Must we really prove, against Karl Barth[41] and other "cultured denigrators"[42] of non-Christian religions, that Egyptian religion also belongs to God's only recognized "elite"? Is there not a danger here that our discipline will be perverted into theology? If it is to count as egyptology, the nature, sphere of action, and meaning of Egyptian gods must first be studied, and one must ask above all how Egyptians themselves saw and understood their gods before even considering any question of evaluation. What is needed is a comprehensive study of Egyptian conceptions of god which will draw on the sources in breadth and in depth; in the flood of writing on ancient Egyptian religion such a work has been lacking.

The lack of such a work provided a challenge that I took up originally in the form of lectures on the Egyptian concept of god in the summer semester of 1965 at the University of Münster in Westphalia and in the summer semester of 1968 at the University of Basel. The immediate stimulus was provided by critical study of two books, published independently by Siegfried Morenz and Eberhard Otto in the same year, 1964, and under the same title, *God and Man*.[43] Both authors chose the singular *God* quite deliberately, and as we have just seen, Mor-

[41]Morenz criticizes him, *Gott und Mensch* 15.

[42][An allusion to the famous work of Friedrich Schleiermacher, addressed as an apologia to the proponents of the Enlightenment: *Über die Religion. Reden an die Gebildeten unter ihren Verächtern* (Berlin 1799) = *On Religion. Speeches to Its Cultured Despisers* (London 1893)—tr.]

[43]E. Otto, *Gott und Mensch nach den ägyptischen Tempelinschriften der griechisch-römischen Zeit* (AHAW 1964, 1); S. Morenz, *Gott und Mensch im alten Ägypten* (Leipzig 1964; Heidelberg 1965). Both authors also studied the Egyptian conception of god in a number of articles: E. Otto, "Monotheistische Tendenzen in der ägyptischen Religion," *WdO* 2 (1955) 99–110; "Zum Gottesbegriff der ägyptischen Spätzeit," *FuF* 35 (1961) 277–80; "Altägyptischer Polytheismus. Eine Beschreibung," *Saeculum* 14 (1963) 249–85; S. Morenz, *Die Heraufkunft des transzendenten Gottes in Ägypten* (SBSAW 109, 2, 1964) = *Religion und Geschichte* 77–119; "Die Geschichte Gottes im alten Ägypten," *Neue Zürcher Zeitung* Oct. 18, 1964.

Before the Second World War the *Wiener Totenbuchkommission* planned a work entitled "Gott und Mensch im Weltbilde der Ägypter"; see G. Thausing, *Der Auferstehungsgedanke in ägyptischen religiösen Texten* (Leipzig 1943) viii.

enz justified his choice with unambiguous clarity; but this justification was itself offered as a hypothesis, and demands the kind of critical scrutiny that inevitably leads to the wider issue of the Egyptian conception of god.

One must ask how ancient Egyptians imagined gods or a single god; whether and in what form they saw or worshiped an impersonal, anonymous power beside or behind the great variety of their deities; and whether their deities can be seen as precursors of monotheistic religions.

Such questions as these mark the beginning of a laborious road that must be traveled by anyone who seeks a correct answer. The information we need must be wrested from sources that are often difficult to interpret and ambiguous; a number of apparently dry and recondite studies are necessary if we are to establish safe and solid foundations for our answer. There is the danger that the chief objectives of research will be lost in the mass of detailed evidence from three millennia and in a labyrinth of minor issues. But I hope always to keep visible on the horizon the broader question whose ramifications extend beyond Egypt to man's understanding of himself and his world: What is a god? What does a god mean to those who believe in him? What does the seeker encounter in so personal a form when he engages in a dialogue with the deity which determines his own existence? There is no need to enter into questions of belief, of the existence or nonexistence of God or of gods. The historical reality of the Egyptian gods is amply demonstrated by the fact that the Egyptians lived with them and carried on a lively dialogue with them for thousands of years. They are legitimate, even necessary objects of an inquiry that does not ask about their existence, their essence, or their value, but about their appearance and their meaning for believers and for the cultures elaborated by those believers.

It was of great value for my study that several new, thorough, and detailed monographs on Egyptian deities appeared during my work on it, providing me with repeated opportunities to reexamine and refine my questions and answers. These studies also remove still more of the obligation to examine the nature of individual deities—Osiris, Amun, Re, Ptah, Anubis, and so forth. Such an examination would involve a separate, lengthy study for each deity. We are concerned here primarily with the features that are common to Egyptian gods in general and to the relationships of Egyptians with individual gods—that is, with the generality of the Egyptian conception of god. I do not, of course, aim to construct an abstract, neutral entity, a schematic super-god; it is always necessary to start from the individual living deities we encounter in our sources.

2 ⟍ Egyptian Terms for God and Their Use

ntr and its basic meaning

Since any study of Egyptian conceptions of god must take as its starting point the original Egyptian texts and representations, it must start with the terminology they used themselves. Le Page Renouf defined this methodological requirement very sharply and clearly:

> Throughout the whole range of [ancient] Egyptian literature, no facts appear to be more certainly proved than these: (1) that the doctrine of one God and that of many gods were taught by the same men; (2) that no inconsistency between the two doctrines was thought of. Nothing, of course, can be more absurd if the Egyptians attached the same meaning to the word God that we do. But there may perhaps be a sense of the word which admits of its use for many as well as for one. We cannot do better at starting than endeavour to ascertain what the Egyptians really meant when they used the word *nutar* [*ntr*], which we translate "god." (*Lectures* p. 92)

This is my first task, and since the reader cannot be assumed to know the Egyptian language, I shall be as sparing with philological argument as possible.

The Egyptian word we translate "god" has the form *nutar* in the writings of le Page Renouf and other early egyptologists. Our present transcription gives it the form *ntr*, in which *t* is a prepalatal stop that is more usually rendered *č*. Our method of

33

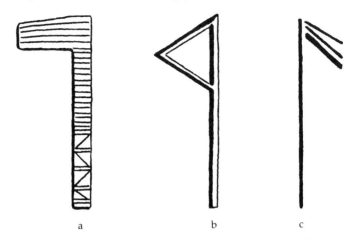

a   b   c

Figure 1. The hieroglyph for "god," "staff bound with cloth."

transcription shows only the consonantal skeleton of Egyptian words, so that it tells us nothing about their pronunciation. In order to make a form such as *nt̲r* pronounceable we join the consonants with *e* and say *netjer*. The true vocalization of Egyptian words is gradually being reconstructed with the help of cuneiform, Greek, Coptic, and other fully vocalized forms; in our case it is roughly *nátjīr* (feminine *natjārat* "goddess").[1]

nt̲r is written with a hieroglyphic sign whose normal form is shown in Figure 1a. Because it has a rare pointed variant, found in earlier periods (Figure 1b), Champollion[2] and some later egyptologists interpreted it as an ax. But Egyptian axes have a quite different appearance,[3] and their handles are not wrapped around as our sign is. For this reason W. M. F. Petrie correctly dismissed the identification as an ax as early as 1892,[4] but some scholars still retained it decades later.[5]

[1]W. Vycichl, *ZDMG Suppl.* 1 (1969) 26.

[2]*Dictionnaire égyptien* (posthumous, Paris 1841) 345.

[3]See E. Kühnert-Eggebrecht, *Die Axt als Waffe und Werkzeug im alten Ägypten* (MÄS 15, 1969).

[4]*Medum* (London 1892) 32.

[5]E.g. Budge, *Gods* I, 63–65, and in other works; Amélineau, *Prolégomènes* I, 284; A. Wiedemann in J. Hastings, ed., *Encyclopaedia of Religion and Ethics* VI (1913) 275; K. Beth, *ZAW* 38 (1920) 92.

The earliest forms of the sign, some of which go back to the predynastic period, are of the type illustrated in Figure 1c, and probably show a staff with streamers.[6] The number of the streamers, which are clearly separated as late as the Third Dynasty, varies between two and four. The sign does not reach its definitive form (Figure 1a) until the Old Kingdom. This form shows a strip of cloth instead of the streamers; carefully executed examples show that the entire staff is wrapped. More recent definitions take account of this; the most precise is that of P. E. Newberry: "a pole wrapped round with a band of cloth, bound by a cord, the end projecting as a flap or streamer."[7] Briefer definitions are those of the Berlin Dictionary (*Wb.* II, 357, 12): "staff wrapped with cloth," or of Alan H. Gardiner: "cloth wound on a pole."[8]

It cannot be disputed that this more recent identification is in principle correct. The Egyptians themselves seem to have interpreted the *ntr* sign in a similar fashion, although the evidence for their view is of the late period or the late New Kingdom at the earliest; its date can scarcely be earlier than 1200 B.C. In the "enigmatic" or cryptographic form of the hieroglyphic script the sign has the value *w* on a number of scarabs; Drioton derived this from *wt* "wrap, bind."[9] From an early period *wt* is the title of an embalmer and the word for mummy wrappings. These can also—not before the late period—be called *ntrj* (*Wb.* II, 365, 14; cf. also II, 363, 19), while the fragmentary Roman period papyrus from Tanis which lists and glosses hieroglyphic signs has for the *ntr* sign *jw.f qrs* "he is buried."[10] Newberry already pointed out these associations,[11] and they provide a concrete background for the practice of calling the

[6]Some are collected by P. E. Newberry, *JEA* 33 (1947) 90 figs. 1–3.
[7]*Ibid.*
[8]*Egyptian Grammar* (Oxford 1927, 3d ed. London 1957) sign list no. R8. In accordance with standard practice, hieroglyphs are cited below by the numbers of this sign list.
[9]*Kêmi* 14 (1957) 22–23.
[10]F. L. Griffith in W. M. F. Petrie, *Two Hieroglyphic Papyri from Tanis* (MEEF 9, 1889) 16 (xv, 2). F. Calice, *Grundlagen der ägyptisch-semitischen Wortvergleichung* (WZKM Beiheft 1, 1936) 35, suggested that *ntr* derived from a common semitic root *kr* "bind, wrap."
[11]*JEA* 33 (1947) 91.

deceased *ntrw* "gods," which is found from an early period: through being wrapped, a practice attested earlier than true mummification, the deceased became a *ntr* in the sense of the wrapped cloth fetish shown by the sign. For Egyptians, who lived in a world of allusions, such associations as these were doubtless very immediate, but for us they are for the moment too vague and hypothetical to allow us to go any further in this direction than to suggest possibilities. In any case, if we pursue this line of inquiry we may gain vital insights into the nature of mummification, but hardly into the nature of the Egyptian conception of god.

There are two alternative interpretations of the significance of the sign, as "cult flag" or as "wrapped fetish." Kurt Sethe, among others, explained the sign as "a sort of flag";[12] the historian of religion Kurt Goldammer also identified it as a "cult flag" or "cloth or flag fetish," in the most comprehensive study of the "god" hieroglyph to date.[13] In this context writers always refer to the tall flagpoles that dominate the entrance towers (pylons) of Egyptian temples. With their fluttering strips of cloth they recall the earliest form of the sign for "god" (Figure 20), and they may already have stood in front of sanctuaries of the early dynastic period.[14] From the Ptolemaic period we know of masts with white, green, and red pennants.[15] The same combination of colors is found once under Amenophis III,[16] but in other colored representations of the New Kingdom we find only white and red strips.[17]

[12]*Urgeschichte* (1930) §10, and before him H. Schäfer, *ZÄS* 34 (1896) 159 n. 3; A. M. Blackman, *The Rock Tombs of Meir* II (ASE 23, 1915) 35.

[13]"Die heilige Fahne. Zur Geschichte und Phänomenologie eines religiösen Ur-Objekts," *Tribus* n.s. 4/5 (1954–5, Stuttgart 1956) 13–55; quotation from p. 16.

[14]From the early dynastic period on (W. M. F. Petrie, *The Royal Tombs of the Earliest Dynasties* II [MEEF 21, 1901] pl. 3A) two flags, which are almost always pointed, are shown in front of the sanctuary of Neith; see the examples collected by G. Matthiae Scandone, *OrAnt* 6 (1967) 145–68.

[15]Junker, *Der grosse Pylon* 79, 9.

[16]Kiosk scene from Theban Tomb 226, Luxor Museum J.134: [J. F. Romano et al.], *The Luxor Museum of Egyptian Art: Catalogue* (Cairo 1979) no. 101 with color pl. VII; the color is very poor, and green has printed as blue.

[17]Checked on the kiosk scenes in Theban tombs (references n. 20 below) and on the columns of shrines for gods; for a colored reproduction cf. Otto, *Osiris*

Several writers have cited ethnographic parallels:[18] until very recently flagpoles were set up at the entrances to holy tombs throughout North Africa and the Sudan as part of a millennia-old tradition, which evidently originated in ancient Egypt. It is significant that, as A. M. Blackman recorded for the Nubians of Derr, the flag is identified with the *numen* itself, the "sheikh"; the sign has reverted to being a fetish.

Strips of cloth are found on other important Egyptian cult objects. They are scarcely ever absent from the common depictions of wooden carrying poles with sacred objects that are charged with power ("standards"), which are found as early as predynastic times; normally there are two strips hanging down from the pole.[19] Similar strips of cloth are attached to the sacred *djed* pillar, which is associated with the cult of Osiris, and are shown in New Kingdom representations of the columns that support both the kiosk surrounding the king on his throne and the shrines of gods.[20] Here too belong the fluttering streamers attached to the royal headgear which give life to Amarna period reliefs in particular, as well as the innumerable long pendant strips that form part of the dress of deities, royalty, and private individuals.[21] All these strips of cloth are certainly more than simply "decorative" in function.

But to interpret the hieroglyph for "god" as a "cult flag" or

---

und Amun pl. III. I was not able to work systematically through the entire material, and may have missed some exceptions.

[18]E.g. P. E. Newberry, *JEA* 33 (1947) 90 n. 2, referring to A. J. Arkell, *JEA* 19 (1933) 175–76 with pl. 30–31; A. M. Blackman, *Man* 10 (1910) no. 11, p. 28; M. A. Murray in *Studies Presented to F. Ll. Griffith* (London 1932) 312–15; Goldammer, "Die heilige Fahne" (n. 13 above) 19 with n. 30.

[19]For a collection of examples see M. Raphael, *Prehistoric Pottery and Civilization in Egypt* (Bollingen Series 8, [New York] 1947) pl. 36.1. Murray and Goldammer also refer to these strips of cloth.

[20]The pictures of kiosks to which Goldammer refers ("Die heilige Fahne," 19) are collected by J. Vandier, *Manuel IV*, 544–71; see also Ali Radwan, *Die Darstellungen des regierenden Königs und seiner Familienangehörigen in den Privatgräbern der 18. Dynastie* (MÄS 21, 1969); K. P. Kuhlmann, *Der Thron im alten Ägypten* (ADIK 10, 1977) 50–101.

[21]I am grateful to Elisabeth Staehelin for a collection of examples on Egyptian clothing; she also refers to the strips of cloth on boats and in the cult of the dead—not to speak of the "handkerchief" in the hands of statues. This material would repay a separate study, and is too extensive to be presented here.

something similar and to cite parallel usages of strips of cloth in Egyptian cult is to blur a significant distinction. The temple flagpoles, the "standards," and the columns are mostly staffs, pillars, or architectural elements derived from plants, to which the strip of cloth is attached, usually at the top.[22] In the hieroglyph for "god," however, the entire staff is wrapped. It is therefore possible that the "cult flag" is a secondary, derived form, and that the primary object is a staff which is wrapped, that is, clothed and hence charged with power. Before the appearance of anthropomorphic forms for gods the wrapped staff, together with animal forms, may have embodied all that was numinous; when the script was invented none of the animal forms may have been sufficiently representative to stand for "god" in general. In the underworld book known as Amduat the name of the hieroglyph for god, *ntrjt*, is determined with the sign of a staff,[23] and thus classified with sacred staffs and scepters.

Goldammer clearly also reckons with the possibility that the "cult flag" is secondary: "the flag probably derived from the wrapped staff" ("Die heilige Fahne," n. 13 above, p. 39). It is not the god himself, but an attribute of him, a signal indicating the place of residence of the god (p. 32).[24] I doubt whether the sacred flag and its precursor should be separated into the two elements of staff and wrappings, each with its own meaning (pp. 27, 38); here Goldammer is partly following M. A. Murray.[25] The *ntr* sign is wrapped all over, forming a unity that must be interpreted as a unity.

The commonest Egyptian hieroglyph for "god" can therefore be interpreted as evidence of the veneration of "inanimate" objects, that is, as a representation of a fetish whose direct descendants are probably the flags and other strips of cloth used in the cult, right down to contemporary national flags.

[22]Below the capital on columns, and on "standards" often in the middle of the carrying pole.

[23]*Amduat* I, 78–79, the only attestation of the Egyptian name of the sign.

[24]On the role of the strips of cloth as signals cf. M. A. Murray, in *Studies . . . Griffith* (n. 18 above) 314.

[25]*Ibid.* 312–15. The occasional use of a tree as a determinative in the Amduat (n. 23 above) would fit this.

a   b

Figure 2. Other hieroglyphs for "god."

In a schematic history of Egyptian religion, such as that of Gustave Jéquier in his *Considérations sur les religions égyptiennes* (Neuchâtel 1946), fetishism is the earliest, most primitive stage, which is followed by the higher stages of zoolatry (the veneration of deities in animal form) and anthropomorphism (the veneration of deities in human form). It is significant that the other two Egyptian hieroglyphs for "god" belong to these two "higher" stages. One of these shows a hawk, one of the most important embodiments of divinity, on a carrying pole (Figure 2a); the most frequent use of this sign is as a semogram or sense sign in the Egyptian cursive script (hieratic), while it is found more rarely in the monumental hieroglyphic script and only occasionally as a logogram for *ntr* "god." This hieroglyph is just as old as the fetish sign; both date back to the invention of the script at the turning point between the prehistoric and historical periods.[26]

The third, anthropomorphic sign for "god," which shows a squatting god with a formless body, wearing the braided di-

[26]Earliest example on the "cities palette" of King Scorpion, shortly after 3000 B.C.: H. Asselberghs, *Chaos en beheersing* (Documenta et Monumenta Orientis Antiqui 8, Leiden 1961) pl. 92 fig. 164. For early examples as a logogram cf. P. Kaplony, *CdE* 41/81 (1966) 90.

Figure 3. Gardiner hieroglyphic sign list, category C.

vine ceremonial beard, is evidently not so ancient (Figure 2b). It occurs in reliefs as early as the beginning of the Old Kingdom (see Chapter 4), but is adopted as a determinative for the names of gods only toward the end of that period;[27] it is used occasionally as a logogram for *nṯr* "god."[28]

Apart from these three general hieroglyphs for god, there is a whole series of pictorial signs for particular zoomorphic and anthropomorphic deities (group C of the sign lists); these were particularly favored in the Ramessid period as abbreviated writings of the names of gods (Figure 3). In studying the problem of the Egyptian conception of god we can disregard these specialized signs. The hieroglyph of a star (N14), which is said in Horapollo to be the sign for "god" (*Hieroglyphica* I, 13; II, 1), acquired this meaning very late, for it is attested only from the beginning of the Ptolemaic period on.

The conclusion, therefore, is that deities occur in the Egyptian script in human, animal, and fetish form. The human form is by several centuries more recent than the other two, which are among the oldest elements in the Egyptian script. The development of the script does not establish any priority of fetishism over zoolatry, as Jéquier proposed in his scheme, and other Egyptian material does not suggest that this idea is likely to be right, although it is not possible to disprove it. The commonest sign for "god" shows a fetish in the form of a wrapped staff and acquaints us with a manifestation of divine power that was important for predynastic and early dynastic Egyptians; but it tells us nothing further about the nature of the Egyptian conception of god.

[27] P. Kaplony, *Or* 37 (1968) 24, n. from 23, refers to examples in the mid-Fifth Dynasty tomb of Ti (e.g. L. Epron and F. Daumas, *Le tombeau de Ti* I [MIFAO 65, 1939] pl. 39 top L). Early cases are mostly in writings of the name Osiris and of the *akh* "transfigured spirit."

[28] Kaplony, *Or* 37 (1968) 23–26. The two similar signs A40 and A41 are often confused in this context, cf. E. Drioton, *ASAE* 44 (1944) 21(a).

One might expect the etymology of the word *nṯr* "god" to be more revealing, but, as with Sumerian *dingir* and semitic *el*, attempts to define the meaning of *nṯr* in etymological terms have not been convincing. The first etymology, "to rejuvenate, renew," which was assumed by de Rougé,[29] Pierret, and many others to be quite obvious, would fit excellently with the Egyptian conception of god; but the writing of *nṯr* with the "year rib," on which it is based, is purely phonetic (the sign has the value *tr*), and so cannot provide evidence for an etymology. After an exemplary, clear, and methodical start le Page Renouf's study turned up a blind alley, because he derived the word from an adjective *nṯrj*, which I shall discuss below and which is clearly a secondary formation deriving from the substantive *nṯr*.[30]

F. W. von Bissing's more recent attempt to derive *nṯr* from "natron" (an ancient Egyptian word), and hence to relate it to cultic purity, is not convincing.[31] M. A. Murray's explanation of the word as *nj-ṯr* "He of the Poplar-Tree" is still more unlikely.[32] M. A. Murray wished to interpret the Egyptian word for "god" as being derived from *ṯrt* "willow" and to link it with tree cults, which are certainly well attested in Egypt;[33] but at no period were they as central to the Egyptian conception of god as her hypothesis would imply. Attempts to find an illuminating etymology for *nṯr* by comparison within the Afro-Asiatic language family have not so far been any more successful. The parallel with *inkira* or *enkera*, meaning "soul, life, demon" in Kushitic languages,[34] is of little use: the difference in time is too great, and the word could be a secondary derivation.

[29]*Revue archéologique* n.s. 1, 1 (1860) 351; P. Pierret, *Essai sur la mythologie égyptienne* (Paris 1879) 8; cf. also H. Brugsch, *Religion und Mythologie der alten Ägypter* (Berlin 1885 and 1891) 93.

[30]*Lectures* 93–100.

[31]*Versuch zur Bestimmung der Grundbedeutung des Wortes NUTR für Gott im Altägyptischen* (SBBAW 1951, 2); see the criticisms of S. Morenz, *OLZ* 49 (1954) 123–25.

[32]*Studies . . . Griffith* (n. 18 above) 314–15.

[33]The material is collected in the unpublished Göttingen dissertation of Ramses Moftah, "Die heiligen Bäume im alten Ägypten" (1959); see also M.-L. Buhl, "The Goddesses of the Egyptian Tree Cult," *JNES* 6 (1947) 80–97.

[34]Calice, *Grundlagen* (n. 10 above) 167; I am grateful to W. Vycichl for the reference.

Finally, it has been proposed that *ntr* did not originally refer to deities, but to the deceased,[35] or more narrowly to the dead king.[36] We shall see at the end of Chapter 4 that the living and perhaps also the dead king could be called *ntr* as early as the early dynastic period, but it would be overly hasty and circular to assume that the Egyptian word for god was restricted to this single usage in the pre- and early dynastic periods. The early dynastic sources, which consist of personal names and titles, do not support the hypothesis of a general equivalence of *ntr* with the deceased, or with the dead king.

The conclusion is virtually inescapable that neither the etymology nor the "original meaning" of the word *ntr* can be established, so that this approach, like the study of the writing, does not provide any insight into the nature of the Egyptian conception of god. We must leave these problems aside and concentrate on the use of the word; this will take us a few steps farther along our road.

The use of the word *ntr*

In the bilingual decrees of the Ptolemaic period, one of which is the famous Rosetta Stone, *ntr* is equivalent to Greek *theos*. Christian Egyptians (the Copts) took the word over in its Coptic form *noute* for the Christian God; the Copts even continued to use the plural form *entēr*, but only in magical spells against demons and in personal names.[37]

Coptic shows that, at least in the latest phase of Egyptian religion, *ntr* = *noute* could be used in a monotheistic sense, and in this respect too is synonymous with *theos*. Our translation "god," which is vague and has a wide range of meaning, is therefore justified, whatever *ntr* may have meant in archaic times.

In Egyptian texts the word occurs in the singular *ntr* (feminine *ntrt*), in the dual *ntrwj* (feminine *ntrtj*) and in the plural *ntrw* (feminine *ntrwt*). The dual need not concern us here; in a

[35]A detailed presentation, based throughout on late evidence, is Amélineau, *Prolégomènes* I, 294–317; see also J. F. Borghouts, *The Magical Texts of Papyrus Leiden I 348* = *OMRO* 51 (1970 [1971]) 45 n. (22).

[36]W. Westendorf, in *Festgabe für Dr. Walter Will* (Cologne etc. 1966) 220–31.

[37]W. E. Crum, *A Coptic Dictionary* (Oxford 1939) 230–31.

usage that is typical of semitic languages, it is applied to two deities who belong closely together, such as Horus and Seth or Isis and Nephthys, and occasionally for pairs of gods.[38]

The plural is more important. It occurs from the early dynastic period down to temple inscriptions of the Roman period, that is, throughout the entire literate history of Egyptian religion. Sir Harold Idris Bell, the expert on Greek papyri from Egypt, remarked that "it is of 'gods' in the plural that we hear most often";[39] even the Christian Copts were willing to tolerate the plural in personal names. Just once there was an attempt to eliminate the plural "gods": Akhenaten, whose religious views we shall encounter several times, occasionally had the plural form of the word erased, in order to satisfy the exclusive claims of his god Aten.[40] For the moment we can disregard this unique case and retain the conclusion that the plural "gods" remained in common use until the end of ancient Egyptian culture. It refers either to a limited number of gods (the gods of a place or a country, or a group of gods) or, mostly in lists, to the virtually unlimited totality of all gods (or of the deceased).

For the question that concerns us here the most important usage is that of the singular "god." Concentrating for the moment on the issue of monotheism, one may say that, if anything can prove the existence of an Egyptian monotheism, this usage of the singular should do so. We must exclude from consideration all cases in which a god who has been named earlier in a text or in some way defined is referred to as *ntr*; these are not relevant to our question of whether there is a monotheistic use of *ntr*. The same applies to cases of *ntr* with a possessive suffix, when a believer speaks of "my god" and means a quite specific god, for example, his city god or the god who is being addressed in a prayer. At Amarna, however, this usage is attested even for the unique God Aten.[41]

[38]W. C. Hayes, *JEA* 32 (1946) 15 n. 9.

[39]*JEA* 34 (1948) 84.

[40]*Urk.* IV, 160, 6; 162, 17; 165, 17; N. de G. Davies, *The Tomb of the Vizier Ramosé* (Mond Excavations at Thebes 1, London 1941) 4 n. 1; Ahmed Fakhry, *ASAE* 42 (1943) 457 (tomb of Kheruef, now republished: The Epigraphic Survey, *The Tomb of Kheruef* [OIP 102, 1980]).

[41]For examples see E. Drioton, *ASAE* 43 (1943) 28–29.

We must study more carefully cases in which _ntr_ is used without discernible reference to a particular god; these are the ones that the proponents of a primary or secondary monotheism in Egyptian religion have used as their chief evidence. This absolute use of _ntr_ is found especially in Egyptian didactic literature, the "wisdom" or "instruction texts"; a second area of use, which I shall discuss first for chronological reasons, is in personal names.

In his _Die Inschriften der ägyptischen Frühzeit_ (I, 379–672)[42] and in a later supplement[43] Peter Kaplony has assembled conveniently all the early dynastic personal names that are known so far. The material he has collected belongs to the period between 3000 and 2600 B.C., and is thus from the earliest stage of Egyptian religion which we can study. One can indeed say that among sources now available Egyptian personal names of the early dynastic period are the oldest of all written evidence of human religiosity. Neither from western Asia nor from the Far East are there comparable sources dating to the first centuries of the third millennium B.C. This is a new, so far unexploited field, which should provide many insights for our problem of the Egyptian conception of god and for a number of other questions. The reading and interpretation of some of these archaic personal names are still disputed, but this scarcely affects the issue at hand because the two signs for "god" which are used (fetish and hawk on carrying pole) are unmistakable.

Among the considerable number of these personal names which are "theophorous," that is, contain a statement about a deity,[44] nineteen use simple _ntr_ "god." I list these names here, followed by parallel name forms that use the names of specific deities (or the divine power of the _ka_), drawn from the same sources. (Numbers are page references to Kaplony, _Inschriften_ I. Most of the renderings follow Kaplony.)

[42]3 vols. (ÄgAbh 8, 1963).
[43]_Kleine Beiträge zu den Inschriften der ägyptischen Frühzeit_ (ÄgAbh 15, 1966) 40–41.
[44]Cf. K. Hoffmann, _Die theophoren Personnamen des älteren Ägyptens_ (UGAÄ 7, 1, 1915); W. Helck, "Zu den theophoren Eigennamen des Alten Reiches," _ZÄS_ 79 (1954) 27–33.

Jm'-jb-ntr "god is well disposed" (418–19), probably two different people. Also *Jm'-jb* "the well-disposed one," name of a princess (417–18); additional names formed with *jm'* (419).

Jndw-ntr "whom god saves" (425). Also *Jnd-n-Ḥnm* "whom Khnum has saved" (425), and similar formations with the goddess Satis and the *ka* (425).

Jrj-ntr "whom god created" (428). Also *Jrj-n-'ḫtj* "whom the horizon god has created" (427), and many similar combinations with Anubis, Satis, Neith, and the *ka*.[45]

Jḫt-ntr "property of god" (432). Also *Jḫt-'* "property of the greatest (god)", *Jḫt-w'* "property of the unique (god)," and similar formations with Neith, the *ka, ba* ("soul"[?]) and the king (*njswt*).

'-b'w-ntr "the might (Kaplony: authority) of god is great" (444). Also *'-dnd-Nt* "the anger(?) of Neith is great" (445); *'-njswt* "the king is great" (444), and many combinations with the synonymous *wr* "great" (467–69).

'nḫ-ntr "may god live" (454). Also "may Ptah live" (452), "may Neith live" (454) and "may (my) *ka* live" (455).

Bnr(t)-ntr, woman's name "the sweet one of god" or "god is gracious" (475).[46] No parallel, apart from *Bnr(t)* "the gracious one" as a woman's name (475).

Mrj-ntr "whom god loves" (497). Many parallels: "whom Anubis loves" and similarly with Wepwawet, Neith, the "two lords," Re, Khnum, Thoth, the *ka*, the king, and various divine epithets.

Nj-'nḫ-ntr "god possesses life" (513). Parallels with Anubis, Hathor, and Sakhmet (uncertain) (512–13).

Nj-ntr-nbtj "god belongs to the Two Ladies" (518–19), name of a prince. It seems to me most unlikely that *ntr* is an abstraction, "divine power," as Kaplony translates. No parallels.

Nfr-ntr-wd-'nḫ "perfect is the god who grants life" (Kaplony: "kindly is the god who lets (me?) live") (545). The order of

[45]With *Jrtj?-ntr-'* (428–29) it is not clear whether the adjective belongs with *ntr* or is an addition to the whole name.

[46]S. Schott, *Hieroglyphen* (AMAW 1950, 24) 123 fig. 15 no. 14, takes the "hawk on pole" here as a determinative.

elements in the name is uncertain; there are no parallels to this precise form, but numerous combinations with *nfr* + divine name (Maat, Min, Sobek, and epithets) (541–50).

Ḥtp-nṯr "god is gracious" (593). Many parallels with Anubis, Nemty, Ptah, Neith, Horus, Khnum, Seshat, Satis, the *ka*, and others (586–98).

Sʾḥ-nṯr "whom the god approaches" (617). No parallels in the early material, but Kaplony compares the Fifth Dynasty king's name *Sʾḥw-Rˁ* "whom Re approaches" and the short form *Sʾḥj* or *Sʾḥw*. The reading seems to me to be certain.

Sjmʾ-nṯr "the one who gladdens god," name of a dwarf (619). Content of the name paralleled in the Sixth Dynasty inscription of Harkhuf, where a dwarf or pygmy is brought who will "gladden the heart" (*sḥmḥ jb, snḥʾḥʾ jb*) of the king through his "god's dancing" (*Urk.* I, 130, 4–5).

Smr-nṯr "companion of god" (624). Kaplony gives later parallels under the short form *Smr*.

Šps-nṯr "god is glorious" (647). Also "Wepwawet is glorious," "the *ka* is glorious," and similar formations (647–48).

Šms-nṯr "the one who follows god" (with a problematic additional element, 649). Corresponding early combinations with the goddess Neith and the *ka*, as well as numerous parallels in later personal names (649–50).

Šdj-nṯr "whom god rears (?)" (651, masculine; 652, feminine). Early parallels with the *ka* and with the god Min (uncertain) (651–52); *šdj* + divine name occurs frequently in later periods, probably with the meaning "save, preserve";[47] here the meaning "suckle, rear," which is attested from the Fourth Dynasty on,[48] seems more likely.

Qʾj-kʾ-nṯr "the god's *ka* is exalted" (653–54). Also "Neith is exalted" and from later periods several other combinations *qʾj* + divine name (653).

In addition to these personal names, there are the Horus names of a king of the Second Dynasty, *Nj-nṯr* "belonging to god," and one of the Third, *Nṯrj-ḥt* "most divine one of the corporation (of gods)." Neither of these names supports the

[47]*Wb.* IV, 563 states that it is attested from the Middle Kingdom on.
[48]*Wb.* IV, 564–65; cf. Junker, *Gîza* I, 225 no. 11; H. Goedicke, *RdE* 11 (1975) 160.

assumption that *ntr* was in origin only the (deceased) king. It is almost unthinkable that *Nj-ntr* proclaimed as the motto of his reign the fact that he belonged to his dead predecessor,[49] while Djoser evidently wished to give himself, the reigning king, a privileged position among a number of beings who possessed the quality of being *ntr*.[50] On the other hand, his Horus name is evidence that the king—whether living or dead—can count as a *ntr*; several of the personal names listed above would also fit this assumption well. The early material does not therefore conflict with the hypothesis that the later use of "god" for the king was already normal. But it would be absurd to conclude that *ntr* referred to the king in all cases.

It is important to note that almost all the names cited have parallels that give not the undefined *ntr* but a particular god's name or the *ka*, the "life force," which is much in evidence in this material. It follows that the characteristics and capacities of *ntr* are not, so far as can be discovered from the personal names, different from those of the individual deities, so that one cannot find here an anonymous "high god" behind the deities. Of the two exceptions here for which no parallels can be cited, one is without significance (*Bnrt-ntr*), but the other is very revealing. *Nj-ntr-nbtj* "god belongs to the Two Ladies" signifies that the vulture and the snake goddesses of the two lands[51] are superior to the *ntr*; in this name he can only be the king or a particular god, for example, the god of a particular place. And, as we shall see in the discussion of divine names, local gods often have no personal names, but are called "he of place A" or "the one upon his lake" or, for a goddess, "the mighty one (feminine)."

The question of whether *ntr* means an abstract divine entity of a higher order or one of the many individual deities can be settled still more decisively in favor of the latter solution. In addition to the nineteen personal names of the early dynastic period that have *ntr* "god" as one of their elements, three contain a similarly undefined feminine *ntrt* "goddess":

---

[49]The same would apply to the uncertain throne name *Jrj-ntr* of the next-to-last king of the First Dynasty; cf. B. Grdseloff, *ASAE* 44 (1944) 287.

[50]On the "corporation (of gods)" see Chapter 7.

[51]Their names, Nekhbet and Wadjet, are not attested before the Old Kingdom.

Wn-k'-ntrt "the *ka* of the goddess exists" (466). In the early dynastic period *ka* is often attributed to the goddess Neith, as in a name like *Wpj-k'-Nt* "the *ka* of Neith is open" (466).

Wr-ntrt "the goddess is great" (467). Uncertain parallel "Mont is great" (467).

Sḥrj-ntrt "the one who keeps the goddess distant" (629). Compare *Sḥrj-m't* "the one who keeps the lioness distant" (629), which gives the explanation of our name: a dangerous and threatening deity, who could harm the newborn child, is to be kept away.

There is much to be said for the assumption that in the first name the goddess Neith is meant and in the last the "lioness," who is later embodied in various goddesses. Nobody will be inclined to understand the "goddess" as an abstract formation, and so such an interpretation for the "god" of the personal names becomes even less likely. When devising a name for a child an Egyptian had in mind a particular one among the many deities. It is quite possible that when he composed a name, *all* divinity—the entire extent of divine action—was incorporated in the single deity who was invoked, who thus became quite simply "god" for him; I shall return to this phenomenon of "henotheism" in Chapter 7. But it is also conceivable that the name giver wanted to leave undefined which of the innumerable deities was responsible for the successful birth and development of the child; I shall give below examples of this undefined use of the word. Because before the Amarna period written Egyptian has no articles, it is always possible to translate *ntr* as "a(ny) god." However that may be, we can exclude one interpretation of the early personal names, and, by analogy, of later ones: *ntr* "god" does not mean a different god, of a higher order than the other gods.

There are other ways in which early personal names replace the actual name of a deity with undefined expressions, for example, with such epithets as "the living one," "the great one," and so forth. Here too belong combinations with *nb* "lord," perhaps better understood as *nb.j* "my lord": *W'd-nb* "(my) lord is one who flourishes" (462),[52] or *Prj-nb* "(my) lord

---

[52]Numbers in brackets are again page references to Kaplony, *Inschriften* I.

is one who goes forth" (477). The use of a personal pronoun referring to the deity is still briefer and less precise: *Jj-n-f* "he has come" (406), *'nḫ-f* "he lives" (452), *Rḏj-f* "he has given" (562), or *Ḥtp-f* "he is content" (587). In all these cases, which date from the beginning of the third millennium B.C., we should certainly not think of the Christian He or of a deity behind the gods, but of a periphrasis for the individual god the Egyptian name giver had in mind, to whom he felt an obligation. This relationship between the name giver and a particular deity also explains why we almost never find personal names containing the plural "gods."[53]

To complete the picture of the use of *nṯr* in Egypt in the earliest historical period I should refer to the Egyptian priestly title *ḥm-nṯr* "servant of god," which occurs first at this time, along with such specific forms as "servant of Khnum" or "servant of the king."[54] By the time of the Old Kingdom the element *nṯr* in the title is invariable, so that priestesses of the goddesses Hathor or Neith are "servants (feminine) of the god"; here *nṯr* is clearly the most general abstract concept, which covers the multiplicity of divine manifestations—"servant of the god" is always the chief priest, irrespective of which deities (there are often several!) he serves on behalf of the king.

I shall now turn to the second group of sources in which the word "god" is used in a sense that appears at first reading to be undefined and general; this is Egyptian didactic literature or "wisdom texts."[55] Here we encounter one of the chief types of evidence cited by proponents of a monotheistic interpretation of Egyptian religion.

[53]Kaplony has only one example: *Sḥ'-ntrw* "whom the gods recall" (630–31).
[54]Kaplony, *Inschriften* II, 1208–10 (index). The uncertain name *Ḥm(t)-nṯr* (572) is omitted from the list above.
[55]See E. Hornung, *Einführung in die Ägyptologie* (Darmstadt 1967) §20. English translations and bibliography are available in Simpson, *Literature*; Lichtheim, *Literature* I–III. Many texts are unpublished or in course of publication. For a recent collection of studies see E. Hornung and O. Keel, eds., *Studien zu altägyptischen Lebenslehren* (Orbis Biblicus et Orientalis 28, Fribourg and Göttingen 1979); see also the review article with extensive bibliography by R. J. Williams, "The Sages of Ancient Egypt in the Light of Recent Scholarship," *Journal of the American Oriental Society* 101 (1981) 1–19. For a recent study of the problem discussed in the following pages see W. Barta, *ZÄS* 103 (1976) 79–88.

In the maxims of the wisdom teachers there are dozens of declarations about "god" which could, if taken in isolation, be thought to come from a tract of one of the monotheistic Religions of the Book. I shall limit myself to a small selection, in order to illustrate the tone of the maxims.[56]

> Do not boast of (your) strength. . . it is not known what will happen, (nor) what god does when he punishes.   (Kagemni)
> Do not do violence to men, for god punishes with the same. . . . Man's plans are never fulfilled. What happens is what god commands.   (Ptahhotpe, Sixth maxim, ll. 115–16)
> One who hears (= obeys) is one whom god loves; the one whom god hates cannot hear.   (Ptahhotpe, Thirty-ninth maxim, ll. 545–56)
> Celebrate the festival of your god and repeat it at its (right) time. Gods are angry if it is missed. . . . (As for) the one who does it, the god will make his name great.   (Ani 3, 3–4, 9)
> A bushel that the god has given to you is better than five thousand wrongly (acquired).   (Amenemope, Sixth chapter)
> Man is mud and straw; the god is his builder. He destroys and he builds daily. He makes a thousand poor men as he wishes and he makes a thousand men into chiefs when he is in his hour of life. How joyful is he who has reached the West (the realm of the dead) and is safe in the hand of the god.   (Amenemope, Twenty-fifth chapter)

In order to avoid constructing a distorted picture from these and many similar declarations about "god" it is necessary to locate them in their general context, in terms both of date and of content. The "instructions" are later than the archaic names and titles we have been considering. The earliest instruction of which some fragments are preserved was composed roughly at the time of the pyramid builder Cheops (2530 B.C.), and is ascribed to Djedefhor, one of the sons of Cheops. A still earlier instruction, which has not come down to us, is connected with the name of the wise man Imhotep, the master builder of the first step pyramid at Saqqara (c. 2600 B.C.). In a chronological list dating to the New Kingdom Imhotep is named as the ear-

---

[56]Unless noted separately, sources are given in Vergote, "La notion de Dieu," and in the books cited in n. 55 above.

liest wisdom teacher, and there are no indications that there was any didactic literature before his date, that is, in the early dynastic period; for various reasons that have to do with the development of the script and the structure of the state, it is most improbable that there were any.[57] It seems, therefore, that the literary genre of "instructions" was created around 2600 B.C. at the earliest,[58] when there was already a tradition of several centuries, at the least, in which proper names and titles used _ntr_ as a deliberately vague or general designation for some quite specific deity.

This simple point of chronology itself raises doubts as to whether the wisdom teachers would have given the word _ntr_ a completely different meaning—a clearly monotheistic one. As we saw in Chapter 1, this interpretation was maintained by early egyptologists and more recently by Drioton and Sauneron,[59] for example—"monotheism is, in fact, a phenomenon restricted to the wisdom texts," as Drioton phrased it.[60] It should, however, be noted that this view is not universally held; Morenz, for instance, considered it possible that the relevant local gods were "tacitly implied when 'god' is spoken of without using a particular name."[61] In order to find a path between these two diametrically opposed views we must examine the primary material, that is, the instruction texts themselves.

This task can be accomplished quite briefly, since Jozef Vergote assembled the statements about god and gods in the instruction texts in a lecture, "La notion de Dieu dans les livres de sagesse égyptiens" (n. 56 above), delivered to the 1962 Strasbourg colloquium on ancient Near Eastern wisdom literature. Vergote offers a detailed critique of Drioton's idea of an Egyptian monotheism, and, very usefully for us, lists in an

---

[57]H. Brunner, _Grundzüge einer Geschichte der altägyptischen Literatur_ (Darmstadt 1966) 11.

[58]The original dates of these texts are disputed by Lichtheim, _Literature_ I, 6, who would place most of them a century or two after the dates of the authors to whom they are attributed, and by W. Helck, _WZKM_ 63–64 (1972) 6–26, who would place them in the first intermediate period (esp. pp. 18–19).

[59]G. Posener, ed., _A Dictionary of Egyptian Civilization_ (London 1962) 109–10.

[60]E. Drioton and J. Vandier, _L'Egypte_ (3d ed., Paris 1952) 63–64; quotation from p. 63.

[61]_Heraufkunft_ 8 = 80.

appendix all the passages in Egyptian instruction texts where "god" in general, "gods" in the plural, or a particular god is mentioned. In the same collective volume a new instruction text of the late period is described by Georges Posener and Jean Sainte Fare Garnot (Papyrus Brooklyn 47.218.135; pp. 153–57). Here, too, Posener refers to the occurrence side by side of p $n\underline{t}r$ "the god" (with the article at this date) and such specific deities as Re, Horus, Thoth, Sia, or the complete group of the "ennead"; he deduces that "in formal terms the context is clearly polytheistic" (p. 156).

Drioton attempted to maintain his monotheistic interpretation of $n\underline{t}r$ despite this significant coincidence in usage, and here Vergote follows him. Both scholars assume that in their texts the Egyptian wise men attempted to take account of the polytheism of the people as well as the "philosophical" monotheism. An immediate objection to this interpretation is that these texts were certainly never intended for the "people," even if a few of them became widely used in scribal schools; they are addressed to a single pupil who is called in Egyptian the "son" of the teacher, or at most to the group of pupils of the wise teacher. They do not need, therefore, to have a dual character of that sort.

But that is not the decisive argument. A much more important point is that, while wisdom teachers do as a rule speak about just "god," they are not deterred from invoking numerous deities of the polytheistic pantheon, and by no means solely in insignificant set phrases. In the Instruction of Ptahhotpe one could explain the "time of Osiris" or the "servant of Horus," who is an obedient son, as set phrases, but in the slightly later Instruction for Merikare, the "lords of eternity" and the "judges" in the next world appear unambiguously in the plural, even the plural "gods" is used once (l. 140), and the "one who came with Osiris" is mentioned (l. 42). There is no clear reason why these phrases should be "concessions to popular belief."

The occasional use of the singular "god" in the Instruction for Merikare is still more informative. At several points the author appeals (as does the later Ani) for the correct performance of the cult of "god," and it is clear that by this he means the various deities of the land; in Egypt there was no cult, temple or priesthood of a _nt̠r_ beside or behind the traditional deities any more than there was the idea of an "unknown god." The same is true of the famous description in the Instruction of the blessed deceased who has been vindicated in the judgment after death, which is the earliest completely clear mention of the judgment: when the deceased is said to be "like (a) god" (_nt̠r_) in the beyond, the word _nt̠r_ certainly does not refer to a "god of the philosophers." I shall return in Chapter 4 to man as the "likeness (_snn_) of god" (l. 132), a phrase that occurs for the first time in this text.

In the slightly later instruction which is put in the mouth of the founder of the Twelfth Dynasty, Amenemhat I, the king is especially favored by the grain god and the god of the inundation. In another passage there is an allusion to the bark in which the sun god travels across the sky. There are similar mythological allusions in the later instruction texts, and the number of deities named in the texts increases in the New Kingdom and late period, no doubt as a result of changes in theology which led to a greater emphasis on visible forms.[62]

The very mixed terminology used by Egyptian teachers of wisdom ("god," "gods," individual gods' names, mythological allusions) does not permit one to speak of any properly defined "monotheism" in their texts, for there is never the exclusivity that must be part of any definition of monotheism. I shall consider below whether one may speak in a weaker sense, with Eberhard Otto, of "monotheistic tendencies" in this literary genre, tendencies that did not result in the exclusion of the multiplicity of polytheistic gods. First one must note that Egyptian religion, which retained its plurality of gods to the end, never became a monotheistic faith, even in its most "philosophically" tinged utterances. The authors of instructions from Ptahhotpe to the demotic texts do not hesitate to use the plural "gods" from time to time or to refer to the plurality of dei-

[62]Amenemope mentions by name the sun god Re (as well as various of his epithets and his uraeus), Khnum, Thoth, and the deities of destiny Shay and Renenet. In Ankhsheshonq, Hapy, Neith and Re are named, and in Pap. Insinger, Hathor, Horus, Isis, Mut, Re, Sakhmet, and Thoth, as well as the sacred bulls Apis and Mnevis.

ties by means of a plural suffix.[63] The instruction texts do not provide confirmation even of a monotheism within the religion that was professed only during particular periods and by particular individuals. Such a monotheism was certainly championed by Akhenaten in the late phase of his reforms, along with and in opposition to the beliefs of the people (see Chapter 7, second Excursus). Monotheism of this sort cannot easily accommodate the use of both singular and plural for gods, as is clearly shown by the case of Akhenaten.

The wisdom teachers' striking preference for the indefinite designation *nṯr* over the names of individual gods does, however, require explanation. We can use as a starting point an important observation by Vergote ("La notion de Dieu," 163). Amenemope, whose Instruction has been dated to the Ramessid period by recent research, makes clear and frequent allusions to Thoth, the god of writing and hence of literature and wisdom, but names him only once; in the other cases he designates him indirectly by invoking his manifestations, such as the ibis, baboon, or moon.

If we read carefully with this example in mind it is easy to observe that the *nṯr* of many instruction texts has clearly solar features, which leads one to suspect that the sun god is meant. Since the late Old Kingdom the sun god had been worshiped under various names as the most important deity and as the creator and sustainer of all creatures and things. In the light of our knowledge of other areas of Egyptian religion, the description in the Instruction for Merikare of *nṯr* as creator and sustainer and the designation of human beings as "images" or "likenesses" (*snn*) of this deity[64] fit the sun god only; an examination of later wisdom texts renders this suspicion a certainty.

In one of his maxims Ani speaks of how one should behave before "god" when he is in procession; then, before a further exhortation to observe the cult, there is the sentence "(The) god of this land is the sun in the horizon, and his images are

[63]Vergote, "La notion de Dieu," gives examples of the first usage; add Ankhsheshonq 2, x + 22; 3, x + 4. For cases with a suffix see Ptahhotpe ll. 118 (Sixth maxim, cited above, which speaks of "god"), 216, 218; Ani 6, 9.
[64]In later periods the "image" definitely describes a relationship of the king with the sun god, cf. Hornung, "Mensch als Bild Gottes."

on earth."[65] Like the author of the Instruction for Merikare, who gives practical instructions for behavior before "god" in the cult, Ani does not mean by *nt̠r* a "god of the philosophers," that is, one who is unknown to the masses, but a specific god with solar attributes who is worshiped in the cult and visible to all in processions; it need not be the old sun god Re, because in the New Kingdom, Amun, Ptah, Osiris, Khnum, and most of the other great gods and even goddesses of Egypt can be understood as solar deities. In the late instruction text in the Brooklyn papyrus the *nt̠r* seems clearly to be Re,[66] and Amenemope uses several times the name and various epithets of the sun god. In the demotic Instruction of Ankhsheshonq there is a litany in column 5, "If Re is angry with a land, then . . . ," which uses the old name of the sun god more than ten times in succession.[67]

Since there are no grounds for assuming that Ani or one of his predecessors introduced a completely new usage of the word *nt̠r* "god," it is possible that in the earlier instruction texts *nt̠r* conceals the sun god Re or another creator god (from the late Old Kingdom on, all creator gods have solar attributes and epithets). One must then, of course, ask why the wisdom teachers normally call him only "god," "your god," or "god of this land," and not Re, Amun, or Ptah. Vergote answers ("La notion de Dieu," 167) that for them the various gods with their individual names are only hypostases or manifestations of the One whom they call *nt̠r*. But if we admit this answer we must assume that the concept *nt̠r* is ambiguous, because it would then refer on the one hand to the deity worshiped in the cult (Ani, Instruction for Merikare, Papyrus Brooklyn 47.218.135), and on the other to the unique divine essence that revealed itself in the cult.

So long as we consider only the instruction texts, Vergote's answer and interpretation, in which he seeks to soften Drioton's harsh juxtaposition of monotheism and polytheism, seems quite possible. The idea that all gods are fundamentally mani-

[65]Volten, *Anii* 111 (7, 16).
[66]G. Posener in *Les sagesses* 156.
[67]S. R. K. Glanville, *Catalogue of Demotic Papyri in the British Museum* II *The Instructions of 'Onkhsheshonqy* (London 1955) 16–17.

festations or hypostases of another god occurs a number of times in Egyptian theology and religious poetry, especially of the New Kingdom. One example is the Litany of Re, first inscribed in tombs around 1500 B.C., which invokes the sun god, as in a litany, in "all his forms." In this case only forms appropriate to the underworld are included, but part of the pantheon, in any case, is thus turned into a set of differentiated manifestations of a single sun god.[68] There are also many hymns in which all deities are seen as forms of the one creator god who is being invoked. Vergote is therefore citing a phenomenon that is well attested in Egyptian religion and which I shall consider in more detail in Chapter 7 under the heading of "henotheism."

It must be said at once, however, that in one respect Vergote's interpretation cannot be retained. The one god who reveals himself in millions of forms and in all other divine names always has a specific, traditional name, whether it is Re, Amun, Ptah, or some other. Even Akhenaten called his unique god the "Aten," never simply "god"; indeed, as we shall see, he was distinctly wary of the designation *nṯr* and avoided or replaced it as much as possible. When, after the Amarna period, the tri-unity of god is postulated for the first time in the Leiden hymn to Amun, the text does not say "god reveals himself in three forms"; the plural form is used: "*All* gods are three: Amun, Re, and Ptah. . . . *His* name is hidden as Amun, *he* is perceived as Re, *his* body is Ptah"[69]—a plural that is taken up again by a singular suffix.

Up till now we have found no examples in Egyptian texts in which the one god who is behind the gods may have been referred to simply as *nṯr* "god." The assumption that the wisdom teachers meant by *nṯr* the one, highest god of the theologians is therefore most questionable, not to say improbable, even if it cannot be rigorously disproved. But in rejecting this explanation we are again confronted by the question of why the instruction texts invoke simply "god" so much more often than any proper name of a god.

In order to find an adequate solution and explanation we

[68]Hornung, *Buch der Anbetung*; Piankoff, *Litany.*
[69]Stanza "300": Zandee, *De hymnen aan Amon* pl. 4, 21–22.

should start from the social context of didactic literature among the Egyptians. The instruction texts are not philosophical treatises and do not seek to make definitive statements about god, the world, and "last things," but are addressed to the pupil who is being introduced to the way of the world and given incidentally practical tips and pragmatic advice about how he should behave. The issue is how one should behave in concrete, precisely defined situations in relation to one's fellow human beings—superiors, colleagues, and subordinates—and also before the gods. The people who moved in official circles, to whom the instructions were addressed, were concerned not just with their local gods, but with a variety of deities. Royal business could take them to the remotest provinces of the country or even abroad, and hence into the often closely circumscribed areas of influence of quite different deities. Even the chief deity of the time could change with a new king or a new royal residence; in the Old Kingdom there was neither an unchanging chief deity nor an unchanging deity of the residence.

As a rule, Egyptian officials did not need to have contact in their work or in private with the totality of the pantheon, but with a particular single deity, who might change from situation to situation. Therefore the wisdom teachers seldom use the plural "gods," and use a divine proper name, such as Khnum, only when a specific characteristic or activity of that deity is meant—in the case of Khnum; his forming mankind on the potter's wheel. Otherwise they fall back on the undefined word "god," not in order to characterize a god of the highest order who is by nature anonymous, but as a neutral term that will cover any individual deity and hence any particular situation that the pupil, and later the official, might encounter.

A statement like "god created humanity" could claim general validity, whether one wished to address Ptah, Re, or Khnum as the creator; "Ptah created humanity," on the other hand, would have been a one-sided theological affirmation that could claim validity only in specific contexts. Because of the wisdom teachers' position in the state (the earliest were all viziers, that is, the highest officials) and because of their aims in writing the texts, they could not restrict themselves to one-sided propaganda for a cult. The "god" they refer to is any god the person being addressed might encounter in a particular situation; or, as Henri Frankfort put it aptly and clearly in 1948, "the god with whom you have to reckon in the circumstances."[70]

In rare cases, as with Ani and his "sun in the horizon," the Egyptian wise men leave one in no doubt as to who they mean by their undefined "god"; but as a rule the reference is deliberately left vague. If we free ourselves from monotheistic preconceptions there is no longer any need to assume that there are completely different usages of the word "god." In addition to its occurrence in instruction texts, personal names and titles, the general, indefinite usage is attested in yet other categories of texts, for example, the Onomasticon of Amenemope. This taxonomic list of the New Kingdom is presented, like the instruction texts, as a didactic work; it is meant to record the entire inventory of living and dead features of the cosmos. In it the general term "god" heads the listing of living beings, and is supplemented by the feminine "goddess."[71] Here, of course, what is meant is all the divine beings of the cosmos (divided into genders); they do not then need to be recorded individually—if they had been, the onomasticon would have extended endlessly. *nt̠r* is the abstract, general concept. Every god is a *nt̠r*, and the word is occasionally placed like a title before the proper name of a god.[72]

If one is saved from danger and is in doubt as to which deity to thank, one addresses in general whichever "god" it was or offers to the "gods" all together; there are many examples of this practice in the stories of the Shipwrecked Sailor and of Sinuhe. On a group of scarabs inscribed with religious maxims the use of "god" is evidently intended to extend the validity of the maxim.[73] In funerary texts the deceased occasionally depart from the normal usage and do not identify themselves with specific deities. Spell 411 of the Coffin Texts contains several occurrences of the statement " 'God' is my name. I do not for-

---

[70]*Religion* 67.

[71]Gardiner, *Onomastica* I, 13*.

[72]G. Roeder, *ASAE* 52 (1954) 341 l. 16 "god Thoth" (Nineteenth Dyn.).

[73]E. Drioton, "Maximes morales sur les scarabées égyptiens," *Latomus* 28 (1957) 197–202. On the scarabs Drioton published in *BSFE* 19 (1955) quite specific deities are addressed as the "lords" of the wearers.

get it, this name of mine" (*CT* V, 236–38). As well as invoking specific deities, the deceased wishes to prove that he is one of them by calling himself *ntr*.

In the biographical inscriptions that were set up in Egyptian tombs from the Fourth Dynasty on, the deceased addresses officials or priests of the royal residence to whom his own local god, whom he may have in mind, very probably means little. Here too the general validity of the word *ntr* is of assistance, just as in biographical inscriptions of officials the "King" under whom they served may be referred to, not the name of a particular king. We must return without reservation to the view formulated by Hermann Kees in 1941:

> In my opinion the general invocation of "god," which is found in the wisdom instructions from Ptahhotpe on, reveals nothing of this special belief [that is, Junker's "primal monotheism"]. This literature laid claim to general validity, so that the speaker did not intend to trouble any local god who was anchored within a local [theological] system. "God" therefore stands simply for "(any) god" . . . . In addition, there are numerous examples in Egyptian texts . . . where the anonymous highest god was not meant, but the author felt it important that the hearer should be free to choose which particular god he understood as being implied by "god."[74]

Kees's argument was directed against the notion of Egyptian primal monotheism proposed by Hermann Junker under the influence of Father Wilhelm Schmidt. But, as Pierre Montet pointed out in the discussion of Vergote's Strasbourg lecture,[75] it applies just as much to Drioton and Vergote's idea of a special monotheism of Egyptian wisdom teachers.

Our survey of the sources has shown that by *ntr* the Egyptians meant "whichever god you wish." Sometimes this is a particular god, such as Amun, Re, Ptah, and so on, in which case a demonstrative pronoun is often added; in the underworld books, for example, the sun god is almost always called "this god" or "this great god." In other cases "god" is used when the hearer or reader may himself choose to put a particular proper name in place of the general concept *ntr*, but with-

[74]*Götterglaube* 273.
[75]In *Les sagesses* 186–87.

59

out excluding the other possibilities, that is, all the remaining proper names of gods.

So far it has not been possible to prove in any example, even in the instruction texts, that an Egyptian meant by "god" either the Only—without there being any other god—or the One and Highest of the gods. Contrary to what is continually asserted in imprecise terms, the Egyptian concept of god never included monotheistic notions within its terminology; even henotheistic or pantheistic notions cannot be certainly identified in the use of the word "god." This observation does not affect the issue of whether the "god" of the wisdom teachers should be considered a monotheistic god because of his attributes. I shall examine this question in Chapter 5, when I turn to the characteristics of Egyptian deities. I shall reserve also for that chapter the study of such designations as "the greatest god" and "the only god," limiting myself for the moment to a consideration of the basic concepts. To establish what a *nṯr* is requires an examination of all his aspects.

Other basic terms for divine forces

Since the word *nṯr* occurs in the earliest written material available to us, the existence of earlier terms for divine forces cannot be proved; those that have been proposed are conjectural. Wolfgang Helck, for example, wished to see in the word *b'w* an older designation of local *numina,* because of the use of *b'w* for the "souls" (as they are conventionally translated) of Buto, Hierakonpolis, Heliopolis, or Hermopolis.[76]

These "souls" have been interpreted in various ways. Sethe considered that they were ancient, deceased kings of these places,[77] while for Kees they were "certain very ancient groups of deities of these places, whose number and nature is not fixed,"[78] so that he does not restrict the terms to kings. Among recent interpretations Louis V. Žabkar's[79] is close to Sethe's;

---

[76]*ArOr* 18 (1950) 139.

[77]*Urgeschichte* §§172–73 and *passim;* also Bonnet, *Reallexikon* 129.

[78]In Bonnet, *Reallexikon* 74; cf. also Kees, *Götterglaube* 188–91. For a survey of opinions see Žabkar, *Ba Concept* 16–17.

[79]*Ba Concept* 15–36.

Elske Marie Wolf-Brinkmann,[80] on the other hand, reaffirms the view of Kees, and probably interprets the material more satisfactorily. As early as the Pyramid Texts (*Pyr.* §1689) the "two enneads (of gods)" seem to form part of the "souls" of Heliopolis, while in the Coffin Texts well-known deities are included among the various "souls."[81] Where the *b*ʾ*w* are personal beings we may therefore take them to be "divine beings" in the broadest sense, who are sometimes identical with the "gods."[82]

There is an older usage of the word *b*ʾ*w*, which is attested in early dynastic personal names and more frequently in the Old Kingdom.[83] Statements are made about the abstract *b*ʾ*w* of particular gods (Khnum, Ptah, Sokar) and goddesses (Hathor, Sakhmet), and about the *b*ʾ*w* of the *ka* and of the king.[84] This *b*ʾ*w* can "manifest itself" (*ḫ*ʾ*j*), and in all clear examples means an efficacy that emanates from the deity; at first it has a quite positive impact on the world, but in later periods it becomes more and more often negative. In the general collapse of the world the author of the Admonitions of Ipuwer can no longer discern the *b*ʾ*w* of the creator god, while an expedition leader of the Eleventh Dynasty ascribes his success to the *b*ʾ*w* of Min.[85] In the New Kingdom, on the other hand, the *b*ʾ*w* of god causes a devastating storm that is recorded in a stela of King Ahmose,[86] and in the New Kingdom and late period *b*ʾ*w* means quite clearly the "anger" or the "rage" of a deity;[87] in Coptic, finally, it means "act of violence, crime."[88]

---

[80]*Versuch einer Deutung des Begriffes 'b3' anhand der Überlieferung der Frühzeit und des Alten Reiches* (Dissertation, Basel 1966; Freiburg im Breisgau 1968) 64–84.

[81]References in Žabkar, *Ba Concept* 29.

[82]As in *Pyr.* spell 217 (cf. Wolf-Brinkmann, *Versuch,* n. 80 above, 77) and *Amduat* II, 63 no. (10).

[83]Examples collected by Wolf-Brinkmann, *Versuch* (n. 80 above) 17–24.

[84]Certain cases in the names of estates, *ibid.* 26–27.

[85]Both cited *ibid.* 87. In *CT* IV, 146m the inundation is the *b*ʾ*w* of the god Hapy.

[86]C. Vandersleyen, *RdE* 19 (1967) pl. 9 l. 14. There too "god" is in the undefined singular.

[87]A. H. Gardiner, *JEA* 48 (1962) 62 n. 3; particularly clear example Edwards, *Decrees* pl. 23 l. 84 (contrasted with *ḥtp*). As early as the Ramessid period the *b*ʾ*w* of the king is "(worse) than death": see M. A. Green, in J. Ruffle et al., eds., *Glimpses of Ancient Egypt: Studies in Honour of H. W. Fairman* (Warminster 1979) 108 (list of examples), 111–12 (with a different interpretation).

[88]*bēu*: R. Kasser, *Compléments au Dictionnaire copte de Crum* (IFAO Bibl. d'Etudes coptes 7, 1964) 9 R.

The original meaning of *b'w* must have been more concrete than is implied by the renderings "fame" or "esteem." As is so often the case, it is probably impossible to find a truly equivalent word in a modern language. Such translations as "might," "will," or more recently "energy, creative power" (Wolf-Brinkmann) do not fit all examples, and at best overlap only to a limited extent with the true meaning of the Egyptian word. It seems certain that *b'w* always refers to an active, visible side of the divine person, and is the vehicle, and perhaps also the cause, of the actions of the gods, just as visible activity is an important characteristic of the conception of the *ba*.[89] The equivalence of action and person, so that deities are termed *b'w*, is certainly not the beginning of the word's history, but is attested from an early period. There is a comparable development in the concept of *z'* "magical protection"; in the Old Kingdom this is a function of deities,[90] but on the apotropaic "magic wands" of the Middle Kingdom it means the protective demons depicted on these objects and alternates with *ntrw* "gods."[91] It is not surprising that terms for the deceased, such as *'hw* "transfigured spirits" or *d'tjw* "underworld dwellers," are also drawn into this circle of interchangeable concepts, for the dead are called "gods" from an early period on.

After *ntr*, *shm* is undoubtedly the next most important Egyptian term for gods. It is normally translated "power," and thus evokes associations with the term *numen* used in the historical study of religions and leads us to the much disputed question of whether there were "powers" before there were "gods."[92] Analysis of the terminology cannot solve this problem; the most we can say is that, like *b'w* and *ntr*, *shm* occurs in the earliest Egyptian texts, and so cannot be proved to be older or younger than the other two words. I have studied elsewhere

---

[89]In the underworld books the *ba* of the deceased is the part that is visibly active, conversing, for example, with the sun god, finding its place in the god's retinue, or going to meet the corpse.

[90]For the Pyramid Texts see van der Leeuw, *Godsvoorstellingen* 27–30.

[91]H. Altenmüller, *Die Apotropaia und die Götter Mittelägyptens* I (Dissertation, Munich 1965) 67.

[92]E.g. Morenz, *Gott und Mensch* 33: "I believe that man knew powers before he comprehended gods."

the later evolution of the meaning of *shm*, which comes to mean "image (of a god)" in the New Kingdom.[93] The oldest clear examples of *shm* seem to refer, like those of *b'w*, to an active emanation of deities or a charisma, so that it embodies an "impersonal power"[94] that can attach to any individual deity and is additionally visible in the *shm* scepter which is held by officials as a symbol of authority. Inasmuch as the deceased becomes a "god," he also acquires the quality of being *shm* (*Pyr.* §§752b–753a). In the Pyramid Texts there are many parallel statements about the *ba* and the *shm* "power" or "might."[95] The name of the goddess Sakhmet shows that she is the "mightiest one," while in later periods Amun in his role as supreme god acquires a similar epithet ("mightiest of the mighty");[96] in the enemy god Seth the same power has a negative effect.[97] Since all deities possess this characteristic of being *shm*, the plural of the word can alternate with the plural "gods";[98] not until the Ptolemaic period is there a clear case of its being used merely for a specific group of deities of a particular locality.[99]

Images of deities are designated by another extensive range of terms which will be discussed in Chapter 4.

The adjective "divine"

From the time of the Old Kingdom Pyramid Texts on, a large number of beings and things are stated to be "divine," through use of the adjective "divine" or of the adjective verb "to be divine" (*ntrj*). This is, of course, an attribute of all deities, but, as with *shm*, some deities are "divine" in greater measure than others; Isis above all is simply "the divine one," or "great of

---

[93]Hornung, "Mensch als Bild Gottes" 137–39.

[94]As van der Leeuw calls it in his study of *shm* in the Pyramid Texts (*Godsvoorstellingen* 22–25).

[95]*Ibid.* 17ff.

[96]New Kingdom and later examples are given in *Wb.* IV, 244, 7; see also E. Drioton, *ASAE* 44 (1944) 14) (Karnak, Ptolemaic).

[97]Moret, *Rituel* 9.

[98]*Pyr.* §894d, cf. P. Kaplony, *Kleine Beiträge zu den Inschriften der ägyptischen Frühzeit* (ÄgAbh 15, 1966) 63 with n. 238.

[99]For the specific deities of a place, such as the ennead of a temple chapel: A. Gutbub, *Kêmi* 17 (1964) 46 with references in n. 4.

divine-ness."[100] Among the range of persons and things that can be "divine" listed in the *Wörterbuch der ägyptischen Sprache* (*Wb.* II, 363–64), only living human beings are absent. Sacred animals, sacred objects, and the blessed dead are often "divine," but here again the terminology preserves the distance between those living on earth and the gods. Even the reigning king, whose titulary makes him a "perfect god" and who receives innumerable divine epithets, is qualified by the adjective "divine" only in rare and exceptional cases.[101]

Characteristic of such exceptional cases is a text that attributes to Queen Hatshepsut the quality *nt̲rj* "divine-ness." At the return of the great trading expedition that Hatshepsut sent to the distant African incense land of Punt, the assembled subjects adore and acclaim the queen "in the instances (*zpw*) of her divine-ness" and "because of the greatness of the marvel that happened for her" (*Urk.* IV, 340, 5–6). This is not an everyday event or action of the queen, but a solemn and exalted moment when her divine-ness is manifest to the whole world, when her vow to the King of the Gods, Amun, that she will make his terrace temple into an incense land in the midst of Egypt, is about to be fulfilled. The queen regnant shows herself to be "divine" through her divine aroma and the golden radiance, both of which emanate from the gods (see Chapter 4). Although clear examples such as this one are rare, it seems to be this special emanation, which can be perceived by humans, that makes human beings, animals, or sacred objects into "divine" entities.

Divine-ness is therefore not a matter of a definition that is fixed by an abstract statement of dogma, but an emanation that can be perceived directly and is produced not only by the gods but also by their images and manifestations. It should not be forgotten, also, that *nt̲rj* is an adjective of the *nisbe* type whose basic meaning is "belonging to (a) god," and therefore can at times have nuances other than "divine."

This divine-ness or state of belonging to god is a quality that

---

[100]For the first epithet cf. *Wb.* II, 364, 22; the second occurs once in the Twenty-first Dynasty: Edwards, *Decrees* 103 no. (1).

[101]E.g. *Medinet Habu* VIII pl. 636 ll. 1–2, in an unusually informal scene with the king.

is always attributed to personal divine forces and their emana-
tions; it never becomes an abstract idea or a personified concept behind, above, or in addition to the gods. For the Egyptians there was nothing that was simply "divine" separate from
the figures of specific gods. This is one reason why we should
exercise great restraint in using this neutral term for the description of Egyptian religion, or, better still, dispense with it
altogether.

We can now pass on from the Egyptian terminology. Although it has helped to provide some illuminating insights,
it has not been able to take us to the heart of our problem.
In order to make Egyptian conceptions of god emerge more
clearly we must turn to the realities for which the terminology
was devised. As with every individual deity, we can attempt to
define the nature of the gods in general, according to the three
criteria of the seventh Platonic letter (342a–b): *onoma* (name),
logos (definition), and *eidōlon* (image), which together provide
epistēmē, true knowledge and insight into the nature of what
we are studying.[102] I shall therefore examine, in a rather different
order from that of Plato, first the names of the gods, then the
image the Egyptians had of the gods and the form in which
they are represented, and finally what the texts say about the
attributes, nature, and actions of the gods.

[102]Cf. E. Otto, *Saeculum* 14 (1963) 271 with n. 55.

3 ∿ Names and Combinations of Gods

Introduction

Many of the names of Egyptian deities allude to particular characteristics of their holders, and the full range of their meaning will therefore be discussed in Chapter 5. Among such cases are very important deities such as Amun "the hidden one" or Sakhmet "the mighty one (feminine)," as well as all the primeval deities, who embody characteristics of the chaotic world before creation: Nun, the "weary" or "inert" primeval flood, Huh "endlessness," Kuk "darkness." Atum, the earliest creator god for whom we have evidence, also seems to have a similar self-explanatory name, which is, however, more difficult to interpret. The verb *tm*, of which the name is a participial formation, can mean "not to be" or alternatively "to be complete." It is not easy to reduce these two to a single formulation, and modern translators of the god's name often resort to detailed definitions. To cite just a few examples, Rudolf Anthes interprets it as "he who is an entirety,"[1] Hans Bonnet as "he who is not yet complete,"[2] and Hermann Kees as "he who is not yet present."[3] I myself believe that "the undifferentiated one" is a more apt rendering because it includes both aspects; but this too is only an imperfect attempt to translate Egyptian

---

[1]*ZÄS* 82 (1957) 2, with further definitions; cf. *id., ZÄS* 80 (1955) 86; *JNES* 18 (1959) 209–10.

[2]*Reallexikon* 71, referring to *CT* II, 174e.

[3]*Götterglaube* 215, and similarly S. Schott, *ZÄS* 78 (1943) 9; but see also Kees, *OLZ* 46 (1943) 404: "that which does not yet exist completely."

terminology into our own. Atum is the god who "in the begin-ning was everything,"[4] complete in the sense of being an undif-ferentiated unity and at the same time nonexistent, because existence is impossible before his work of creation.

Of the most important Egyptian gods only a small number have names whose meaning is more or less clear and assists us toward a better understanding of their nature and function; most have names of quite uncertain meaning. No convincing etymology has yet been given for Re, Min, Ptah, Osiris, or Seth, although many hypotheses have been put forward. The Egyptians themselves relished wordplay and the coincidence of words and concepts, and they too tried their hand at providing etymologies for these names,[5] so that Osiris was interpreted as "the strong one" or "the many-eyed one,"[6] and Re as "the one who ascends."[7] Papyrus Jumilhac gives examples of the fantas-tic wordplays and explanations concocted by Egyptians of the Ptolemaic period; Anubis is interpreted as, among other things, the "wind-water-mountain."[8]

In form and meaning the modern "scientific" etymologies are no more credible than these Egyptian "folk etymologies"; Osiris, for example, has been interpreted variously[9] as "seat of the eye," "the occupier-of-the-throne" (that is, king),[10] "he with the forelock,"[11] or as an offshoot of a foreign deity like the

[4]Goethe, *Faust* Part I, l. 1349; this is the implication of the phrase *jtmw nb tm*, CT III, 27b.

[5]For the importance of the name in general see H. Brunner, in H. von Stieten-cron, ed., *Der Name Gottes* (Düsseldorf 1975) 33–45; Piankoff, *Litany* 3–9.

[6]Plutarch, *De Iside et Osiride* 37: J. G. Griffiths, *Plutarch's De Iside et Osiride* (University of Wales 1970) 176–77, *ombrimos*, from *wsr* "strong"; 10 (Griffiths 132–33): *polyophthalmos*, from *ʿš'-jrt* "many-eyed." The former derivation has been proposed again by J. G. Griffiths, *The Origins of Osiris and His Cult* (SHR 40, 1980 [1st ed., *The Origins of Osiris* (MAS 9, 1966) 60]) 94–95. F. Zimmer-mann, *Die ägyptische Religion nach der Darstellung der Kirchenschriftsteller* (Pader-born 1912) 42 n. 2, gives examples of the wordplay *Wsjr/wsr*.

[7]Wordplay with *(j)ʿr* "ascend, approach," e.g. *Amduat* I, 20, 1–2; Moret, *Rituel* 135 ll. 10–11.

[8]J. Vandier, *Le papyrus Jumilhac* ([Paris 1961]) 102–3, with further interpreta-tions.

[9]Survey in Griffiths, *Origins* (n. 6 above) 87–99.

[10]H. S. K. Bakry, *ASAE* 59 (1966) 1, following M. A. Murray.

[11]P. Kaplony, *Kleine Beiträge zu den Inschriften der ägyptischen Frühzeit* (ÄgAbh 15, 1966) 69–70; see the criticisms of W. Barta, *BiOr* 25 (1969) 176.

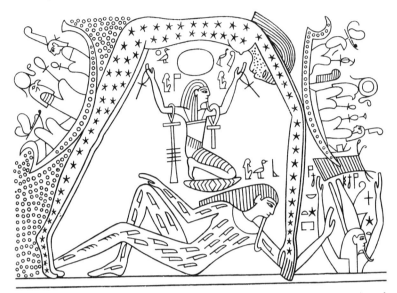

Figure 4. Shu separates the sky and the earth (shown in the form of Geb and Nut).

Assyrian chief god Assur. These are all at best "vague speculations," and scholars have not been able to offer anything better; the same is true of interpretations of the name Ptah.[12] Both the "origin" of Osiris, Seth, or Ptah and the meaning of their names remain enigmas to us.

It is striking that the names of the "cosmic" deities of Egypt, unlike those of Greece, are not the same as the words for the elements in the cosmos which they embody. The earth is *t'* but the earth god is Geb, and the sky is *pt* but the sky goddess is Nut (Figure 4); the sun god Re stands beside *jtn*, the term for the sun disk, and the moon is called *j'ḥ*, while the two early moon gods are Thoth (*Dḥwtj*, no plausible etymology) and Khons (probably "the wanderer"). This distinction between names and phenomena should warn us against hastily dubbing a deity a "moon god" or an "earth god"—the nature of Egyptian cosmic deities is much richer and more multifarious.

---

[12]M. Sandman Holmberg, *The God Ptah* (Lund 1946) 7–11. On comparable efforts with the name Seth cf. te Velde, *Seth* 3–7.

Apart from these divine names whose meaning is no longer clear, there were from the beginning of history "divine names with clear conceptual reference," whose holders are often, following Hermann Usener,[13] termed "special gods" (*Sondergötter*). In his *Die ägyptische Religion nach der Darstellung der Kirchenschriftsteller* (Paderborn 1912), Friedrich Zimmermann devoted a separate chapter to Egyptian "special gods," among which he included gods in plant form and the decans. But other egyptologists have not adopted Usener's terminology of "special gods" and "momentary gods" (*Augenblicksgötter*), and rightly so, for it is ill suited to the nature of Egyptian deities. Only personified functions, such as the "tetherer" who ties up the damned in the underworld, the "destroyer" who destroys them, the "devourer of the dead," and similar demonic beings[14] can be considered "special gods" in Usener's sense, and these too the Egyptians tended to see not as independent deities but as manifestations of the "great" gods. These latter, however, are not restricted to a single concept, as Usener's "special gods" are: the "mighty" Sakhmet, for example, or the cataract god Khnum, whose name is probably connected with the word for "well," are many-sided and so cannot be categorized as "special gods."

In the case of Khnum, on the other hand, there arises the question of geographical restrictions, which are certainly more relevant to Egyptian deities than conceptual restrictions. Khnum is the local god of Elephantine, the large island in the Nile north of the rapids of the first cataract which was for millennia the southern frontier of Egypt. His main sanctuary was in the southern part of the island,[15] where the goddesses Anukis and Satis were worshiped along with him. These deities are invoked especially in the countless inscriptions of quarrying ex-

[13]*Götternamen: Versuch einer Lehre von der religiösen Begriffsbildung* (Bonn 1896, 3d ed. Frankfurt a.M. 1948). On "special gods" see pp. 75ff.

[14]The god of fishing Khededu (*Ḥddw*, see B. Grdseloff, *BIFAO* 45 [1947] 181 with n. 1; Baines, *Fecundity Figures* §2.3.2 n. 1) may belong here, if the category has any validity.

[15]H. Ricke and S. Sauneron, *Der Tempel Nektanebos' II in Elephantine* (Beiträge Bf 6, 1960). On Khnum see Ahmad Mohamad Badawi, *Der Gott Chnum* (Glückstadt etc. 1937). For preliminary reports on the recent excavations see W. Kaiser et al., *MDAIK* 26ff. (1970ff.).

peditions in the first cataract region; for the expedition leaders and their subordinates they were protective deities of the area, within whose sphere of influence the expeditions were working. The other places with cults of Khnum and the two goddesses are not so significant.

The results of the recent excavations suggest that Elephantine was of some importance in the early dynastic period, but from the time of King Huni (c. 2580 B.C.) it became politically and strategically much more prominent. We do not, however, encounter Khnum, or the goddesses associated with him, in the cataract area until much later.

The generally accepted view is that locally based deities acquired a wider currency only gradually, through shifts in political and religious power, but the opposite can be shown to be true of the deities of the cataract area. In inscriptions and especially in personal names of the early dynastic period Khnum is named with striking frequency,[16] but no special connection with Elephantine can be seen. Satis is also found several times in the same material;[17] only Anukis, who was later considered to be the daughter of the other two,[18] appears to be absent. This means that these apparently local deities were already important in the early centers of royal rule, Memphis and Abydos, and must doubtless have possessed cults there. Khnum also occurs quite often in the names of servants of the Fourth and Fifth dynasties.[19]

One must therefore be careful not to interpret the history of Egyptian religion as the gradual rise of local deities to universal acceptance in the entire land, concomitant with a continuing extension of their natures until they acquired a universal meaning. The example of the Khnum/Satis illustrates how acceptance could be universal—chiefly in the royal residence and

[16]Kaplony, *Inschriften* I, 463, 468, 498, 546–47, 550, 604 etc.; see also I, 376 with n. 1863; I, 406–11, and *Supplement* (ÄgAbh 9, 1964) 11, 13; E. Schott, *RdE* 21 (1969) 77–83.

[17]Kaplony, *Inschriften* I, 425, 428–29, 597, 644(?), 655.

[18]Labib Habachi, *ASAE* 50 (1950) 501–7.

[19]B. L. Begelsbacher-Fischer, *Untersuchungen zur Götterwelt des Alten Reichs* (Orbis Biblicus et Orientalis 37, Fribourg and Göttingen 1981) 43–45.

among the intellectual elite of the court—at the very beginning of recorded history.

Other examples of this phenomenon abound. The goddess Neith (perhaps "the terrifying one"), whom we connect primarily with Sais, her chief cult center in the Nile delta, had from the First Dynasty on a dominant role at the royal court, a role that survived a number of religious and political changes. Even relatively minor deities are revealed on close inspection to have a surprisingly wide currency. Jacques Vandier presented an unusually full documentation for the "Heliopolitan" goddesses Iusaas and Nebethetepet,[20] showing how much importance was accorded, in all the temples of the land, to these deities who at first sight seem to have a strongly local character. It would, of course, be possible in this case to cite in explanation the geographical and intellectual proximity of the royal residence; similarly, a "political" explanation of the position of the goddess Neith has been attempted—that she is the representative at the residence of Lower Egypt, which had been placed in subjection by Upper Egypt. Thus Khnum and Satis provide a more telling example, because in their case no "political" explanation can be found. Elephantine first gained great political importance under its potentates of the late Sixth Dynasty, and although the source of the Nile was located there, as a religious center it never had a discernible influence on the country as a whole.

There were of course in Egypt's long history deities whose importance was at first purely local and who gradually—or suddenly—became dominant in the entire land, and, as a visible sign of their new position, placed the kingship under their protection. This is the case with the hawk-headed god Mont, who was worshiped in the Theban nome, and whose first occurrence in royal inscriptions is in the Sixth Dynasty. The earliest certain examples of his name[21] are all from the reign of Phiops I

[20]*RdE* 16 (1964)–18 (1966), also published as a separate volume; supplement *RdE* 20 (1968) 135–48. See especially the remark *RdE* 16, 123: "It seems thus that the goddesses of Heliopolis had a more important role in the cosmogony of theologians than in local religion."

[21]*Pyr.* §§1081a–b, 1378b; cylinder seal, H. Goedicke, *MDAIK* 17 (1961) 80–81 (no. XII).

(c. 2292–2260 B.C.), whose widespread building activities display a newly kindled interest in the provinces and their deities. The earliest known representation of Mont dates to the end of the Sixth Dynasty (c. 2200).[22] For the Theban Eleventh Dynasty of a century later, which united the country a second time, Mont occupied the leading position among all deities—until he was displaced by Amun. The rise of Re, Osiris, and Amun[23] to a dominant position in Egyptian religion was as sudden as that of Mont, but I think it is meaningless to interpret these complex, universal deities as having originally been local deities. The emphasis on local cults, which has prevailed since the time of Carl Richard Lepsius,[24] is too one-sided and needs correcting. In addition to clearly local gods, whose existence should certainly not be denied, there is a circle of gods, attested from the earliest inscriptions of the thirtieth century B.C., who were current at the royal court as well as having their own cult places, which may already have been spread over the whole country.

Genuinely local deities can often be recognized by a particular form of name, which is derived directly from the place where they are manifest. Thus the vulture goddess of Nekheb (el-Kab) is called Nekhbet, the heron god of the delta city Buto (ḏbˤw) is Djebauti, and the anthropomorphic god of the ninth Lower Egyptian nome (ˤnḏt), who was assimilated early to Osiris, is Anedjti. Other local and nome deities owe their names to specific topographical features—"he who is on his lake" (Ḥrjšf, Greek Harsaphes), for example, is the name of the chief god of Herakleopolis—or to typical features of their manifestation, as with Pakhet, "tearer apart," who was worshiped as a lioness at the mouths of wadis. Khentamenti, "foremost before the Westerners" (later a manifestation of Osiris) who was worshiped at Abydos, has as a name a paraphrase that

---

[22]In the mortuary temple of Phiops II, see G. Jéquier, *Le monument funéraire de Pepi II* II (Service des Antiquités de l'Egypte, Fouilles à Saqqarah, Cairo 1938) 47. A Second Dynasty example (Kaplony, *Inschriften* I, 467) is very doubtful.

[23]According to F. Daumas, *BIFAO* 65 (1967) 213–14, the earliest certain example of the "Theban" Amun also dates to the time of Phiops I; but see D. Wildung, *MDAIK* 25 (1969) 212–19.

[24]*Götterkreis* 173 = 17: "Nowhere was the influence of local cults on general priestly theology so strong as in Egypt."

leaves the deity fundamentally anonymous. These indefinite, general name forms show that the influence of these deities is restricted in space but never channeled into specialized areas of activity; it acquires an all-encompassing breadth, and represents the entire extent of divine power,[25] as it were focused by a lens on a single point in the world.

By an early date the Egyptians had created a still more general term, which means simply "local god."[26] The earliest known example is the early dynastic statue of a cloaked anthropomorphic deity in the Kofler-Truniger collection in Lucerne, which has a hieroglyphic inscription *njwtj* "belonging to the city."[27] There was thus available a phrase—one that occurs very frequently—comparable in its indefiniteness and generality with the use of "god" in personal names and instruction texts. Criminals could be handed over to "the judgment of the king, Osiris, or their local god"[28] without its being defined more closely who was responsible for the judgment, or visitors to tombs could be addressed as devotees of their own local gods (*Urk.* I, 268, 13); as with the *ntr* of the wisdom teachers, one could thus avoid referring too narrowly to a particular deity. An indication that the significance of local gods should not be interpreted strictly as confined to a particular place is their occurrence in the Pyramid Texts (*Pyr.* §891a), the royal burial ritual of the Old Kingdom.[29]

One must distinguish clearly between the old local deities with their often indefinite, descriptive names, and the local manifestations of the "great gods," such as Amun of Karnak,

---

[25]Paraphrasing Bonnet, *Reallexikon* 218, where there are further penetrating remarks about local deities.

[26]*ntr-njwtj*, literally "town god," although *njwt* means not just "town" but any settlement: see M. Atzler, "Erwägungen zur Stadt im Alten Reich" (Dissertation, Leipzig 1968). There is no monograph on the phenomenon of the "local god" and its meaning.

[27]H. W. Müller, *Ägyptische Kunstwerke, Kleinfunde und Glas in der Sammlung E. und M. Kofler-Truniger, Luzern* (MÄS 5, 1964) 40–41; also illustrated in W. Wolf, *Frühe Hochkulturen* (Belser Stilgeschichte 1, Stuttgart 1969) fig. 21.

[28]*Urk.* I, 305, 15–306, 1. The "local god" is also named as a judge in *Urk.* I, 78, 9.

[29]"Local gods" and "nome gods" are also named in the plural in a list of the entirety of the gods in *Pyr.* §1522c.

Re of Sakhebu, or the various provincial Horuses. These forms do not constitute a distillation of the function and significance of all divine power, but focus on a quite specific deity for the benefit of a limited "congregation." In many cases, however, one may suspect that local forms like these adopt the heritage of local deities and gain a universal meaning that is similar to theirs.

Personifications

Localities and nomes may also be personified. If a particular place was experienced in personal form, a personification could be created anew at any time during the historical period. Thus in the Eighteenth Dynasty there appears a goddess Khefther-nebes personifying the Theban necropolis, whose name she bears. She is important in the papyri of the Twenty-first Dynasty,[30] but then disappears from texts and pictures. Even so short-lived a deity as this should not be called a "free invention" or an "empty abstraction";[31] ancient cultures had a capacity, which is difficult for us to comprehend, for encountering their environment in personal form—for seeing the face of a deity in a salient or even an insignificant feature of the landscape, such as a tree or an animal.

In Egyptian religion there are other, much older "personifications" who remained the objects of belief for millennia. The most important is the goddess Maat (Figure 5), the personification of the order of the world which was established at the time of creation, who was for Adolf Erman "no more than an empty

[30]A. Piankoff and N. Rambova, *Mythological Papyri* (ERT 3, 1957) *passim*; E. Chassinat, *BIFAO* 3 (1903) 142. See also A. H. Gardiner, *The Wilbour Papyrus* II (London 1948) 27 n. 2; W. Helck, *MDAIK* 23 (1968) 119–20. Helck also documents a personification W'st-nḫtt "victorious Thebes," who is found from the second intermediate period on (*id.*, *Historisch-biographische Inschriften der 2. Zwischenzeit* . . . [Kleine Ägyptische Texte, Wiesbaden 1975] 45 l. 5 of original), but she can scarcely be a development of Thebes, as he suggests; she is more likely to be an independent goddess.

[31]Erman, *Religion* 1st ed. 24, 3d ed. 57, on the personification of Maat. B. Grdseloff still followed him (*ASAE* 40 [1940] 193), and even J. Vandier suggested that the goddess Iusaas, like the ennead, was "created in Heliopolis by theologians" (*RdE* 18 [1966] 120 n. 4).

74

Figure 5. The goddess Maat.

abstraction." But this "empty abstraction" was imbued with the reality of a cult, having her own priesthood from the Fifth Dynasty at the latest,[32] and, in the New Kingdom, temples in a number of different places. In the Theban area we find a "scribe and overseer of the cattle of Maat" in the cortege of the vizier Ramose,[33] and the "herds" of her temple in Thebes are mentioned in a Ramessid tomb.[34] Evidence for a cult of her in the delta includes the title "scribe of the temple of Maat" on a stela from the delta capital of the Ramessids now in Hildesheim[35] and the offering formula on the door jamb of the vizier Paser,[36] both

[32]C. J. Bleeker, *De beteekenis van de egyptische godin Ma-a-t* (Leiden 1929) 77 with n. 1, gave a few references. Viziers in particular are attested as "prophets of Maat" from the Fifth Dynasty on, but the title is found with other legal officials: W. Helck, *Untersuchungen zu den Beamtentiteln des ägyptischen Alten Reiches* (ÄgFo 18, 1954) 74; W. C. Hayes, *The Scepter of Egypt* I (New York 1953) 106, 110. The title occurs as late as the Twenty-fifth Dynasty: J. Leclant, *JNES* 13 (1954) 163, 166 n. 73 with pl. 13. See also P. Vernus, *BIFAO* 75 (1975) 105 n. (d).

[33]N. de G. Davies, *The Tomb of the Vizier Ramosé* (Mond Excavations at Thebes 1, London 1941) pl. 27 lower.

[34]Theban Tomb 409: M. Abdul-Qader Muhammed, *ASAE* 59 (1966) 180. On Maat at Thebes see also A. Varille, "Inventaire d'objets cultuels d'un temple thébain de Maat," *BIFAO* 41 (1942) 135–39.

[35]G. Roeder, *ZÄS* 61 (1926) 61; Labib Habachi, *ASAE* 52 (1954) 488.

[36]Labib Habachi, *ASAE* 52 (1954) 480 with pl. 20.

dating to the reign of Ramesses II. There are also personal names in which Maat is referred to as a goddess.[37]

"Conceptual personifications"—or, to avoid this dangerously misleading term, deities whose names are identical with a religious concept—may therefore acquire a cult, but they do not necessarily do so. The creator god has at his disposal three special powers that help him to plan and execute his work of creation: Sia, "percipience" in planning the work; Hu, creative "utterance"; Hike, the "'magic'" that brings the world into being out of the creative word (see Chapter 6). All three occur as divine beings in human form, as when they accompany the sun god in his journey across the sky and through the underworld. Hu and Hike play an active part as early as the Coffin Texts, in which they "fell" the snake enemy of the sun god, in order that he may appear again unopposed on the horizon.[38] But of these three similar helping gods only Hike acquired a cult, which is documented by priesthoods in the Old Kingdom[39] and late period.[40] Hu and Sia, on the other hand, remained without a cult, so far as we know.[41] The circle of these "gods who aid the realization of the divine will" (Siegfried Schott) is enlarged in the later New Kingdom by the addition of "sight" (*Jrj*) and "hearing" (*Sḏm*);[42] they occur first as aides of the scribes of the gods Thoth and Seshat in the temples of Sethos I and Ramesses II at Abydos, and later are often associated with Hu and Sia. Because they were depicted in reliefs in the main temples, all four were able to partake in the general cult of the gods, even though they did not have their own priests or rituals.

One might be tempted to follow Eberhard Otto and call such figures "conceptual gods" (*Begriffsgötter*); Otto wished also to

[37]Morenz, *Gott und Mensch* 138.

[38]*CT* VII, 466. On the enemy (Apopis) see Chapter 5.

[39]See evidence cited by H. G. Fischer, *ZÄS* 90 (1963) 39 nn. 4–5.

[40]E. Otto, *ZÄS* 81 (1956) 115 (Memphis, Ptolemaic); on the cult of Hike alongside that of Sakhmet in the third Lower Egyptian nome see H. de Meulenaere, *BIFAO* 62 (1964) 170–71. Hike is the third member of the divine triad in the temple of Esna (Graeco-Roman period), cf. S. Sauneron, *Esna* (Publications de l'IFAO, 1959–) *passim*.

[41]For other aspects cf. A. H. Gardiner, *PSBA* 38 (1916) 43–54, 83–95.

[42]E. Brunner-Traut in *Fragen* 125–42.

include Atum, Amun, and Ptah under this heading.[43] I believe, however, that the term is excessively narrow, and positively misleading, even for the deities of this sort who have no cult. In the Book of Gates Sia appears as the sun god's herald who stands at the bow of the solar bark, a function that can scarcely be traced back to the concept *sj'*.[44] Hike departs still further from the concept *ḥk'*, as when he is worshiped as a moon god.[45] Such reservations apply still more strongly to the highly complex natures of Atum and Amun. Like all others, these deities have a life of their own which does not necessarily submit to the laws of the concepts they "personify."

A number of deities who are manifest in the cosmos or in nature are often considered to be "personifications." In the case of sky and earth we have already seen that the words "earth" and "sky" are different from the names of the deities, but the "empty" space between them appears as the god Shu (Figure 4), an "abstraction" derived from the verb *šwj* "to be empty"; by the Old Kingdom Shu played an important part in creation, and from the Ramessid period at the latest he was worshiped widely in the cult.[46]

There is a striking lack of personifications of waterways or stretches of water in the Egyptian pantheon. The so-called "Nile gods," more recently termed "fecundity figures" (Figure 6),[47] personify general concepts of abundance and its causes, among which the most prominent is the inundation. They may bring offerings to the king in his mortuary temple, or with the king they bring them to the gods in a normal cult temple; they can scarcely be termed deities. There is neither a river god of the Nile (there are of course no other rivers in Egypt), nor deities

[43]*Saeculum* 14 (1963) 255. For H. Stock, on the other hand, Atum is a "speculation": *Saeculum* 1 (1950) 622.

[44]This placing may reflect in part Sia's precedence over Hu, which is visible as early as the Pyramid Texts (*Pyr.* §§267–68); cf. H. Kees, *StG* 19 (1966) 125.

[45]P. Derchain in *La lune* (Sources orientales 5, Paris 1962) 51.

[46]A. de Buck, *Plaats en betekenis van Sjoe in de egyptische theologie* (Mededeelingen der Kon. Nederlandsche Ak. van Wetenschappen, Afd. Letterkunde n.s. 10, 9, Amsterdam 1947). On the name see G. Fecht, *ZÄS* 85 (1960) 104ff. For an alternative etymology see P. Derchain, "Sur le nom de Chou et sa fonction," *RdE* 27 (1975) 110–16.

[47]Baines, *Fecundity Figures,* esp. §2.2.2.

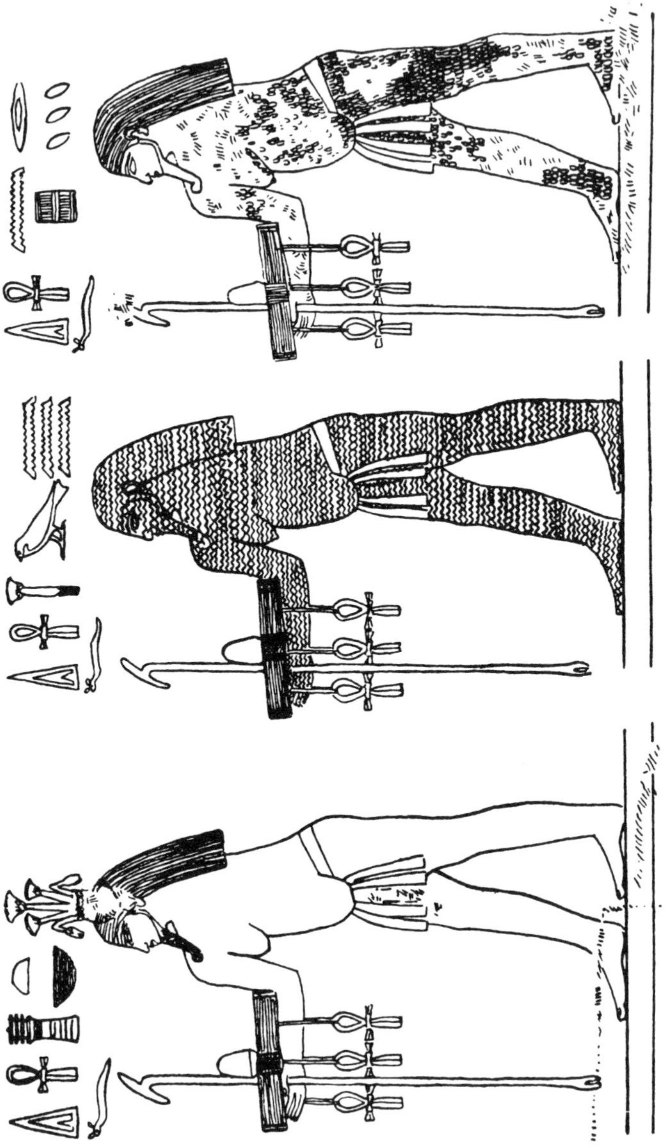

Figure 6. Fecundity figures.

of the larger lakes, although the Faiyum with the Birket Qarun, and the delta branches of the Nile, are found among fecundity figures, as are probably the bitter lakes to the east of the delta.[48] There is no god of the sea before the New Kingdom, when a semitic god was "imported" for the purpose.[49] The only fecundity figure who takes on an independent existence as a deity is the inundation, Hapy.[50] Otherwise, waters are under the tutelage of gods in crocodile form, especially Sobek (Greek Suchos), who is the lord of the fishes,[51] while the ram god Khnum is the patron of the first cataract with its mythical caverns, which were considered to be the sources of the inundation. It is noteworthy that, apart from the goddess Hatmehit "she who is before the fishes,"[52] we find no deities in fish form comparable with the countless gods in bird form. This lack probably reflects a partial and selective taboo on fish. Nevertheless, fish can be manifestations of some major deities: Atum may be an

[48]Baines, *Fecundity Figures* §2.3.1, g, l, p, q. For the Birket Qarun (*wꜣḏ-wr*) see Farouk Gomaà, *Chaemwese* (ÄgAbh 27, 1973) 85, 122 (no. 54). The delta branches of the Nile (*jtrw ꜥꜣ, pꜣ mw n pꜣ Rꜥ* etc.) are attested in series of fecundity figures from the Nineteenth Dynasty on, and the bitter lakes(?) and swamp areas of the country (*pḥww*) from the reign of Hatshepsut on: E. Naville, *Deir el Bahari* V (Egypt Exploration Fund, London n.d.) pl. 128; P. Lacau et al., *Une chapelle de Hatchepsout à Karnak* I (Service des Antiquités de l'Egypte and IFAO, Cairo 1977) 88–91.

[49]Yamm, the god of the sea, occurs only in the myth of the "Astarte papyrus"; see R. Stadelmann, *Syrisch-palestinensische Gottheiten in Ägypten* (PÄ 5, 1967) 125–31. The *wꜣḏ-wr* that occurs among fecundity figures from the Fifth Dynasty on (Figure 6) may be a personification of the delta lagoons (Lakes Mariut, Idku, Burullus, and Manzala) rather than of the open sea. Cf. also W. Helck, "Meer," in Helck et al., eds., *Lexikon der Ägyptologie* III (Wiesbaden 1980) 1276–79.

[50]The fundamental study is A. de Buck, "On the meaning of the name ḤꜥPJ," in *Orientalia Neerlandica* (Leiden 1948) 1–22. On the god of the inundation in the Graeco-Roman period cf. D. Bonneau, *La crue du Nil* . . . (Etudes et Commentaires 52, Paris 1964) pt. 3.

[51]E. Edel, *Zu den Inschriften auf den Jahreszeitenreliefs der "Weltkammer" aus dem Sonnenheiligtum des Niuserre* II (NAWG 1963, 5) 144.

[52]Worshiped in the delta, especially in the nome of Mendes (no. 16), and also in the third nome and in the Iseum of Behbeit el-Hagar (P. Montet, *Kêmi* 10 [1949] 45). On the identification of the fish (possibly a *lepidotus*, previously thought to be a dolphin) see L. Keimer, *Bulletin de la Société archéologique d'Alexandrie* 41 (1956) 97–101; I. Gamer-Wallert, *Fische und Fischkulte im alten Ägypten* (ÄgAbh 21, 1970) 98–101.

eel[53] (evidently by analogy with his form as a snake) and Neith a *lates* fish.[54]

Like the waterways, the elements fire, earth, air, and water were never personified in Egypt, and I doubt very much whether there was in ancient Egypt a doctrine of the four elements similar to that of the Greeks.[55] There are of course large numbers of "fiery" deities, such as snakes who spit fire, but there is no god of fire or of water. Air and earth are also shared among several deities: Shu as "empty" space, Amun as air in motion or the vivifying breath of wind, and Seth in the destructive might of storms; in addition to Geb, Aker and Tatenen (also called Ptah-Tatenen), at least, there are other gods who embody the earth. According to a recent study, Tatenen is the god of the depths of the earth or the "primeval earth" (*Urerde*), and is linked only secondarily with the primeval hill; as Ptah-Tatenen he embodies the earth in a much more general fashion.[56]

The Egyptians conceived of only a few of the most important stars and constellations as deities. Apart from the sun and the moon, only Sothis, the brightest fixed star Sirius, acquired a cult as the herald of the inundation. From the early dynastic period on she was worshiped in cow form,[57] but was soon felt to be a manifestation of Isis, just as Osiris was recognized in Orion (Egyptian *Sꜣḥ*). The names of the planets show that they were believed to be manifestations of the god Horus; they occur as deities only in astronomical scenes. Even the morning and evening stars had no cult; nor did the Pole star (α Draconis in the early Old Kingdom), despite its great importance as the fixed pole of the sky and the goal of the dead king's ascent into the sky.[58] For the Egyptians the great mass of other stars was

---

[53]For the animal forms of Atum see K. Myśliwiec, *Studien zum Gott Atum* I (HÄB 5, 1978).

[54]For an old survey of the worship and avoidance of fish see Kees, *Götterglaube* 63–69; more recently Gamer-Wallert, *Fische und Fischkulte* (n. 52 above).

[55]B. H. Stricker, *De geboorte van Horus* II (MVEOL 17, 1968).

[56]H. A. Schlögl, *Der Gott Tatenen nach Texten und Bildern des Neuen Reiches* (Orbis Biblicus et Orientalis 29, Fribourg and Göttingen 1980).

[57]G. Godron, *BIFAO* 57 (1958) 143–55; parallel in Kaplony, *Inschriften, Supplement* (ÄgAbh 9, 1964) 20 with fig. 1008. For arguments against an early identification with Isis see R. Anthes, *ZÄS* 102 (1975) 3–5.

[58]R. O. Faulkner, "The King and the Star-Religion in the Pyramid Texts," *JNES* 25 (1966) 153–61.

a metaphor for vast numbers[59] and also embodied the souls of the dead. Because these souls counted as "gods," the stars were considered to be gods in the latest periods of Egyptian religion, and the word "god" came to be written with a star (see Chapter 2).

The funerary papyrus of a chantress of Amun of the Twenty-first Dynasty contains a number of interesting scenes, one of which is quite exceptional: against a background of stars stands a winged snake with two pairs of legs, its snake body terminating in front in a bearded human head and behind in a jackal's head.[60] As a caption tells us, it is "death, the great god, who made gods and men"—a personification of death as a creator god and an impressive visual realization of the idea that death is a necessary feature of the world of creation, that is, of the existent in general (Chapter 5, Excursus). But this is the only occurrence of death as a deity which has so far been identified from Egypt; in a whole series of texts, death is called a "robber" "who sees but is not seen," who snatches men away from life stealthily and suddenly, but this usage is no more than a metaphor.[61]

Nor did the Egyptians experience other fundamental attributes of human life—emotions such as love, fear, terror, and so on—as deities. Feelings proceed from the deity and belong to every god and his relationship with humanity,[62] but they are not perceived as forms separate from the gods.[63] Nor are all the

[59]Examples cited by R. A. Caminos, *The Chronicle of Prince Osorkon* (AnOr 37, 1958) 98–99. The "many faces that are in the sky" (*CT* VI, 92n) may also be the stars.

[60]Papyrus of Henuttawy, BM 10018, reproduced by S. Schott, *Zum Weltbild der Jenseitsführer des Neuen Reiches* (NAWG 1965, 11) 195 with pl. 4; *Egyptian Mythology* (London etc.: Paul Hamlyn 1965) 26. See also K. Myśliwiec, *Studien zum Gott Atum* I (HÄB 5, 1978) 103.

[61]On death as a "robber" see H. Grapow, *ZÄS* 72 (1936) 76–77; P. Derchain, *CdE* 33/65 (1958) 29–32; id., *Le papyrus Salt 825* 177 no. (136); E. F. Wente, *JNES* 21 (1962) 126(a), 127. It is possible that all the examples identified so far refer only to a premature death as "theft." The article by G. Thausing, "Über die Personifikation des Todes," *AÄA* 1 (1938) 215–21, deals with the demon *Nbḏ*, and is not relevant here. Quotation from Wente, p. 124 (translation), p. 127 (text).

[62]W. K. Simpson, "Amor dei: *nṯr mrr rmt m t3 w3*," in *Fragen* 493–98.

[63]Among fecundity figures there are occasional examples of *'wt-jb* "well-being" (Baines, *Fecundity Figures* §2.3.1, a) *snb* "health," and *'nḫ* "life" (§2.3.1, f). In

main features of the cosmos experienced in personal form as gods. There is, for example, no trace of a personification of night before the fifth century B.C.; then, during the Persian domination of Egypt, we find a couple Grḥ/Grḥt "night," or perhaps "cessation," among the pairs of primeval deities in the temple of Hibis in el-Kharga oasis.[64]

This example comes from a period when new, speculative figures appear more frequently, often as personifications of concepts, but are hardly current outside the confines of a priestly science of the divine.[65] I shall therefore not deal with similar phenomena in temple texts of Graeco-Roman times, but limit myself to earlier periods.

Although animal form is characteristic of the iconography of Egyptian deities—and will be discussed in Chapter 4—there are only a few gods with animal names, all of whom are minor figures during the historical period. One example is the "hare" goddess Wenut in the Hermopolitan nome, who may, however, not have been interpreted as a hare until the Graeco-Roman period, and may originally have been a snake goddess Wenut "the swift one."[66] More certain animal names are those of the ichneumon god Khatery[67] and the millipede Sepa. Other deities have names that are not words for animals but epithets describing their animal natures; among these are the lioness Pakhet "tearer apart," and a number of other deities, including per-

the Graeco-Roman period the "active" quality of snḏ "fear" or "fearfulness" was also personified, among others: E. von Bergmann, "Der Sarkophag des Panehemisis," *Jahrbuch der Kunsthistorischen Sammlungen in Wien* 1–2 (1883–84) 11 no. 7.

[64]N. de G. Davies, *The Temple of Hibis in el Khargeh Oasis* III (Metropolitan Museum of Art, Egyptian Expedition Publication 17, New York 1953) pl. 21, 33. In both cases the couple occurs with the pair of primeval gods called "darkness."

[65]There were, however, popular cults of Shay "destiny" and Mestasytmis "the hearing ear" in the Graeco-Roman period; see J. Quaegebeur, *Le dieu égyptien Shaï* (Orientalia Lovaniensia Analecta 2, Louvain 1975); G. Wagner and J. Quaegebeur, "Une dédicace grecque au dieu égyptien Mestasytmis de la part de son synode," *BIFAO* 73 (1973) 41–60.

[66]Assmann, *Liturg. Lieder* 306 n. (4). For earlier collections of material about Wenut see Jéquier, *Considérations* 123ff., esp. pp. 152–53; Bonnet, *Reallexikon* 841–42.

[67]E. Brunner-Traut, *Spitzmaus und Ichneumon als Tiere des Sonnengotts* (NAWG 1965, 7) 150–57.

haps the panther Mafdet, the "runner,"[68] and the scorpion goddess Selkis (*srqt* "the one who causes to breathe").[69] These epithet-style names are commoner than pure animal names, but they cannot be used as evidence for an original phase of zoolatry in Egyptian worship. The names of the gods do not provide any support for a hypothetical stage of development in which all gods were animals; it is more plausible that fetishes, animal powers, and abstract powers of nature existed side by side. Jéquier's scheme of the development of Egyptian religion from fetishism through zoolatry to anthropomorphism[70] undoubtedly simplifies excessively the early history.

Before concluding this chapter we must examine three additional characteristics of Egyptian divine names: feminine doublets to masculine names of gods, multiplicity of names, and syncretism. This examination will enrich significantly our understanding of Egyptian conceptions of god.

Female doublets

These name forms, which are distinguished from the corresponding masculine names of gods only by their feminine endings, and probably by a different vocalization, seem to be another manifestation of the desire for differentiation, which was so highly developed in Egypt. The most characteristic doublings are the four pairs of primeval deities, each of which gives form to a category of the world before creation (primeval flood, darkness, boundlessness, and others).[71] In the couples that represent these negative categories the goddesses clearly have

[68]W. Westendorf, *ZÄS* 92 (1966) 137, who also discusses the identification of the animal (leopard?); *id.*, *ZDMG* 118 (1968) 248–56; on earlier identifications see H. de Meulenaere, *BiOr* 7 (1950) 104. The hawk god whose name was formerly read Anty "he with claws" is now read Nemty "wanderer": O. D. Berlev, *Vestnik drevnej istorii* 1 (107) (1969) 3–30.

[69]The full form of the name is *Srqt-ḥtjt* "she who causes the throat to breathe"; cf. Bonnet, *Reallexikon* 196–97, 722–23. The name may be apotropaic in meaning.

[70]*Considérations* 14–25.

[71]See the fundamental study of K. Sethe, *Amun und die acht Urgötter von Hermopolis* (APAW 1929, 4). The names were evidently not rigidly fixed, for there are many variations.

no independent role. The couples did not receive a cult, at least until the late period; the Egyptians probably felt that their nature was too abstract for worship. This is not true, however, of the pair Amun/Amaunet, which was integrated into the system of the ogdoad only at the beginning of the late period.[72] The doublet Amaunet cannot be described in Usener's words as "more a play of language than a religious conception,"[73] for she was made the object of a cult at a relatively early period. There are several priests of this goddess attested from the Eighteenth Dynasty, including even a "second prophet of Amaunet."[74] This evidence shows that the cult of Amaunet must have been served at that time by at least two high-ranking priests ("prophets"), as well as lector priests and humbler *wab* priests.[75] Tutankhamun had a colossal statue pair of the divine couple Amun and Amaunet set up in the temple of Karnak,[76] and her cult survived into the late period, at least in Thebes. Horakhbit, the high priest of Amun at the beginning of the Twenty-sixth Dynasty, was also prophet of Amaunet in the temple of Karnak,[77] and the Ptolemaic buildings of Thebes contain a number of representations and mentions of the goddess.[78]

In the New Kingdom even the sun god Re acquired a female doublet Raet (or "Raet of the Two Lands"), who occurs in the most varied mythological contexts,[79] and does not at all give the

[72]As observed by P. Barguet, *Le temple d'Amon-Rê à Karnak* (IFAO RAPH 21, 1962) 20, and G. A. Wainwright, *JEA* 49 (1963) 21–23, whereas Sethe believed that Amun came originally from Hermopolis and its ennead.

[73]*Götternamen* (n. 13 above) 31.

[74]On funerary cones in the Metropolitan Museum of Art: W. C. Hayes, *The Scepter of Egypt* II (New York 1959) 54.

[75]For a *wab* and lector priest of Amaunet see Nina M. Davies, *Scenes from Some Theban Tombs* (Private Tombs at Thebes 4, Oxford 1963) 17 with pl. 19. Amaunet is attested earlier, in the Twelfth Dynasty, in a context that already implies a cult: P. Lacau and H. Chevrier, *Une chapelle de Sésostris Ier à Karnak* (Service des Antiquités de l'Egypte, Cairo 1956–69) 85 §215, scene 16, pl. 19.

[76]Hari, *Horemheb* 271–72.

[77]R. A. Parker, *A Saite Oracle Papyrus from Thebes* (Brown Egyptological Studies 4, Providence, R.I. 1962) 29.

[78]Sethe, *Amun* §§54-62; cf. E. Drioton, *ASAE* 44 (1944) 154; A. Gutbub in *Mélanges Mariette* (IFAO BE 32, 1961) 336.

[79]Queen Hatshepsut as Raet: *Urk.* IV, 332, 11. On a Twenty-second Dynasty stela there is even a *R't-Jtmwt*, a female doublet of Re-Atum: J. Vandier, *RdE* 20

impression of a forced, artificial, or abstract creation. She becomes associated with Mont as his consort and is known in this role from various temples in the Theban area, in reliefs of the late New Kingdom and later;[80] in the late and Graeco-Roman periods she was the mother of the young sun god Harpre.[81] There is also some documentary evidence for a cult of her. Six generations of "prophets" of Raet are known from the central delta during the Twenty-fifth and Twenty-sixth dynasties,[82] and a Theban temple of hers was still flourishing under Hadrian (A.D. 117–38) and Antoninus Pius (138–61).[83] The cult of this goddess was surely more important than can easily be seen from these stray pieces of evidence.

The female doublets of the gods of the dead Anubis and Sokar are rather more peripheral to the pantheon. A Sokaret appears in the ritual of burial,[84] while an Input plays some part in the cults of the Seventeenth Upper Egyptian nome[85] and is occasionally depicted.[86] None of these deities was ever a cult figure of the first rank, but their role in religious life is too important for them to have been no more than learned priestly speculations.

(1968) 138. See also J. Leclant, *Recherches sur les monuments thébains de la XXVe dynastie dite éthiopienne* (IFAO BE 36, 1965) 261.

[80]E.g. Twentieth Dynasty reliefs in the temple of Khons at Karnak: The Epigraphic Survey, *Scenes of King Herihor in the Court* (The Temple of Khonsu I, OIP 100, Chicago 1979) pl. 37, 88, 93; common in the Graeco-Roman period, see especially M. T. Derchain-Urtel, *Synkretismus in ägyptischer Ikonographie. Die Göttin Tjenenet* (GOF 8, 1979) 55ff.

[81]In the Twenty-fifth Dynasty she suckles the king in the form of Harpre (Leclant, *Recherches* [n. 79 above] 88–89, pl. 55); for Graeco-Roman material see J. Vandier, *RdE* 18 (1966) 113.

[82]Labib Habachi, *CdE* 42/83 (1967) 30–40. She appears there next to Ptah and is equated with Werethekau.

[83]S. V. Wångstedt, *Orientalia Suecana* 12 (1963) 55 (Hadrian); 16 (1967) 40–41 (Antoninus Pius). The goddess is here "Raet of the Two Lands," and has at her disposal a "god's father" and *wab* priests.

[84]J. Settgast, *Untersuchungen zu altägyptischen Bestattungsdarstellungen* (ADIK 3, 1963) 55 with n. 3. On the bark personification *Skrt* see J. C. Goyon, *RdE* 20 (1968) 67 n. 2.

[85]H. Kees, *MIO* 6 (1958) 170–75.

[86]A. Mariette, *Dendérah* IV (Paris 1873) pl. 80. J. Leibovitch, *BIE* 25 (1943) 187–88 with fig. 6, studied this scene, referring to a statuette of the goddess in Turin.

Multiplicity and hierarchy of names

Multiplicity of names is a fundamental feature of the gods which is common to all polytheistic religions. In particular the great gods, such as Amun, Re, and Osiris, are not content with presenting themselves to their worshipers under only one name. The "lord of all" Atum is found already in the Coffin Texts as "with many names in the mouth of the ennead" (*CT* VII, 469d): the host of gods surrounding him (the "ennead") knows about the many names that all refer to the one god Atum, and both priests and laymen are careful not to limit this number in a dogmatic fashion. Litanies are sung to "Osiris in all his names,"[87] and these names are collected in long lists; from an early date Osiris has the epithet '*š'-rnw* "he of many names."[88] Hymns credit Amun with a similar multiplicity of names, "he of many names, the number of which is not known."[89] In the Graeco-Roman period the goddess Isis was still simply *the* "one of many names," as was appropriate to the richness and diversity of her nature.[90]

Everywhere and at all periods the gods thrive on an abundance that tolerates no dogmatic restriction. The multiplicity of names, of manifestations, and of possible ways of encountering these deities is an outward sign of this abundance. But the innumerable names, in which the richness of the gods' unrestricted nature is manifest, are not all of equal value and status. The Egyptians were familiar with a hierarchy of names which found its classic formulation in a New Kingdom mythological story, known as Isis and Re, that occurs on Ramessid

[87]R. O. Faulkner, *JEA* 40 (1954) 34–39, and, more fully, *id.*, *An Ancient Egyptian Book of Hours* (Oxford 1958).

[88]E.g. at the beginning of the great hymn to Osiris, Louvre C286: A. Moret, *BIFAO* 30 (1930) 725–50; Assmann, *ÄHG* no. 213; Lichtheim, *Literature* II, 81.

[89]Grébaut, *Hymne* 23–24.

[90]On Isis *polyōnymos* see H. I. Bell, *Cults and Creeds in Graeco-Roman Egypt* (Liverpool Monographs in Archaeology and Oriental Studies, Liverpool 1953) 16. An altar at Mons Porphyrites was dedicated to Isis *myriōnymos*: A. Boeckh and J. Franzius, *Corpus Inscriptionum Graecarum* III (Berlin 1853) 353–54 no. 4713b; see further H. Lewy, *ASAE* 44 (1944) 228 l. 21 (Greek inscription at Kalabsha).

Figure 7. Isis and Osiris.

papyri and ostraca.[91] The story describes the aged sun god in graphic terms and, as his opponent, the great magician goddess Isis, who knows everything "in the sky and on earth" except the sun god's (true) name. But even this most secret knowledge of all will not remain hidden from her any longer. By means of her magic arts she creates a poisonous snake whose "fire" makes the god suffer acute agony. Only Isis the magician can release Re from his agony through her knowledge of a powerful spell against snake bite, but she demands to know his name before she will use it, for "a man lives if he is addressed by his name." The sun god then enumerates a long list of epithets that are his due as creator and guarantor of the world, ending with his three chief manifestations: "Khepry in the morning, Re at midday, Atum in the evening." But the poison remains in his body, because his true name is not any of these appellations. In his agony he finally whispers this last, most secret name into Isis' ear, and then the poison leaves the "burning god," releasing him from his pain. Isis, the cunning magician, has achieved her purpose and learned the most secret thing of all; she is even permitted to share her knowledge with her son Horus.

The story, which was intended as an effective spell against snake bite, shows clearly that the chief god, at least, possesses secret names in addition to those he bears in cult and myth. Some texts give the impression that there was a ritual prohibition against pronouncing some divine names; Ramesses IV asserts on his stela from Abydos that "I have not pronounced the name of Tatenen."[92] It is unlikely that the name referred to is the well-known name Tatenen itself; it must rather be another name which is to be kept secret.

As early as the Pyramid Texts (*Pyr.* §394c) it is said of the deceased king at the end of his journey to the sky, when he appears among the gods as the highest god, that "his mother does not know his name"; like the sun god before he was tricked, the deceased king shares with no one the knowledge of

---

[91]Translation and bibliography: Piankoff, *Litany* 56–59; *ANET* 12–14. Text of passage translated: Gardiner, *Chester Beatty* pl. 65, 3, 2.

[92]M. A. Korostovtsev, *BIFAO* 45 (1947) 158 l. 17 = KRI VI, 23, 13. On the name taboo see also Morenz, *Religion* 22–23 = 21–22.

his name. In this way he eludes the mysterious and automatic annexation of power that we call "magic" and the Egyptians termed *hike* (*ḥkꜣ*). It can operate only if the name and nature of the object of the action is known; knowledge of the name gives the magician the power both to repel evil and to coerce other beings.[93]

In the New Kingdom this magical importance of the name led to the invention of fantastic name forms of a type very familiar from magical papyri of the Graeco-Roman period and from Gnostic texts. One of the thousands of ostraca from the workmen's village at Deir el-Medina combines the story of Isis and Re with a list of "exotic" divine names such as Hetebteni and Asembeni, the bizarre forms of which, composed of the most varied elements, prefigure Graeco-Roman ones. It is clear that this is a novel, "abnormal" category of names, because a word *nr*, otherwise almost unattested, is applied to them; this may be a form of the normal word *rn* "name," "perverted" by metathesis and evoking associations with words for "terror" and "protection."[94] One motive for the invention of all these artificial forms was certainly the desire to find the right name, whatever the circumstances and however fantastic and unfamiliar that name might be. The same desire may be present, consciously or unconsciously, in the pious worshiper who uses as many names as possible when he addresses his god in his prayers.

For Egyptian conceptions of god, however, the *reality* of the name, even outside the context of magic, is more important. For the skeptical man in the Dispute of a Man with his *ba*, the name is the only thing that certainly survives death;[95] like *maat*, it has a substance and is an "effective nourishment" for the deceased,[96] forming part of the nature and substance of every

---

[93]"I know you, I know your names": CT III, 133e; similar: CT IV, 67e. On the general importance of the name cf. Piankoff, *Litany* 3ff.; on the importance of the name in Greek magical spells from Egypt see D. Wortmann, *Bonner Jahrbücher* 168 (1968) 96.

[94]G. Posener, *Catalogue des ostraca hiératiques littéraires de Deir el Médineh* II, 2 (IFAO DF 18, 1952) no. 1212; *id., RdE* 16 (1964) 214.

[95]W. Barta, *Das Gespräch eines Mannes mit seinem BA* (MÄS 18, 1969) ll. 36–37.

[96]Berlin leather roll with a later copy of an inscription of Sesostris I: A. de Buck in *Studia Aegyptiaca* I (AnOr 17, 1938) 50.

living being. Thus in the case of divine names and epithets, the nature and sphere of influence of a god are extended as the number of his names increases. By using many epithets the believer testifies to the abundant nature and rich and powerful substance embodied in the god who is addressed. Just as every visible image enhances the reality of the god (Chapter 4), so also does every name or epithet that is applied to him—hence the tendency of hymns and litanies to cloak great gods such as Re, Osiris, or Amun in a mass of epithets, and to address and praise them with ever more names. Among the many examples, the beginning of a Ramessid hymn to Osiris, which is known from a number of copies, should suffice as an illustration:

> O . . . Osiris, foremost of the westerners . . . justified god, lord of endlessness, ruler of eternity, oldest son whom Geb begot, the first one of the womb of Nut, lord of Busiris, ruler of Abydos, sovereign over the land of silence (the realm of the dead), possessor of splendor, great of terror, sacred ram before Naret, divine king, content with Maat, greater than his father, mightier than his mother, lord of what came into being through himself, greatest of the great, chief of his brothers, son of the white crown, whom the red crown bore, lord of lords, ruler of rulers, sovereign, god of gods. . . .[97]

These are not mere glorifying phrases for the god who is being worshiped; behind every name and every epithet there is a reality of myth or cult, which is often incorporated more directly into the invocations by means of wordplay. But just because these epithets have a reality they are not necessarily restricted to a particular deity; almost all of them can be applied to other gods. The most varied gods, including ones of the second rank, may even be termed "greatest god" or "unique god" (Chapter 5, end). Divine epithets are attracted to different gods like the iron filings in a magnetic field, and because of their greater powers of attraction, the leading gods acquire the most epithets.

If Egyptian gods of quite different character are called, for example, "lord of the sky," this attribute and this reality of

[97]Ramadan el Sayed, *Documents relatifs à Sais et ses divinités* (IFAO BE 69, 1975) 14–16.

being "lord of the sky" are common to all of them. The natures of the individual gods are not clearly demarcated, so that aspects of one god can be identical with those of another. Here we encounter a phenomenon that is of the greatest importance for Egyptian religion and its deities: "syncretism."

Syncretism

Anybody who studies Egyptian syncretism is much indebted to Hans Bonnet's fundamental contributions to the topic.[98] Although Bonnet aptly characterized syncretism as the realization of the "idea of 'inhabiting' (*Einwohnung*),"[99] one still continues to read statements that syncretism means that gods are "fused," "equated," or "identified." Even "inhabiting" is seldom lasting; rather it is transitory, and the link can be dissolved at any time. The syncretistic formula Amon-Re "simply observes that Re is in Amun" (*ZÄS* 75, 45)—the degree of intimacy and the duration of the combination vary from case to case. Bonnet gave another excellent definition of the formula Amon-Re in his *Reallexikon der ägyptischen Religionsgeschichte*:

> The formula Amon-Re does not signify that Amun is subsumed in Re or Re in Amun. Nor does it establish that they are identical; Amun does not equal Re. It observes that Re is in Amun in such a way that he is not lost in Amun, but remains himself just as much as Amun does, so that both gods can again be manifest separately or in other combinations. (p. 239)

We then face the problem of how and why such syncretistic formulas arose and one god came to "inhabit" another. The sun god provides perhaps the best illustration of the process. The sun god Re gained steadily in importance throughout the central period of the Old Kingdom; the earliest evidence for this development dates to the Second Dynasty.[100] Most of the

[98] "Zum Verständnis des Synkretismus," *ZÄS* 75 (1939) 40–52; *id., Reallexikon* 237–47. Among later works see especially Morenz, *Religion* 147ff. = 140ff.; Junker, *Geisteshaltung* 130ff.; W. Schenkel, *SAK* 1 (1974) 275–88.

[99] *ZÄS* 75 (1939) 45; *Reallexikon* 239.

[100] Royal name Raneb "Re is (my) lord"(?). On further personal names of the period that may contain the element Re see Kaplony, *Inschriften* I, 422, 555, 561, 604.

names of the kings of the Fourth and Fifth dynasties contain
the element Re; the ground plan of the sphinx temple was
adapted to the sun god's journey through the hours of the
day and the night;[101] from the time of Djedefre, the successor of
Cheops, the kings considered themselves to hold their office as
"son of Re."[102]

In the Fifth Dynasty the dominance of the sun god was made
visible architecturally in special solar temples, and in the Sixth
he was so much the true creator god that other gods who
were thought of as creators appeared to believers as X-Re—
combined syncretistically with the sun god. The Pyramid Texts
speak of a god Re-Atum (*Pyr.* §145b–c and *passim*), meaning
Atum as creator, that is, as Re.[103] From the Middle Kingdom on
such links become much commoner; examples are Sobek-Re
and Khnum-Re, and, the most familiar, Amon-Re, the new
state god Amun in his solar and creator aspect as Re.

These syncretisms may be interpreted as meaning that Egyptians recognize Re in all these very different gods as soon as
they encounter them as creator gods, just as they "recognize"[104]
the great hawk of the sky Horus in the most various gods who
have hawk form. It is also clear that every deity whom another
deity "inhabits" acquires an extended nature and sphere of
action. But all these formulations are no more than initial attempts to grasp the meaning of syncretism. In order to achieve
a deeper understanding first we must place the phenomenon
of syncretism in context with other ways of combining gods
and not view it in isolation, and then we must demarcate the
rich variety of its forms more precisely.

In Egyptian religion there are many ways of formulating a
link between two deities, and these formulations seem to be
chosen very carefully or devised anew to suit each case. Apart

[101]S. Schott, "Le temple du Sphinx à Giza et les deux axes du monde égyptien,"
BSFE 53–54 (1969) 31–41; *id.*, "Ägyptische Quellen zum Plan des Sphinx-
tempels," in Beiträge Bf 10 (1970) 51–79; R. Anthes, "Was veranlasste Chefren
zum Bau des Tempels vor der Sphinx?" in *Aufsätze zum 70. Geburtstag von
Herbert Ricke* (Beiträge Bf 12, 1971) 47–58.
[102]H. W. Müller, *ZÄS* 91 (1964) 131. On this formula see Chapter 5, end.
[103]Here the "older" god Atum is placed second. In the other common combination of solar gods, Re-Harakhte, Re is again in first position.
[104]Formulation of H. Bonnet, *ZÄS* 75 (1939) 46.

from syncretism the following types can be distinguished, each having subdivisions of its own:

1. Kinship: a deity may be the son, spouse, brother, or the like, of another.

2. Statements that a god (or the king) is the "image," "manifestation," or *ba* of another. A revealing example of this type occurs where it is said of Amun in his syncretistic form as Amon-Re that he "made his first manifestation (*ḫprw*) as Re":[105] quite apart from his syncretistic form, in which he assumes features of Re, Amun can be manifest for a moment completely as Re. When we study the manifestations of the gods in Chapter 4 we shall consider in more detail what is meant by the "image" or "manifestation" of a deity.

3. Finally, there are occasional complicated theological statements about the union of two gods. Apart from the Leiden hymn to Amun, in which Re and Amun are united,[106] these statements relate to the union of Re and Osiris, the theology of which was evidently rethought repeatedly; in the late period the union was even enacted in the cult.[107] In the Coffin Texts a common formulation is that Osiris has "appeared as Re" (*CT* I, 191g–192a), while elsewhere it is said that the *ba*s of Osiris and Re meet each other in Mendes and there become the "united *ba*" (*CT* IV, 276–81); according to the stela of Ramesses IV from Abydos this united *ba* speaks "with one mouth."[108] A well-known relief in the tomb of Nofretiri is virtually an illustration of this idea (Plate I). It shows a ram-headed mummy between Isis and Nephthys captioned "This is Re when he has come to rest (*ḥtp*) in Osiris" and "This is Osiris when he has come to rest in Re";[109] it is thus deliberately left open which god has come to rest in the other.

[105] Abd el Mohsen Bakir, *ASAE* 42 (1943) 87 with pl. 4 ll. 13–14, in a hymn of the end of the Eighteenth Dynasty; Assmann, *ÄHG* no. 88.

[106] Stanza "200": Zandee, *De hymnen aan Amon* pl. 4, 13. The sentence "Re himself is united in his (Amun's) body" may mean that Re, in the entire richness of his nature, is present in Amun (as Amon-Re).

[107] Derchain, *Le papyrus Salt 825* 35–37, 153–56.

[108] M. A. Korostovtsev, *BIFAO* 45 (1947) 158 l. 10 = KRI VI, 23, 1. The name "united one" in the Litany of Re also belongs in this context: Hornung, *Buch der Anbetung* I, 1, 122, 179, 180, 239; II, 61, 77, 84, 92.

[109] These phrases are from the Litany of Re: Hornung, *Buch der Anbetung* I, 178; II, 83 = Piankoff, *Litany* 35; for the scene cf. Hornung II, 53–54, 60.

Plate I. Re and Osiris united, between Isis and Nephthys.

Similarly, in programmatic scenes above the entrances to Ramessid royal tombs Isis and Nephthys worship the sun disk, acclaiming both Re and their brother Osiris in the one heavenly body. In the Book of the Dead the two gods are felt to be a unity to such an extent that in many passages their names appear to be interchangeable,[110] while in the Amduat the corpse of the sun god is at the same time the corpse of Osiris.[111] At the judgment of the dead it is not clear which of the two entirely different gods properly should preside. One might think that the syncretistic formula Re-Osiris would be suitable here and would resolve all the difficulties and variations in naming. But the Egyptian "theologians"—here, for once, the word is appropriate—deliberately avoided viewing this link between Re and Osiris as a syncretism.[112] This careful discrimination is a great help to us when we try to separate syncretism from other ways of combining gods.

The correct approach is suggested by a Ramessid variant of the formula in the tomb of Nofretiri which describes the union of Re and Osiris in the ram-headed mummy. In this variant the text is followed by the adverb "daily,"[113] thus showing how it should be understood: Re enters into Osiris and Osiris enters into Re daily, and the combination is dissolved again daily. The Egyptians encounter in the form of the murdered god Osiris the ineluctable fate of death, from which even the gods are not

[110]Especially *Urk.* V, 15, 12ff.; see also the gloss 88, 15–16.

[111]Sixth hour, cf. *Amduat* II, 124, with further bibliography on this combination, which I wrongly termed "syncretism" (corrected in *Amduat* III, 64). See also C. Lalouette, *Fidèles du soleil* (Faculté des Lettres et Sciences Humaines de Paris, Groupe d'études égyptologiques, 1963) 52ff.; E. Feucht-Putz, *Die königlichen Pektorale* (Dissertation, Munich; Bamberg 1967) 123–25; J. Zandee, *An Ancient Egyptian Crossword Puzzle* (MVEOL 15, 1966) 27–28; Žabkar, *Ba concept* 36–39; Assmann, *Liturgische Lieder* 101–5.

[112]In the Twenty-first Dynasty the form "Re-Osiris, the greatest god" occurs for the first time: A. Piankoff and N. Rambova, *Mythological Papyri* (ERT 3, 1957) no. 7, scenes 3, 5.

[113]Theban Tomb 290; see the color reproduction in R. Boulanger, *Ägyptische und altorientalische Malerei* (Weltgeschichte der Malerei 2, Lausanne 1961) 28 lower. For further parallels to the scene in Tombs 335 and 336 cf. B. Bruyère, *Rapport sur les fouilles de Deir el Médineh (1924–1925)* (FIFAO 3, 3, 1926) 136 with figs. 67, 92; on the formula in the Book of the Dead see Assmann, *Liturgische Lieder* 101–5.

exempted (Chapter 5). Through the generalization of an originally royal privilege every deceased person of the Middle Kingdom and later became an "Osiris," bearing the god's name like a title or designation of role in front of his own. This usage does not betoken a genuine identity with the ruler of the dead; rather, it means that through his own efforts the human being takes on a previously determined role that bears the name Osiris.[114] Similarly, in his daily descent into the realm of the dead the sun god Re must also become "Osiris," for he dies and appears in the underworld as a "corpse." But in this case the Egyptians imagine that there is a true union. Unlike the rest of the deceased, Re does not assume the title "Osiris"; instead he incorporates the ruler of the dead into his own being so profoundly that both have one body and can "speak with one mouth." Osiris does indeed seem to be absorbed into Re, and becomes the night sun, which awakens the underworld dwellers from the sleep of death.

But this linking of the two great gods is of short duration. When the sun god appears again on the horizon in the morning he is no longer Osiris, and is free from all the fetters of death. An "image" of him is left behind in the depths of the underworld—the outward shell of the god who was Re and Osiris in one.[115] This daily reenacted union of two gods, the duration of which is clearly defined, is a different phenomenon from the syncretistic combination Amon-Re.

Simply because of its multiplicity of names and forms, polytheism poses the problem of relations between gods—whether or not it attempts to order them in a larger system (see Chapter 7). The Egyptians evidently felt this difficulty, and attempted to solve it by means of a multiplicity of carefully ranked formulas. The most important, and one of the oldest,[116] of these formulas is syncretism. Because it does not imply identity or fusion of the gods involved, it can combine deities who have

[114]For references see my *Geschichte als Fest* (Darmstadt 1966) 24 with n. 55.

[115]*Amduat* II, 193 (fourth scene).

[116]There may be a combination Horus-Min as early as the Second Dynasty, see Zaki Saad, *CdE* 21/42 (1946) 198; Junker, *Geisteshaltung* 132–33. For Bonnet "syncretism is not a development [of the historical period]; it is fundamental to Egyptian thought" (*ZÄS* 75 [1939] 41).

different forms[117] and even, on occasion, ones of opposite sex.[118] Quite often not just two but three or four gods form a new unit that is the object of a cult. Beside tripartite forms such as Ptah-Sokar-Osiris there are quadripartite ones like Amon-Re-Harakhte-Atum[119] or Harmachis-Khepry-Re-Atum (*Urk.* IV, 1542, 17). In such cases one is reminded of chemical compounds; like them, syncretistic combinations can be dissolved at any time into their constituent elements, which can also form part of other combinations without sacrificing their individuality.

Is the purpose of these combinations a clever priestly "equalization" of conflicting religious claims, as Bonnet, like his predecessors, assumed?[120] Must gods be "equated" with one another until one finishes with a vague, solar-tinged pantheism? Such an interchange of attributes, which leads toward uniformity, is un-Egyptian; if anything it is Hellenistic. The Egyptians place the tensions and contradictions of the world beside one another and then live with them. Amon-Re is not the synthesis of Amun and Re but a new form that exists along with the two older gods. In this case one could, if necessary, provide arguments for an "equalization" required by religious politics—however questionable such a method may be—but what could be the purpose of "equalizing" Horus and Sothis or Harmachis, Khepry, Re, and Atum? In the last example, the three daily forms of the sun god are evidently present together in the Great Sphinx (Harmachis): the sun is Khepry in the morning, Re or Harakhte in the middle of the day, and Atum in the

[117]The hawk-form Horus, for example, can be combined with the most various of deities. Cf. Bonnet, *ZÄS* 75, 45: "Inhabiting is not identity, and does not require identity of form."

[118]Bonnet excluded this possibility (*ZÄS* 75, 47), but occurrences have since been found of Neith-Osiris (Amduat I, 188 no. 803), Mut-Min (H. G. Fischer, *Inscriptions from the Coptite Nome* [AnOr 40, 1964] 38; H. Goedicke, *JARCE* 3 [1964] 45), and Horus-Sothis (Edwards, *Decrees* 24 with n. 12, 114: Sothis-Horus, the later form). Thus this unusual type of combination is not restricted to androgynous deities such as Neith.

[119]P. Barguet, *Le temple d'Amon-Rê à Karnak* (IFAO RAPH 21, 1962) 256 (Eighteenth Dynasty); *Medinet Habu* VI pl. 430B col. 1; with the last two elements reversed: M. Plantikow-Münster, *ZÄS* 95 (1969) 120(a).

[120]*Reallexikon* 237, cf. also 238: "cult-political considerations." E. Otto spoke more cautiously of "exchange," but also of "union" (*Saeculum* 14 [1963] 272).

97

evening. The deity's human partner—not just the priest, but believers in general—recognizes in the divine image of the Great Sphinx both the sun god in his threefold form, in the universality of his daily journey across the world, and the Sphinx, which is itself a manifestation of the sun god. Together the tetrad of names and forms produces a single new partner for the worship and cult service of mankind; for the cult, too, something new arises from the syncretistic combination.[121]

It is clear that syncretism does not contain any "monotheistic tendency," but rather forms a strong counter-current to monotheism—so long as it is kept within bounds. Syncretism softens henotheism, the concentration of worship on a single god, and stops it from turning into monotheism, for ultimately syncretism means that a single god is not isolated from the others: in Amun one apprehends and worships also Re, or in Harmachis other forms of the sun god. In this way the awareness is sharpened that the divine partner of humanity is not one but many.

The names of the gods, which may be obscure in meaning or may be periphrases that leave their possessors fundamentally anonymous, can tell us little about Egyptian conceptions of god. But the accumulation of names, syncretism, and the interchangeability of epithets lead straight to the problem of the one and the many. Together with multiplicity of forms discussed in Chapter 4, they make up a trait of the Egyptian conception of god which Gerardus van der Leeuw[122] and Henri Frankfort[123] called its "vagueness." The form, name, and epithets of an Egyptian deity seem to be variable almost at will, and are largely interchangeable with those of other deities. The deceased Egyptian who takes on the role of a god in the next world also wishes to assume many forms and appear under many names; the numerous "transformation spells" in the mortuary texts help him to achieve this goal.

We shall find repeatedly that Egyptian deities do not pre-

---

[121] According to J. Spiegel, *Das Werden der altägyptischen Hochkultur* (Heidelberg 1953) 622–23, the first element in the combination is the form in which the god is to be worshiped in the cult. As Junker showed (*Geisteshaltung* 131–32), this is true only to a limited extent.

[122] *Godsvoorstellingen* 120.

[123] *Religion* 26.

sent themselves to us with as clear and well defined a nature as that of the gods of Greece. The conception of god which we encounter here is fluid, unfinished, changeable. But we should not impute to the Egyptians confused conceptions of their gods; such an idea is contradicted by numerous specific details and clearly defined statements throughout the texts. There must be other reasons for the vagueness of this conception of god, which can be discovered only by studying the Egyptian notion of existence (see Chapter 5).

It is evidently unnatural for Egyptian gods to be strictly defined. Their being remains a fluid state to which we are not accustomed; it escapes every dogmatic, final definition and can always be extended or further differentiated. The combinations gods form with other gods are transitory in many respects and can be dissolved at any time. This fluidity leaves no room for monotheism, which bases itself on unambiguous definitions. Let us now see whether the study of the manifestations and characteristics of Egyptian gods confirms this initial impression.

4 ➘ Depiction and Manifestation of the Gods

The first stages

The names of the gods are a source for the study of Egyptian conceptions of god as far back as the beginning of literacy around 3000 B.C. Representations of divine powers can take us back another millennium, which is as near as we can get to the putative origins of these conceptions.

The true neolithic period in Egypt (Merimda and Faiyum cultures) has not so far produced any representations that can be interpreted with certainty as depictions or symbols of divine powers. No conclusions can be drawn from this lack of evidence, because the art of the time consists of pottery vessels and the first cosmetic palettes; there are no depictions of human beings, animals, or objects. It is, for example, impossible to establish from archeological evidence whether in neolithic times there was a worship of fetishes made of perishable materials. The absence of animal burials seems to me to be more revealing. Here, too, new finds could suddenly change the picture, but the worship of sacred animals was probably not so important as it was in later Egyptian religion.[1]

The chalcolithic period, lasting in Egypt for much of the fourth millennium B.C., brings the first clear evidence for a belief in gods, which is already at this early stage surprisingly

---

[1] Contrast the clear evidence for a belief in life after death at this time; selected material in M. A. Murray, "Burial Customs and Belief in the Hereafter in Predynastic Egypt," *JEA* 42 (1956) 86–96.

100

multifarious and highly differentiated. The main sites are, in Lower Egypt, Maadi and Heliopolis, and, in Upper Egypt, Badari and Naqada. Animal burials have been found in all these places, most commonly of gazelles and dogs (or jackals), and more rarely of cattle and rams.[2] The care with which these animals were buried and provided with grave goods is evidence for a cult of sacred animals or of divine powers in animal form. The cosmetic palettes now assume animal form, and finally, at the end of the predynastic period, they are richly decorated with animal figures in relief, the most notable examples being the "animal palettes" in Oxford and in the Louvre.[3] From the Naqada I period there are also figures of animals on decorated vases and in the form of clay statuettes.

In view of the numbers of these representations and of the evidence for animal burial, there can be scarcely any doubt that in the last centuries of prehistory the Egyptians for the most part worshiped divine powers in animal form. But even in that period there was no pure zoolatry. From Naqada II times and from the beginning of the historical period the animals on "standards" and archaic objects of uncertain character which were carried on poles are evidence for the worship of sacred objects.[4] To judge by the representations, this fetishism was much less important than animal worship, but because of the chances of preservation and other factors they may be an imperfect record. The later nome standards evolved formally from the predynastic carrying poles, and, as we saw in Chapter 2, the commonest hieroglyph for "god" shows a fetish of a similar type.

It is disputed whether the third stage of development posited by Gustave Jéquier (cf. p. 39—anthropomorphism or the wor-

[2]For a summary of the subject see *StG* 20 (1967) 74–75, with the most important references in nn. 51–52 (especially H. Behrens, "Neolithisch-frühmetallzeitliche Tierskelettfunde aus dem Nilgebiet und ihre religionsgeschichtliche Bedeutung," *ZÄS* 88 [1963] 75–83).
[3]In e.g. H. Asselberghs, *Chaos en Beheersing* (Documenta et Monumenta Orientis Antiqui 8, Leiden 1961) figs. 122–24, 127–30.
[4]On the standards see W. Kaiser *ZÄS* 84 (1959) 119–32; 85 (1960) 118–37; P. Munro, *ZÄS* 86 (1961) 61–74. For the material see M. Raphael, *Prehistoric Pottery and Civilization in Egypt* (Bollingen Series 8, [New York] 1947); Vandier, *Manuel* I (1952), esp. the collection of examples p. 341 and fig. 231.

ship of deities in human form—was reached in predynastic times. Human figures of clay and ivory are occasionally found in the Badari culture and become common in the Naqada cultures; these have been interpreted repeatedly as deities. They have even been explained as figures of the "great mother goddess," even though by no means all of them are clearly female, there are no attributes of divinity, and a nude "mother goddess" is quite unknown in Egypt in the earlier historical period. One should be equally skeptical about the attempt to identify naked, bearded figures as gods.[5] In reliefs and paintings of the time pointed beards of the sort found on several figurines are often worn by enemies, while in late predynastic and early dynastic times nakedness is reserved for subjugated enemies of Egypt. The fragile material of the clay figurines also decreases the probability of their representing deities. No attributes that are comparable to those of deities have been found so far.

A monograph by Peter J. Ucko deals with the problems of authenticity, dating, and interpretation raised by these figures.[6] After a careful analysis Ucko rejects the interpretation of them as idols. He refers to the wide variety of uses and meanings that such figurines can have in other cultures, and assumes that there was a comparable diversity in Egypt. Some could be dolls, others magically efficacious images that were used for various rituals or as votive offerings. He considers the possibility that some were pieces of equipment used in initiation rituals, but does not find adequate reasons for identifying any of them as images of deities. There is, therefore, no certain

[5]Beards are used as a tentative criterion of divinity ("The pointed beard may indicate divine status.") by W. Needler, "Six Predynastic Human Figures in the Royal Ontario Museum," *JARCE* 5 (1966) 11–17 with pl. 5–9 (quotation from p. 15). Beards are fairly widespread in late predynastic sculpture and relief and occur on some figures that are probably neither enemies nor divine, such as the animal keepers on the recto of the Narmer palette, in e.g. K. Lange and M. Hirmer, *Ägypten/Egypt* (4th ed., Munich 1967/London 1968) pl. 4.

[6]*Anthropomorphic Figurines of Predynastic Egypt and Neolithic Crete, with Comparative Material from the Prehistoric Near East and Mainland Greece* (London 1968; for the interpretation see pp. 409–44); id., *Journal of the Warburg and Courtauld Institutes* 26 (1963) 205–22 (with H. W. M. Hodges); id., "Anthropomorphic Ivory Figurines from Egypt," *Journal of the Royal Anthropological Institute* 95 (1965) 214–39.

evidence for the worship of anthropomorphic deities in pre-dynastic Egypt. Deities such as Min, Neith, and Onuris, whom we encounter in human form at the beginning of history, were most probably worshiped already in the Naqada period,[7] but their human iconography is known only from historical times and thus tells us little about the earlier period.

It is in the nature of the nonliterate evidence from prehistory that the information it provides about the gods is sparse and ambiguous. Only a few of the historical deities of Egypt can be traced back for any distance into prehistory. The "standards" document the existence of early hawk cults, but they do not show whether the gods are Horus or other hawk gods. Nor can the opponent of Horus, the violent and destructive Seth, be made out with certainty in the gloom of prehistory.[8] Finally, the goddess in cow form, who is found on the Narmer palette (Figure 9), and about three centuries earlier on a palette from Girza,[9] is iconographically closer to Bat, a goddess who was later worshiped in the seventh Upper Egyptian nome,[10] than to the better-known Hathor; the stars added to the image show that she is already a sky goddess.

The predynastic Egyptians' view of the relationship between animal and human being can probably be seen most clearly in the "Battlefield" palette, of which there are fragments in London and Oxford (Figure 8).[11] The recto of this cosmetic palette shows a battlefield covered with the contorted bodies of de-feated enemies; other enemies are being captured and led away

[7]Certain only for Neith and for Min, whose fetish (not yet convincingly iden-tified) is found, like the crossed arrows of Neith, on predynastic standards (Vandier, *Manuel* I, 340–41) and on the "Scorpion" mace head (J. E. Quibell, *Hierakonpolis* I [Egyptian Research Account 4, London 1900] pl. 26c, 1). On the problem of the colossi of Min see below.

[8]Te Velde, *Seth* 7–12.

[9]W. Kaiser, *ZÄS* 91 (1964) 119.

[10]H. G. Fischer, "The Cult and Nome of the Goddess Bat," *JARCE* 1 (1962) 7–23; 2 (1963) 50–51. I owe this reference to E. Staehelin, who studied Bat and the *bat* pendant in her *Untersuchungen zur ägyptischen Tracht im Alten Reich* (MÄS 8, 1966) 128–35.

[11]There is a probable third fragment: J. R. Harris, *JEA* 46 (1960) 104–5; H. W. Müller, *Ägyptische Kunstwerke, Kleinfunde und Glas in der Sammlung E. und M. Kofler-Truniger, Luzern* (MÄS 5, 1964) no. A3.

Figure 8. The "Battlefield" palette, obverse.

in fetters. Naked and without weapons, the subjugated party—
in human form—is an image of utter defenselessness. The vic-
tors, to whom the defeated surrender helplessly, are shown as
animal powers: lion, bird of prey, and standards surmounted
by birds. The figure on the extreme right, of whom only the
lower part is preserved, partakes of animal potency at least
through its clothing; without the missing part of the palette
we cannot know whether it was "disguised" with other attributes as an animal, as are the human hunters on the other

104

palettes of the time and in predynastic rock drawings.[12] But it seems certain, at least, that men of this period (c. 3000 B.C.) felt themselves defenseless without an animal disguise. Animals still appear to be the most powerful and efficacious beings, far superior to men in all their capacities. This probably explains why in late predynastic times the powers that determine the course of events were mostly conceived in animal form.

At the beginning of the historical period this view of man's position and of the superiority of animals changed radically. The earliest kings of a unified Egypt still have animal names: Scorpion, Catfish, Kite (?), Cobra, "Wing-spreader" (that is, probably, "bird of prey"). Toward the end of the First Dynasty (c. 2800 B.C.), however, this type of name disappears for good. In the extraordinary exertions of intellectual and physical power which produced the first civilizations, man also achieved a new self-awareness. He ordered the world creatively and subjected it to his planning and interpreting mind, no longer feeling himself to be the plaything of incomprehensible powers. This process may be related to the fact that the powers that were worshiped as deities came more and more to show a human face, and their original animal or inanimate form changed into a human one.

This evolution "from dynamism to personalism"[13] took place between 3000 and 2800 B.C. There are certainly many repetitions of it and parallels for it in the history of religions, but only in Egypt can its history be observed and documented. The "anthropomorphization of powers" (*Vermenschlichung der Mächte*), as it has been termed more aptly, produced the first gods in human form, but other methods of depicting this anthropomorphization appear at the same time. The cow heads that crown the Narmer palette (Figure 9) contain a human face that looks at the viewer, and the subjugated "land of papyrus" has a human head; this personal mode of encounter with a foreign

---

[12]Cf. E. Hornung, *StG* 20 (1967) 73 with n. 43.
[13]As A. Bertholet termed it, in W. J. Kooiman and J. M. van Veen, eds., *Pro regno pro sanctuario* (Nijkerk 1950) 35ff. The fundamental treatments of the subject in Egypt are Sethe, *Urgeschichte* §§30–37; S. Schott, *Mythe und Mythenbildung im alten Ägypten* (UGAÄ 15, 1945) 88–97.

105

Figure 9. The Narmer palette, verso.

country is also shown on a stela fragment of King Khasekhem of the Second Dynasty.[14]

Most of the earliest depictions of gods in human form show a body without separate limbs. The use of this iconography certainly does not reflect a lack of artistic skill, but must have some other, as yet undiscovered, meaning. Mummy form, which is depicted in similar fashion, cannot have been the model because mummification was not practiced until some centuries later; it is, indeed, more likely that the mummy form of the deceased, who become "gods," relates to the archaic form of the earliest anthropomorphic gods. I should rather seek an interpretation in another direction, in the deliberate concentration on essential and unavoidable features of the human form, and ignoring of all dispensable details, which can be seen so clearly in sculpture at the beginning of the early dynastic period. This same schematic outline is used in the Egyptian script, which was invented at the same time, as a classifier for all words that mean "representation" or, more generally, "image." The archaic figure of a god shows no more and no less than is necessary to evoke an image in human form; there are early parallels in the images of divine animals, such as a hawk or a cow, which are drawn with similarly schematic outlines. Should we see here a deliberate restraint, in which no more is said about the gods than is absolutely necessary? The only firm conclusion that we can draw is that their appearance can be human from now on.

At first the number of these gods in human form is small. From the First Dynasty the annal stone in Palermo records the making of a statue of Min which already has the familiar human form of the god with a raised flail and erect penis (line 2); in line 5 the production of a statue of Min is recorded again, in the Third Dynasty.[15] Strictly speaking, however, this is not contemporary evidence. The annal stone, which records years down to the Fifth Dynasty, is based on a late copy from early records, so that its sign forms may be influenced by later

[14]J. E. Quibell and F. W. Green, *Hierakonpolis* II (Egyptian Research Account 5, London 1902) pl. 58; W. B. Emery, *Archaic Egypt* (Harmondsworth 1961) 100 fig. 64.
[15]H. Schäfer, *Ein Bruchstück altägyptischer Annalen* (APAW, Anhang 1902).

models. But it is much more likely to be genuine ancient tradition than a matter of chance that in the late period the Egyptians placed Min at the beginning of history, creating a link between him and the legendary founder of the state "Menes."[16]

The colossal "archaic" statues of Min from Koptos are of uncertain value as evidence. As monumental sculpture in stone they can scarcely be earlier than the Third Dynasty, and were even dated down into the first intermediate period by E. J. Baumgartel.[17] But an image of Ptah incised on a stone vase from Tarkhan can definitely be placed in the early dynastic period (Figure 10, extreme right).[18] For other deities such as the goddesses Neith and Satis there is so far only the evidence of early personal names, and we can do no more than guess that they assumed human form during the first two dynasties.[19] Relief fragments in Turin provide an example of Geb in the early Third Dynasty;[20] like him, the other cosmic deities are in human form (Figure 4): Nut (the sky), Shu (air), and Atum, the god of the primeval beginning. We can assume that in the Third Dynasty, at the beginning of the Old Kingdom, all these deities were already familiar to Egyptians in the form that was later normal for them, although our fragmentary evidence does not so far provide proof of this point.

[16]See the posthumous article of S. Morenz, "Traditionen um Menes," ZÄS 99 (1973) X–XVI = Religion und Geschichte 162–73.

[17]ASAE 48 (1948) 533–53; cf. also J. Černý, Ancient Egyptian Religion (Hutchinson's University Library, London 1952) 28. Vandier, Manuel I, 986 dates them to the Second or Third Dynasty.

[18]For another early dynastic picture of Ptah see P. Lacau and J.-P. Lauer, La pyramide à degrés V (Service des Antiquités de l'Egypte, Fouilles à Saqqarah, Cairo 1965) 18–19 fig. 28; eight early calcite vases with representations of Min are referred to on pp. 19–20.

[19]For Neith this development can be dated more precisely between kings Djet (c. 2840) and Ninetjer (c. 2700 B.C.), see S. Schott in E. Edel et al., Das Sonnenheiligtum des Königs Userkaf II (Beiträge Bf 8, 1969) 125–26. In Munich there is an early dynastic statuette of a goddess(?) from Abydos: Staatliche Sammlung ägyptischer Kunst (Munich 1976) 34, AS 1512.

[20]From a building in Heliopolis, published by R. Weill, Sphinx 15 (1912) 9–26; W. S. Smith, A History of Egyptian Sculpture and Painting in the Old Kingdom (2d ed., London 1949) 133–37 figs. 48–53. Seth, too, evidently has a human head in this series, which uses the same iconography for all the deities shown (Smith fig. 50, 3).

Figure 10. Figures of gods on early dynastic objects.

During the first two dynasties the group of purely anthropomorphic deities appears in addition to the gods in purely animal form, who are still predominant—Horus and Seth, the Apis bull, and the baboon-form "great white one." What is lacking at the beginning of the early dynastic period is the "mixed form" of gods, combining human and animal elements, which is so characteristic of Egypt. Toward the end of the Second Dynasty the first gods in human form with animal heads (hawk and the fabulous Seth animal) appear on cylinder seal impressions of King Peribsen (Figure 10); the earliest examples show the god Ash, "lord of Libya."[21] The first example of the mixed form with a hawk's head is on a Third Dynasty stela in the Louvre;[22] this is the god Horus, who in the First Dynasty had been shown exclusively in animal form. There is also a pair of figures with birdlike heads and ram's horns on a very early, but not precisely datable, small stone shrine.[23]

The "mixed form" and its interpretation

Although this fusion of human body and animal head never superseded the representation of gods in purely human or

[21]Kaplony, *Inschriften* III pl. 76–80.

[22]E 25982: J. Vandier, *CRAIBL* 1968, 16–22; *id., Musée du Louvre, le département des antiquités égyptiennes, guide sommaire* (Paris 1973) pl. 2, 2.

[23]H. W. Müller, *Ägyptische Kunstwerke . . . Sammlung . . . Kofler-Truniger . . .* (n. 11 above) no. A31.

purely animal form, but added a valuable new type, it has widely been taken as what is most characteristic of the Egyptian depiction and conception of god.[24] As I showed at the beginning of the first chapter, this type was what caused the early and passionate rejection of Egyptian religion. Egyptian gods are certainly not all "dog-headed" or equipped with other animal heads, but this iconography is so characteristic of and important for the Egyptian image of the gods that we should study it in more detail. We must not treat this mixed form in isolation, but must view it in the context of all the possible ways of representing a deity.

There is an astonishingly rich variety of possibilities; only to a very limited extent can one speak of a canonically fixed iconography of a god. The goddess Hathor is a good example (Plate II). Her normal iconography, which is familiar to us, shows a slim woman who wears a wig covering her head and on top of it a pair of cow horns with a sun disk between them. There are, in addition, three more ways of imagining Hathor. In direct contrast to her completely human form, the goddess may have a pure animal form, as, for example, in the Hathor shrines of Deir el-Bahri, where she is depicted as a cow from whose udder the king drinks or as a cow stepping forth from the western mountains of Thebes and taking the deceased into her protection. In between there is the unusual form of the capital of a Hathor column or pillar (Figure 11), which is well known to everybody who visits the temples of Deir el-Bahri or Dendara: a cow head with human face, whose ears are animal and whose eyes, nose, and mouth are human. Finally, the form of human body with animal head is not lacking; Hathor is indeed less commonly shown as a woman with a cow's head than in other forms, but without searching too far one can find many examples in two and three dimensions (as in Plate III, which shows Mehetweret rather than Hathor).[25]

[24]On the mixed form in general see R. Merz, *Die numinose Mischgestalt* (Religionsgeschichtliche Versuche und Vorarbeiten 31, Berlin 1978).

[25]Bronze statuettes of the late period in Cairo: G. Daressy, *Statues de divinités* (CGC, 1905) nos. 39133 (Mehetweret?), 39134–39140bis (Hathor); Morenz, *Gott und Mensch* 107 fig. 31; see also W. B. Emery, *JEA* 56 (1970) pl. 9.1 (published as Isis); in Brooklyn: Frankfort, *Religion* fig. 14; in Leiden: C. J. Bleeker, *Hathor and*

Plate II. The king before Hathor.

Plate III. Mehetweret with the head of a cow.

All these very different forms show the same goddess Hathor, and her iconography appears still richer when one recalls that she is also imagined as a lioness, a snake (uraeus), a hippopotamus, and a tree nymph. Although the various forms are not all equally old,[26] we are not observing a historical development in which one form replaced another; at all periods different ways of depicting the goddess simply existed side by side. A most unusual group statue in the Louvre brings together in a curious fashion cow, lion-headed goddess, uraeus, and goddess with sistrum on her head, showing four forms of the goddess next to one another.[27]

We should not, therefore, assume that the Egyptians imagined Hathor as a woman with a cow's head. It is more plausible to see the cow as one possible manifestation of Hathor, and the cow's head and cow's horns as attributes that allude to a manifestation of the goddess or a part of her nature. In Hathor there is the maternal tenderness of the cow, but, among many other characteristics, also the wildness of the lioness and the unpredictability of the snake. Any iconography can be no more than an attempt to indicate something of her complex nature. I shall review some examples which show still more clearly that

---

Thoth (SHR 26, Leiden 1973) pl. 3a. The earliest examples in relief date to the Ramessid period; tombs of Tawosret (Mehetweret, Plate III here) and Ramesses III; stela showing Hathor as a tree goddess with a cow's head: S. Bosticco, *Museo archeologico di Firenze, Le stele egiziane del nuovo regno* (Rome 1965) no. 48 = Ramses Moftah, *ZÄS* 92 (1965) 44 fig. 4; shrine: W. M. F. Petrie and G. Brunton, *Sedment* II (BSAE, 27th year 1921, 1924) pl. 74; lintel in Brooklyn: J. Berlandini-Grenier, *BIFAO* 74 (1974) pl. 3. As Hathor-Hecate the same form is found on magical gems of the Graeco-Roman period: P. Delatte and P. Derchain, *Les intailles magiques gréco-égyptiennes* (Bibliothèque Nationale, Cabinet des médailles et antiques, Paris 1964) 155–56. There are several examples of Isis in the form in the Graeco-Roman period (she has cow's horns as early as *CT* I, 215b).

[26]Tree nymphs and the mixed form with a cow's head are not attested before the New Kingdom, but the suckling Hathor cow occurs in the Twelfth Dynasty, while cow's horns with inset sun disk are familiar from the Old Kingdom (e.g. the triad statues of Mycerinus).

[27]J. Vandier, *La revue du Louvre et des musées de France* 19 (1969) 49–54 with fig. 14; *id.*, "Une groupe du Louvre représentant la déesse Hathor sous quatre de ses aspects," *Mélanges de l'Université Saint-Joseph* 45 (Beirut 1969) 159–83; Ptolemaic(?).

113

Figure 11. Hathor pillar.

pictures of gods should not be understood as illustrations or descriptions of appearances, but rather as allusions to essential parts of the nature and function of deities.

A variation in iconography between completely animal form

114

and the combination of animal head and human body can be observed not only for Hathor but also for Anubis (canine form), Thoth (ibis and baboon form), and many other deities. Even the further possibility of alluding to the animal element by means of the ears only is, although unusual, not restricted to the iconography of Hathor. The demon "violent of face" (*mds-ḥr*) in the seventh hour of the Amduat has a cat's head in later copies, but in earlier ones he has a human head and cat's ears.[28] A punishing demon with cat's head also appears in the Book of Caverns (fourth section, bottom register),[29] and the sun god himself can take on the form of the "great tomcat" (Figure 12) in order to punish his enemies.[30]

As with mammals and birds, so also with amphibians and reptiles the Egyptians do not hesitate to combine a human body with the relevant animal's head; the long tripartite wig worn by almost all gods neatly disguises the transition between human and animal nature (Plate IV). The goddess Heqet, who helps woman in childbirth, appears as a frog or with a frog's head, while among crocodile-headed gods Sobek (Greek Suchos) is predominant; among the many snake goddesses I shall confine myself to the harvest goddess Renenutet, who is shown with a snake's head in relief and even in sculpture.[31] Here too the long wig disguises the transition, but the figure's appearance verges nonetheless on the grotesque; one step further, for example, to gods with insect heads, and the sphere of the eery or the ridiculous would be reached.

The Egyptians themselves also felt that forms such as this one were at the limit of what was acceptable in this type of iconography. "As elsewhere, the Egyptians' feeling for dignity

---

[28]No. 495 (cf. *Amduat* II, 128).

[29]A. Piankoff, *Le livre des quererts* (Cairo 1946) 43.

[30]Shown in a well-known vignette to chap. 17 of the Book of the Dead (e.g. Hornung, *Totenbuch* 69), and earlier on a Middle Kingdom "ivory wand" in the Metropolitan Museum of Art: W. C. Hayes, *The Scepter of Egypt* I (New York 1953) 249 fig. 159.

[31]Statuette of Renenutet suckling, from Sa el-Hagar: G. Michailidis, *BIE* 33 (1952) 153 with pl. 1; 37, 1 (1956) 191ff. with pl. 4. The best-known versions of the motif in relief are in the tombs of Khaemhat (Theban Tomb 57, reign of Amenophis III) and Ramesses III; cf. also J. Leibovitch, *JNES* 12 (1953) 73–113. There are also pictures of Renenutet in purely reptile form. See in addition J. Broekhuis, *De godin Renenwetet* (Assen 1971) chap. 2.

Plate IV. The god Khepry.

and moderation, which is always characteristic of them and kept them from indulging in crude fantasy, did not desert them" (Hans Bonnet).[32] Where insects, plants, or inanimate objects share in the divine essence or allude to gods, the Egyptians chose other methods of representation. It is exceptional for the god Khepry to have a beetle in place of a head (Plate IV); normally this matutinal, newly existing manifestation of the sun god carries the scarab (the hieroglyph for "to become, to come into existence") above his human head. Similarly, the goddess Selkis always carries a scorpion on her head, while Nefertem carries the lotus flower in which he is embodied, and the tree goddess sometimes carries her tree.[33] The same applies to the throne with which the name of the goddess Isis is written (Figure 7). Still other deities have hieroglyphs on their heads: Geb has a goose, Maat an ostrich feather, the goddess of the west the sign for "west," and Nephthys her entire name ("mistress of the house"). Here the distinction between caption and attribute or between picture and writing becomes blurred.

Marginal cases such as these should warn us once more against taking Egyptian representations of gods as pictures of them. Henri Frankfort proposed much more aptly that they should be taken as "ideograms"[34] or as pictorial signs that convey meaning in a metalanguage (see Chapter 8). The gods may indeed inhabit these representations as they may inhabit any image, but their true form is "hidden" and "mysterious," as Egyptian texts emphasize continually. Attributes may allude to the natures of deities and indicate that a deity is present, but no god is comprehended totally in his attributes. The same is certainly true also of other religions and conceptions of god.

The Egyptian iconography of gods acquires an unmistakable individuality through a rule that I should like to term the "interchangeability of head and attribute." Here again, the Egyptians brought the rule into harmony with their well-developed sense

[32]*Reallexikon* 220, where there are other pertinent remarks on the Egyptian iconography of deities.

[33]E.g. tomb of Nakht (mid-Eighteenth Dynasty): A. Mekhitarian, *Egyptian Painting* (Geneva etc. 1954, London etc. 1978) 18; Baines, *Fecundity Figures* §1.3.2.2.

[34]*Religion* 12.

of moderation, order, and beauty. They very rarely created monstrous effects, and then only in areas that were in any case liminal in relation to the ordered world. Birth and the bed on which the mother suckles her child are surrounded by the grotesque but helpful deities Bes and Thoeris, while the mysterious desert houses fabulous animals, such as the griffon or the Seth animal of indeterminate species; above all, the deceased is in danger of falling into the clutches of monstrous demons of the next world.

The limit set by aesthetic sensibility is exceeded much more frequently in the third intermediate and late periods. The Egyptians' feeling for moderation and for what is appropriate to divine majesty becomes uncertain, and mummiform coffins come to be covered with demons who have feathers, torches, and other objects in place of heads; often there are several heads belonging to different animals emerging from a single neck. Careful observation in any of the larger Egyptian collections will reveal countless of these grotesque creations among this material, which has not been worked through and is largely unpublished.[35]

From the New Kingdom, however, I know only of isolated, quite exceptional cases where an object is shown in place of a god's head. I was puzzled by one of these strange figures for some time before the riddle was solved by a coincidence; the figure is also another clear and convincing example of the rule that the heads and attributes of deities are interchangeable. At two points in the underworld book Amduat, a divine being is shown who has two strange protuberances in place of a head (Plate V). Like earlier commentators, I was unable to explain the nature and meaning of these "arteries" in my edition of the

[35]For a good example see the coffin Grenoble Inv. 3572, G. Kueny and J. Yoyotte, *Grenoble, Musée des Beaux-Arts. Collection égyptienne* (Inventaire des collections publiques françaises 23, Paris 1979) 83–86 no. 108, on which figures have instead of heads the name of Nefertem, the Hathor cow emerging from the mountain, and a pair of arms holding a sun disk; see also A. M. Blackman, *JEA* 5 (1918) with pl. 6 (bread or vegetable for head); Piankoff, *Litany* 66–128. The sanctuary in the temple of Hibis (fifth century B.C.) contains numerous comparable figures: N. de G. Davies, *The Temple of Hibis in el-Khargeh Oasis* III (Publications of the Metropolitan Museum of Art Egyptian Expedition 17, New York 1953) pls. 2–5.

Plate V. Figure of a god in the Amduat.

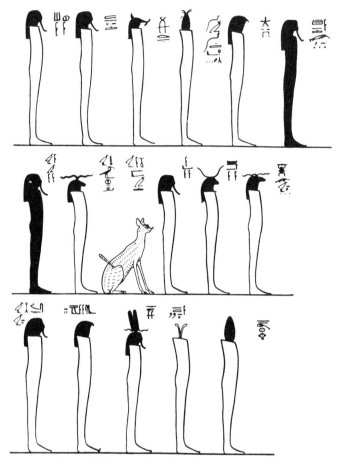

Figure 12. Figures of gods in the Litany of Re.

book.[36] Only later[37] did I encounter a figure with the same protuberances among the seventy-four manifestations of the sun
god depicted in the contemporary Litany of Re (Figure 12 bottom). It was now easy to interpret the figure, whose caption in
the Litany is the revealing name "he who fetters." The apparent "arteries" proved to be ropes, an attribute that indicates the

[36]*Amduat* II, 87 no. 310; 165 no. 710.
[37]Corrected in *Amduat* III, 63; cf. Hornung, *Buch der Anbetung* II, 118 n. (178).

120

function of this being, which is to bind the damned in the underworld. The underworld demon *Njkw* does the same thing; in the top register of the seventh hour of the Amduat he grips the rope that fetters the damned, who are lying helpless before Osiris, the judge of the dead. This demon carries in his hand the attribute that is appropriate to his function and nature, while the demon with the "arteries" has it in place of a head.

The principle that the outward appearance of deities is distinguished by attributes that they carry in their hands was not applied consistently until the advent of Greek religion. As the crook and "flail" in the hands of Osiris show, it was not foreign to the Egyptians, but from the early dynastic period on, the hands of the great Egyptian gods hold different, more general attributes that are common to all gods: the hieroglyphs for "life" (*'nḫ*) and "power" (*w's*), the most important benefits that the gods dispense to the world of creation. The deceased man who wishes to take on the role of the creator god, the "lord of all," takes hold of these attributes, showing that he is the "lord" of life, who has control over life and can dispense it to other beings.[38] I shall consider in Chapter 6 the significant pictorial motif of a deity holding the sign of life to the king's nose. Here all that need be recalled is that the hands of Egyptian deities hold only the general attributes of their divinity, and that specific attributes are therefore placed elsewhere: on the head or in place of a head.

The dress of Egyptian deities is also relatively uniform, seldom allowing the viewer to distinguish one from another. At all periods goddesses wear a long close-fitting garment with shoulder straps, while gods mostly wear an archaic short kilt which is sometimes combined with a shirt with shoulder straps. The entire bodies of Osiris, Ptah, Min, and some other gods disappear within a close-fitting wrapping. In Egypt only gods who are considered to be children are shown nude, for example, Harpokrates or the sun child on the flower; in addition,

---

[38]*CT* VII, 467b–d. In addition to the king and the queen, both of whom hold the sign of life relatively often, especially when deceased, there are rare examples with private individuals: H. G. Fischer, "An Eleventh Dynasty Couple Holding the Sign of Life," *ZÄS* 100 (1974) 16–28; Abd el Hamid Zayed, *RdE* 20 (1968) 152 with pl. 8a: deceased "singer of Amonrasonther."

the sky goddess Nut is depicted nude.[39] Egyptian deities are exempt from the vagaries of fashion. Only very rarely can the spirit of the times be seen in their dress, as when the elaborate, completely diaphanous garments of the late Eighteenth Dynasty occur exceptionally on a set of statues of goddesses, whose style is influenced by that of Amarna.[40]

More distinctions are possible among the crowns of the gods than in the rest of their clothing (Figure 7). Motifs such as feathers, horns, and sun disk allude to the nature of the wearers, and render their divinity visible.[41] But crowns are only seldom restricted to a particular deity, and one can observe in later periods an increasing tendency to mix elements and a preference for composite crowns, in which the individuality of the wearer is lost in the plethora of symbols of divine power.

In the iconography of other religions we find many ways of linking a deity pictorially with an attribute. The Greeks and Romans tended to put the attribute in the deity's hand, while the Hittites placed deities on animals that relate to their nature and manifestation—a tradition that can be traced back through the decoration of seals of the Akkad dynasty to the beginning of Sumerian civilization.[42] Mesopotamian deities can have a hu-

[39]E.g. on the ceilings of Ramessid royal tombs and on post–New Kingdom coffin lids. The goddess of the west (i.e. Hathor) is occasionally shown nude on the floors of late period coffins; there is an example in the Basel Museum für Völkerkunde (Inv. III, 130c).

[40]The protective goddesses from the canopic shrine of Tutankhamun, see e.g. I. E. S. Edwards, *Treasures of Tutankhamun* (U.S.A. exhibition catalogue, Metropolitan Museum of Art, New York 1976) no. 43, pls. 24–25; *Tutanchamun* (exhibition catalogue, Ägyptisches Museum, Berlin 1980) no. 1.

[41]See below. On crowns see the general studies of Bonnet, *Reallexikon* 394–95; Abd el Monem Joussef Abubakr, *Untersuchungen über die altägyptischen Kronen* (Glückstadt etc. 1937). There is no study of the crowns of gods and their development. De Rochemonteix collected forty-eight types of divine crown: *Rec. trav.* 6 (1885) 29–35 with pl. 2.

[42]For the earliest case (c. 3200 B.C.) see H. J. Lenzen, *XXI. vorläufiger Bericht . . . Uruk-Warka* (Deutsches Archäologisches Institut, Abteilung Baghdad, Berlin 1965) pl. 19, a seal impression on a clay cone (reference and interpretation supplied by M. A. Brandes). I am grateful to R. Opificius for many examples from the Akkad and Old Babylonian periods; for Assyria and Urartu cf. H. Demircioğlu, *Der Gott auf dem Stier* (Dissertation, Berlin 1939); H.-V. Hermann, *Jahrbuch des Deutschen Archäologischen Instituts* 81 (1966) 92ff.

Figure 13. "Soul" birds.

man head that sits on an animal body. In all these cultures the gods appear in human form after the "anthropomorphization of the powers," and the animal, vegetable, or inanimate attribute serves to define the figure more precisely; the way in which the two are combined is irrelevant to the nature of the deity. Here too the Egyptians were never dogmatic, but kept several possibilities open. The combination of a human body with an attribute for head may be claimed to be specifically Egyptian, but it is not the only alternative and should not be equated with the Egyptian image of gods.

The opposite solution, which was elaborated more thoroughly in Mesopotamia, is best known from Egypt in the form of the sphinx;[43] here the animal body is crowned by a human head, which may in extreme cases have the ears and mane of the animal, so that only the face remains human. The iconography of one Egyptian "soul" concept, the *ba,* also has the mixed form in reverse: the "soul bird" has a human head and often human arms, which it uses in a gesture of adoration or when scooping up water (Figure 13). This form is used more frequently for personified objects. The executioner's tools (*šms*), which go in front of the sun god, who acts as judge, and his bark on his nightly journey through the underworld, have human heads, showing that they are personal, independent powers.[44] The underworld books of the New Kingdom, in particular, are full of similar personifications. The stelae that surround the

[43]Cf. in general H. Demisch, *Die Sphinx. Geschichte ihrer Darstellung von den Anfängen bis zur Gegenwart* (Stuttgart 1977).
[44]*Amduat* II, 146, with addendum III, 65. The personified birth brick with human head in pictures of judgment after death belongs here, cf. C. Seeber, *Untersuchungen zur Darstellung des Totengerichts im alten Ägypten* (MÄS 35, 1976) 83–88.

"lake of fire" in the Book of Gates and the graves of the gods in the seventh hour of the Amduat—all such things that are experienced as persons can be seen to look at us with human faces. The verso of the Narmer palette, with its enemy country personified in the same way, shows that this mode of representation is even older than the "normal" mixed form of human body and animal head, and that its origin is a direct product of the "anthropomorphization of the powers" (Figure 9).

Whatever combination the Egyptians chose, the mixed form of their gods is nothing other than a hieroglyph, a way of "writing" not the name but the nature and function of the deity in question. The Egyptians do not hesitate to call hieroglyphs "gods,"[45] and even to equate individual signs in the script with particular gods;[46] it is quite in keeping with their views to see images of the gods as signs in a metalanguage. As is true of every Egyptian hieroglyph, they are more than just ciphers or lifeless symbols; the god can inhabit them, his cult image will normally be in the same form, and his priests may assume his role by wearing animal masks—Pierre Lacau even assumed that this priestly animal costume was the origin of the mixed form for gods.[47]

But none of these animals, plants, and objects that are related to the manifestation of deities gives any information about the true form of a deity. According to the texts the true form is "hidden" and "mysterious"; the Coffin Texts tell us that only the deceased may know the true form of a god (CT VI, 69c, 72d). No thinking Egyptian would have imagined that the true form of Amun was a man with a ram's head. Amun is the divine power that may be seen in the image of a ram, among many others, as Horus shows himself in the image of the hawk whose wings span the sky and Anubis in the image of the black canine ("jackal") who busies himself around the tombs in the desert. Similarly, Christian saints, especially the four evange-

---

[45]*Urk.* I. 7.11; Junker, *Gíza* XI, 84–85.

[46]Winter, *Untersuchungen* 76–84; Baines, *Fecundity Figures* §1.3.2.2.

[47]See J. Sainte Fare Garnot, *Aspects de l'Egypte antique* (Publications de l'Institut français d'archéologie, Collection Eôs, Cairo 1959) 21.

lists, may be shown in animal form or with the head of an animal.[48]

None of these images shows the *true* form of a god, and none can encompass the full richness of his nature—hence the variable iconography of Egyptian gods, which is seldom reduced to a fixed, canonical form. Every image is an imperfect means of making a god visible, characterizing his nature, and distinguishing him from other deities. In the early days of egyptology Lepsius already perceived that this intimate and wholly successful fusion of attribute and human, personal manifestation was the essence of the mixed form: "[The gods] can be distinguished easily, partly through the many symbols they wear on their heads or in place of a head, and partly through their names, which are always written next to them."[49]

Multiplicity of forms and pantheism

Every image can constitute a powerful but, in the last analysis, limited and imperfect expression of the nature and reality of the deity who is shown. This imperfection is the root of the multiple forms of Egyptian gods, which is analogous to the multiplicity of their names (see Chapter 3), for a name, too, can express only one aspect of a god's complex nature. This multiplicity of forms renders the iconography of Egyptian gods often difficult and confusing. Scarcely any important deity is restricted to a single form and manifestation. The canine form of Anubis and the mixed crocodile, lion, and hippopotamus form of Thoeris are relatively fixed, but the rest of the major deities are true to their common epithet "rich in manifestations" and behave, to quote another epithet, as "lord of manifestations,"[50] in which the word "lord" means that they have power over some-

[48]Cf. Demisch, *Die Sphinx* (n. 43 above) 218–19 with figs. 598–99 (evangelists), 600 (Christ).

[49]*Götterkreis* 1–2 = 157–58.

[50]*CT* V, 211f, referring to Atum; further examples in Assmann, *Liturg. Lieder* 216–17 no. (46). In the sun hymn that Assmann translates and comments upon, even this "multiform" appearance of the sun god is only one of his many manifestations (*ḫprw*). Contrary to Assmann, I would see the epithet as marking a further intensification of this aspect of the god.

thing. Parallel epithets refer to the multiplicity of "faces" (*ḥrw*) which the gods have at their disposal; the most varied gods are termed "many-face"[51] or are "lord of faces."[52] The iconography of the gods shows that epithets such as these refer to a well-known reality: a deity shows many faces to an Egyptian and presents himself to him in many forms.

Thus the god Thoth appears as an ibis, a baboon, or the moon, but also in purely human form or in a mixed form consisting of some of these elements, which can never exhaust the full richness of his nature. With deities who are combined syncretistically with other deities (Chapter 3), and so may take on the form of other gods, the range of possibilities is vastly wider. Apart from his own pictorial forms of human being, ram, and Nile goose, Amun acquires the sun disk from Re and ithyphallic form from Min. And Isis, whose "many names" and "many forms" continue to be emphasized in the Graeco-Roman period, hides her nature in a bewildering number of attributes and forms, from a mother suckling her child to snake, scorpion, and bird, and appears as well in the forms of the goddesses with whom she is combined syncretistically;[53] from the New Kingdom on, Isis and Hathor can often be distinguished only by the captions giving their names, not by their iconography.[54]

"What a confusion!" one might cry in the words of Adolf Erman. The one creator god "made himself into millions" (see Chapter 5), into the differentiated richness of the pantheon, whose forms may be exchanged at will. As we have seen, only a few gods are fixed in their iconography, while conversely a single animal or object can be a manifestation of many deities. For example, how many gods and goddesses may be embodied in the form of a lion—or in the sun, in which one may adore almost any of the great deities, including even Osiris!

[51]*Amduat* II, 119; additional references from the Coffin Texts to Philae in L. Kákosy, *ZÄS* 90 (1963) 67.

[52]J. C. Goyon, *RdE* 20 (1968) 89 no. (4), gives reference for Sokar—parallel to "rich in manifestations"—and other gods.

[53]For a collection of material, which could easily be extended, see Münster, *Isis* 201–3.

[54]*Ibid.* 119–20; this is, however, certainly not "random."

In the Eighteenth Dynasty Litany of Re the sun god is equated with the most various deities.[55] The first editor of the text, Edouard Naville, saw these equations as the product of a pantheistic view,[56] and for Breasted too "solar pantheism" was one of the basic elements in the Egyptian conception of god.[57] For Alfred Wiedemann, not only is Amon-Re a "pantheistic deity," but Ptah-Sokar-Osiris is "a being who is viewed pantheistically and who rules and encompasses everything."[58] Van der Leeuw,[59] Bonnet,[60] and many other recent and contemporary authors speak of Egyptian pantheism; the *Lexikon für Theologie und Kirche* still sees "the Egyptian cult of the gods and of the dead" as being "pervaded by pantheistic conceptions."[61]

At a first glance gods such as Re, Amun, and Ptah, with their multiplicity of names and manifestations, might seem to be identified with everything that exists. But if one examines the material more closely, there emerge clearly the constraints that rendered impossible any steady progress toward pantheism in the sense of the deification of everything and the "essential identity of God with everything that exists."[62] The number of manifestations of a god is limited; Amun may appear in the most various forms, but never as the moon, a tree, or a

[55]Piankoff, *Litany*; Hornung, *Buch der Anbetung*, where I demonstrate (II, 30–36) that the figures in the litany were originally no more than illustrations to the invocations to the sun god, which were then reinterpreted secondarily as manifestations of the god.

[56]*La litanie du soleil* (Leipzig 1876) 6, 122. According to his *Religion,* the Heliopolitan cosmogony (pp. 115–16 = 135–37) and some solar hymns (p. 124 = 146–47) are pantheistic in character.

[57]*Development* 360, and a "national pantheism" pp. 312, 357, 362.

[58]*Religion* 139 = 260; 76 = 136. Elsewhere in the book Wiedemann speaks several times of pantheism, esp. pp. 166ff. = 301ff.

[59]"Altägyptischer Pantheismus," in H. Frick, ed., *Rudolf-Otto-Ehrung* = *Quellenstudien zur Religionsgeschichte* (Aus der Welt der Religion n.s. 1, Berlin 1940) 16–38. The article is essentially a commentary on spell 215 of the Pyramid Texts, but the vital line §147b can be interpreted differently as "Atum (and) every god"; the two do not have to be identified.

[60]*Reallexikon* 244, with reservations. S. A. B. Mercer, *The Religion of Ancient Egypt* (London 1949) 308, correctly points out that pantheism is not cultic in character and is therefore un-Egyptian.

[61]S. Pfürtner in vol. 8 (1963) col. 27.

[62]Definition from *Lexikon für Theologie und Kirche* 8 (2d ed., Freiburg 1963), art. "Pantheismus."

stretch of water. And, as Wiedemann already saw, amid all the "fusion" Egyptian gods never sacrifice their separate natures: "The result is a general fusion of forms that should logically have led to pantheism. This did not happen, because the Egyptians did not want to sacrifice the individuality of each figure, even though they were identified with one another."[63]

So although in Egyptian religion the accumulation of manifestations and combinations of deities produced phenomena that are reminiscent of pantheism, the resemblance is coincidental and superficial. The Egyptians never had the inclination or the wish to deify everything. The Egyptian creator god may manifest himself in his creation, but he is not absorbed into it. His nature may be extended by new forms and epithets, but it never becomes identical with the "all," which for Egyptians certainly included realms that are not divine. Therefore one cannot speak of pantheism, in the strict sense, in Egyptian religion.

The gods in their "true" appearance

If the depiction of the gods is not a picture of their bodies but a characterization of their nature, a sign, or a hieroglyph in a metalanguage, what, then, is their true form? In order to know the true form of the gods one must have seen them. So we must first pursue the question of how and in what form deities manifest themselves to mankind. The sources that tell us about this are literary, because we cannot use pictorial forms as evidence for the "true" appearance of the gods. This situation may seem paradoxical, but follows from our understanding of the nature of the Egyptian iconography of gods.

Egyptian gods do not mingle freely with people on earth; they may be encountered only in liminal areas where the world of mankind and the world of the gods come into contact—on a distant island, for instance, as in the story of the Shipwrecked Sailor, or in a dream. But a systematic review of the texts produces a good many other cases in which a theophany is described, especially in hymns and in literature about the hereafter.

[63]*Religion* 139 = 260; 76 = 136. Retranslated here.

The description of the god's appearance in the story of the Shipwrecked Sailor[64] contains important details, and is noteworthy also because the deity who is revealed is new and previously unknown to the protagonist. An Egyptian official has been shipwrecked while sailing through the Red Sea and thrown "by a wave of the sea" onto a lonely island. He spends three days there, finds vegetable and animal nourishment in great abundance, and makes a burnt offering in order to thank the "gods" for his rescue. Then the atmosphere grows strange, and he relates:

> Then I heard a noise of thunder; I thought it was a wave of the sea; trees cracked and the earth quaked. I uncovered my face (again) and found that it was a snake coming. It was thirty cubits (long, about fifteen meters), and its (divine) beard was more than two cubits (one meter). Its flesh was gilded and its eyebrows were of genuine lapis lazuli.

The snake god threatens the intruding castaway with death by fire, and the man faints out of fright. But then the deity proves to be friendly and full of prophetic insight into the future. He dismisses with a laugh the material offerings that the rescued man promises him, because he lives in plenty and his rule on earth is only transitory: the shipwrecked man will never see the island again, for it will "become water." The god does not say what will happen to him then, but he has already recounted the destruction of his seventy-four relatives, which he alone survived, in a story within the story. We must assume that the snake god, too, is a mortal, transitory being, and this may relate to the only favor he asks of the shipwrecked man on his return home, which is to make him known in Egypt. The god is not named at any point, and he is only indirectly spoken of as a _ntr_ "god"—otherwise he is called simply a snake (a masculine word in Egyptian)—but the story leaves us in no doubt that the shipwrecked man sees in him the manifestation

[64]Text: _MES_ 41–48; passage quoted below 43, 5–9; translations: Simpson, _Literature_ 52; Lichtheim, _Literature_ I, 212. On the god cf. M. T. Derchain-Urtel, _SAK_ 1 (1974) 83–104, who relates the seventy-four relatives to the seventy-four manifestations in the Litany of Re (n. 55 above).

129

of a god and the revelation of a hitherto unknown deity in distant lands. The form in which the god appears to the man is that of an animated cult image of the finest materials (gold and lapis lazuli), complete with a divine attribute (a beard).

The appearance of known and familiar deities, which may occur in a dream, is rather different. The fact that for the Egyptians there were dreams "by night and by day" probably indicates that the concept of a "dream" (*rswt*) also includes "visions," *epiphaneia*,[65] especially since the word strictly means "awaking."

The best-known dreams or visions are those of New Kingdom kings. Hunting in the desert while still a prince, Tuthmosis IV lay down at midday in the shadow of the Great Sphinx at Giza, and slumber "seized" him. Then "he found the person of this noble god speaking with his own mouth, as a father speaks to his son. . . ." Thus he heard the mouth of the Great Sphinx speaking. For the Egyptians the Sphinx was Harmachis ("Horus in the Horizon"), a manifestation of the sun god, but Tuthmosis IV does not seem to have considered it to be a specific form of the god—at least this is not stated in the inscription to be the case (*Urk.* IV, 1542).

Gods were manifested to other New Kingdom kings in dreams on their campaigns, but the descriptions of these are even shorter. "The person of this noble god" Amun appears to the sleeping Amenophis II "in order to give valor to his son" (*Urk.* IV, 1306–7). King Merneptah receives a similar encouragement from his favorite god, Ptah.[66] From the appearances in dreams we learn something about the actions and statements of the gods, but nothing about their forms. The dream book in the Nineteenth Dynasty Papyrus Chester Beatty III shows that Egyptians—not just the king, but anyone—could sometimes see a deity in a dream.[67] Among the many phenomena one can

---

[65]Cf. F. Daumas, *BIFAO* 56 (1957) 54–55. Even if Merikare l. 137 (Volten, *Politische Schriften* 75) is translated differently, the fact of daydreaming remains established.

[66]G. Posener, *De la divinité du pharaon* (Cahiers de la Société asiatique 15, Paris 1960) 85; S. Sauneron in *Les songes* (Sources orientales 2, Paris 1959) 24–25.

[67]Gardiner, *Chester Beatty* I, 12, II pl. 5 (recto 2, 14); cf. also Posener, *Divinité* (n. 66 above) 86.

see in a dream is "seeing the upper (or: chief?) god: good. It means much food." Here the god does not act but is seen—in what form is not stated.[68] Manifestations in dreams are generally ill-suited to giving us clues about the true apearance of the gods, even though in the Egyptian view the sleeper dwells in the world of the gods, in the next world, as Adriaan de Buck demonstrated.[69] In order to make progress in this matter and to complement the information from the story of the Shipwrecked Sailor, we must search out texts that are directly concerned with the next world and the appearance of gods in the world of the dead. There we are in a world in which the gods are at home (cf. Chapter 7), from which they emerge into this world only on specific occasions.

The first stanza of the notorious "cannibal spell" in the Pyramid Texts (spell 273–74) runs:

The sky is clouded, the stars disturbed,[70]
the "bows" quake, the bones of the earth god tremble.
But those who move are still when they have seen the King
with (his) soul manifest, as a god
who lives on his fathers and feeds on his mothers.

As in the story of the Shipwrecked Sailor, a great commotion in nature announces the appearance of the deity (who is here the deceased king). In other texts, too, the quaking of the earth or of the heavenly bodies accompanies the appearance of deities,[71]

---

[68]For a case in which Hathor appears in a dream to a private individual see J. Assmann, *RdE* 30 (1978) 22–50.

[69]*De godsdienstige opvatting van den slaap* (MVEOL 4, 1939) esp. p. 29.

[70]All recent translators, including R. O. Faulkner, *The Ancient Egyptian Pyramid Texts* (Oxford 1969) 80, and H. Altenmüller, in *Fragen* 20, follow the *Wörterbuch's* suggested rendering of *jhj* "to become dark(?)" (*Wb*. I, 121, 8), although the word is a passive participle of *hwj* "to strike, drive, heave"; compare also the writing with the "striking man" in *CT* VI, 177b. Roeder's translation "quake" [*beben*] (*Urkunden zur Religion des alten Ägypten* [Jena 1915] 191) is also possible. The meaning is best expressed by Schiller's "In the sky is busy movement" (*Wallensteins Tod* 5, 3, l. 3405). My rendering is followed by M. Lichtheim, *Göttinger Miszellen* 41 (1980) 67.

[71]References to the Pyramid Texts in J. S. Karig, "Die Landschaftsdarstellung in den Privatgräbern des Alten Reiches" (Dissertation, Göttingen 1962) 146. Cf. also *CT* II, 209d; VII, 252a; *BPf* 242 and *passim*. There are countless parallels in

reflecting the huge amount of power which emanates from them—power that the dead king hopes to possess himself in his role as a god. On the sarcophagus of the "god's wife" Ankhnesneferibre (sixth century B.C.) the deceased appears in the role of the goddess Hathor of Dendara as the destructive eye of the sun: "no man and no land sees her . . . if she is seen, a million cubits of fire are on all her ways."[72]

Characteristic of a god's approach is that monstrous events announce him, and his form is defined by the signs of power that are at his disposal and surround him like an aura. In the "cannibal spell" quoted above they are part of the deceased's epiphany:

> The *ka*s of the King are around him, his *hemusets* at his feet.
> His "gods" (crowns?) are on him, his uraei are on his brow,
> the "leading snake" of the King is on his forehad. . . ,
> the powers (*wsrw*) of the King are in their place. (*Pyr.* §396)

In the same spell the king swallows crowns in the next world in order to annex their powers, for the attributes are not just signs, but carriers of divine strength. Spell 422 of the Pyramid Texts describes in great detail all these symbols of power which are part of a god's manifestation:

> Your *ba* is yours within you,
> your might is yours around you,
> your *wrrt* crown is yours, on you,
> your *mjzwt* crown is yours on your shoulder,
> your face is before you, your adoration is before you,
> the retinue of a god is behind you, the noble ones of a god are
>   before you,
> performing "A god comes, a god comes. . . ." (*Pyr.* §§753a–754b)

---

the history of religions—from 1 Kings 19:11–12 to Goethe's "Poetische Gedan-ken über die Höllenfahrt Jesu Christi" (1765)—but there is no need to cite them here.

[72]C. E. Sander-Hansen, *Die religiösen Texte auf dem Sarg der Anchnesneferibre* (Copenhagen 1937) 126 ll. 407–10; for an earlier parallel see *Amduat* I, 90–91; II, 103: the "secret way of the land of Sokar" is "full of flames from the mouth of Isis."

Jan Assmann has collected this passage and a number of similar ones from the Pyramid Texts and Coffin Texts[73] in his *Liturgische Lieder an den Sonnengott,* and compares them with similar descriptions in solar hymns of the New Kingdom. In all the texts the awesome quality of the god's manifestation is expressed by listing an accumulation of visible and invisible symbols of power. These are the vehicles of power, and to represent them is to evoke that power. The attributes we have encountered in the iconography of gods also form part of their true appearance, in which they are vehicles of power; but in addition to these outward signs there are presentiments, feelings, and effects that cannot be depicted. Radiance and aroma, which are the "mildest" signs of divine presence, can be identified only in textual sources.

When the god Amun approaches the sleeping Queen Ahmose in order to beget the later Queen Hatshepsut by her, "the palace is flooded with divine aroma."[74] The aroma wakes the queen and indicates to her that the god is present, even before he lets her see his true "form of a god" (*jrw n ntr*; he has taken on the form of her husband Tuthmosis I).[75] We are not given any more details, but this much is clear, that the manifestation of the god produces a pervasive aroma "like that of (the incense land) Punt." The divine aroma is well attested elsewhere, among Christian martyrs, for example,[76] and it is the "ozone of a god" that Dr. Riemer in Thomas Mann's *Lotte in Weimar* senses around the great prince of poets, Goethe.[77] Already in the early dynastic period an unguent has the name "aroma of Horus,"[78] and in the Ptolemaic temple of Horus at Edfu we still read "the throat breathes from your aroma."[79] In the great Eighteenth Dynasty hymn to Amun in the Cairo Museum the god is the one

[73]*Pyr.* §§1089b–d, 1374–75; *CT* V, 392e–i.

[74]Restored from a parallel: H. Brunner, *Die Geburt des Gottkönigs* (ÄgAbh 10, 1964) pl. 4, fourth col. at right, pp. 35–58; on the god's aroma see p. 51.

[75]*Urk.* IV, 220, 1; Brunner, *Die Geburt* (n. 74 above) pl. 4, third col. at right. The terminology distinguishes clearly between the god's true and assumed forms.

[76]T. Baumeister, *Martyr Invictus* (Forschungen zur Volkskunde 46, Münster 1972) 44.

[77]In *Gesammelte Werke* II (Frankfurt a.M.: S. Fischer Verlag 1960) 445.

[78]Kaplony, *Inschriften* I, 291.

[79]*Edfou* I, 293, 1–2 (cf. Otto, *Gott und Mensch* 150, 18 with no. 329).

"whose aroma the gods love when he comes from Punt,"[80] while the deceased, too, as "Osiris" or as "god," achieves a divine fragrance.[81] In the underworld books, however, it is often difficult to distinguish between the "aroma" of divine beings and the "stink" of decaying corpses, because the Egyptian always speaks of *stj* "smell," literally "what pours forth."

Next to aroma, radiance is what betrays the presence of Egyptian deities. When Queen Hatshepsut receives the expedition to Punt on its return home and enters the role of a god[82] with "myrrh on her limbs," and divine fragrance pouring forth from her, "her aroma mingled with (the divine incense of) Punt. Her skin was gilded with white gold, glittering, as the stars do, within the festival hall, before the entire land" (*Urk.* IV, 339, 13–340, 2). A related idea, attested from the Middle Kingdom on, is that the "flesh" of the gods is of gold and their bodies of the most precious materials.[83] The bark in which the sun god travels is golden and radiant,[84] and the blessed deceased wishes to become "one body" with the god and hence to partake in his precious, radiant substance.[85]

A god may be sensed and seen not only in his attributes of fragrance, radiance and power, but also and more forcefully in the way he affects men's hearts—in the love, fear, terror, respectful awe, and other feelings that his presence evokes. In his *Liturgische Lieder an den Sonnengott,* which I have already cited several times, Jan Assmann has analyzed with a sure touch how a god is experienced in the human heart—leaving aside the problem of his objective existence.[86] In these cases the

[80]Grébaut, *Hymne* 6.

[81]Sander-Hansen, *Die religiösen Texte* (n. 72 above) 44. The "sweet smell" of the blessed is also stressed in the Book of Gates (*BPf* 289), but this probably relates to the prevention of bodily decay.

[82]The subjects acclaim her "in the instances of her divine-ness." (cf. p. 64). Thus the text emphasizes that she makes her appearance and acts as a "god"; for the king in the role of a god see also below.

[83]References in P. Seibert, *Die Charakteristik* (ÄgAbh 17, 1967) 121–22; Assmann, *Liturg. Lieder* 81 with n. 16; J. Yoyotte, *Annuaire de l'Ecole pratique des Hautes Etudes, Ve Section* 79 (1971–72) 165.

[84]A. Massart, *MDAIK* 15 (1957) 184, verso V, 7.

[85]Cf. Assmann, *Liturg. Lieder* 101 (his n. 57 also gives references for the mummy as the "body of the god").

[86]Esp. *Liturg. Lieder* 64–68, 250–62.

invisible god may be grasped as a subjective reality, whereas he can be made visible to the believer only in images, because his true appearance has no fixed contours and is suffused with blinding radiance.[87] Unlike Jewish and Muslim believers, Egyptians are not forbidden from making an image of a god, but they distinguish carefully between the image and the "true form," which is revealed to human eyes only in the most exceptional cases. In the next world it may be possible to see the true form and hence the god himself, but here on earth the believer must fall back on images and intermediaries, and lives in an unsatisfied longing to behold the "perfection" (*nfrw*)— which often means the physical manifestation—of the god.

Images of gods; the king

According to the systematic theology of the New Kingdom, as formulated, for example, in the Leiden hymn to Amun,[88] the god is in the sky in order to illuminate the world,[89] his body rests in the underworld, and on earth among men images of him bear witness to his presence. These images too may be the "bodies" of the gods, into which they "enter."[90] The most important are the cult images, that is, the temple statues on which the daily cult is performed. In order to resemble the true body of the god as closely as possible they were made of the most precious materials, and almost all have succumbed to human greed; only very rarely have the originals been preserved over the millennia. The cult image normally partook in the invisibility of the deity; it was set up in the dark sanctuary and was accessible only to the officiating priest, who daily celebrated the ritual on it and before it. During the great festivals the

[87]A unique figure of a winged "angel" of uncertain identity in a scene of judgment after death in a Ramessid tomb is surrounded by flickering lines that could indicate the radiance of a divine presence or the rapid fluttering of wings (there are other "normal" figures of deities in the scene): W. S. Smith, *The Art and Architecture of Ancient Egypt* (Pelican History of Art, Harmondsworth 1958) pl. 16B; C. Seeber, *Untersuchungen zur Darstellung des Totengerichts im alten Ägypten* (MÄS 35, 1976) 206 n. 10, with references.

[88]Zandee, *De Hymnen aan Amon* pl. IV, 16–17.

[89]*Urk.* IV, 1676, 19, referring to Amun.

[90]Junker, *Götterlehre* 65.

Figure 14. The cult statue of a god in procession.

portable image of the god was carried out into the outside world on the shoulders of priests (Figure 14), gave oracles and was thus accessible to human concerns; but even then, to judge by the reliefs, it remained invisible in its covered shrine.[91] Even to see a god's image was a special privilege that was accorded daily only to the officiating priest, after he had opened the shrine of the god's image.[92]

Just as a god may reside in a cult image of stone or wood, so he may reside in the body of an animal. The best known of these living cult images is the Apis bull in Memphis, which was worshiped as a separate deity by the early dynastic period, and later as an embodiment of the god Ptah. Here, as with

[91]An exception is the unshrouded cult image of Amenophis I on the west bank at Thebes, see J. Černý in R. A. Parker, *A Saite Oracle Papyrus from Thebes* (Brown Egyptological Studies 4, Providence, R.I. 1962) 42–43.

[92]Cf. the chapter of the daily temple ritual "seeing the god," which comes after the opening of the shrine: Moret, *Rituel* 55–56. For references to "seeing" the god in the realm of the dead see *Amduat* II, 16–17; III, 59.

other bull cults in Egypt,[93] we see the worship of a single member of a species; only when all members of a species are worshiped can one speak of "animal cults."

In animal cults, as in names and manifestations, we encounter the ability of Egyptian gods to extend their existence almost endlessly—to be manifest not just in one ibis or crocodile, but in all ibises or all crocodiles. This multiplication is another example of a tendency we have encountered several times in the Egyptian conception of god; but even in this form the tendency does not lead to pantheism, for only certain species are related to a deity, and they are often worshiped in only one locality. The multiplication of visible images makes the god more accessible and visible for the believer, and brings him close on earth, so that the concerns of individuals can reach him more easily. Animal cults are therefore part of a popular piety, and may be compared in many respects to the Catholic cult of relics, whose proliferations they also share. Here we need not go any further into Egyptian animal cults[94] because their logical extension, which was not put into practice before the late period, teaches us a misunderstanding rather than a genuine comprehension of the Egyptian conception of god. Individual animals are not the god, but the god may take up his abode in them; they allude to him and are images and vessels of him. This is why, despite innumerable manifestations in animals, Egyptian deities only rarely have animal names: their nature is not subsumed in these manifestations.

For simple worshipers image and deity may merge, and they may encounter the god Thoth personally in every ibis, but the theology of the priests always distinguishes carefully, in formulations that vary from period to period, between animal and deity. For the priests the animal remains a symbol in the fore-

[93]E. Otto, *Beiträge zur Geschichte der Stierkulte in Ägypten* (UGAÄ 13, 1938); S. Morenz, "Rote Stiere—Unbeachtetes zu Buchis und Mnevis," in O. Firchow, ed., *Ägyptologische Studien* [Grapow Festschrift] (Deutsche Akademie der Wissenschaften zu Berlin, Institut für Orientforschung, Veröffentlichung 29, Berlin 1955) 238–43 = *Religion und Geschichte* 360–65; A. Hermann, "Der letzte Apisstier," *Jahrbuch für Antike und Christentum* 3 (1960) 34–50.

[94]See E. Hornung, "Die Bedeutung des Tieres im alten Agypten," *StG* 20 (1967) 69–84 (with earlier references).

ground, an intermediary between man and god. As "speakers" or "heralds" of the god the sacred bulls may dispense oracles in which the god reveals his will. All sacred animals are the *ba* of a deity,[95] the visible manifestation of an invisible power, as the wind is the *ba* of the air god Shu and the visible sun is the *ba* of the sun god. At the end of the pagan period in Egypt Celsus still held them to be sacred signs of deities, *aenigmata*.[96]

Human beings are also "images of god"; rare but unambiguous references show that this is true of all human beings. In the stories of Papyrus Westcar even a criminal condemned to death is one of the "sacred herd" of god.[97] In the Instruction for Merikare (first intermediate period, c. 2060 B.C.) mankind, this "herd of god," is said to be "his likenesses (*snn*) who came forth from his flesh,"[98] and for the teacher Ani of the end of the Eighteenth Dynasty, "Men are the equals (*sn-nw*) of god (because of) their custom of listening to a man who brings a plea. Not only the wise man is his equal, as if the rest (were) so many cattle. . . ."[99] Thus all men may be god's children from birth (Merikare), or may prove by their actions that they are images of god; the man with knowledge is also said elsewhere to be a "likeness (*mjtj*) of god"[100] and sons "images" of their fathers;[101] in these cases what is meant is not a simple similarity but a fundamental kinship of action, nature, and rank.

But the reigning king is the prime son and image of the creator god; almost all Egyptian references to man as the "image of god" relate to him. From the Fourth Dynasty on—that is, from the time of the Great Pyramid at Giza—the king is the "son" of the sun god, and in the course of the Middle Kingdom

[95]Morenz, *Religion* 165–66 = 157–58; E. Otto, *Saeculum* 14 (1963) 259–60.

[96]Cited by T. Hopfner, *Fontes historiae religionis aegyptiacae* (Fontes historiae religionum 2, Bonn 1923) 352 (Origen 3, 19).

[97]K. Sethe, *Ägyptische Lesestücke* (2d ed., Leipzig 1928) 30, 24–31, 2. For translations see Simpson, *Literature* 24; Lichtheim, *Literature* I, 219.

[98]Volten, *Politische Schriften* 73 ll. 131–32.

[99]Volten, *Anii* 161–63.

[100]*Amduat* I, 22, 2–3; III line 13; Volten, *Anii* 171 (10, 15). For the various Egyptian terms for "image" and the differences between them cf. Hornung, "Mensch als Bild Gottes."

[101]*Urk.* IV, 1383, 11, in the text about the installation of the vizier Useramun, cf. Hornung, "Mensch als Bild Gottes" 152 with n. 46.

and second intermediate period a new definition of the king as the "image" of the same deity was developed. I have analyzed the meaning of this in detail elsewhere.[102] For the Egyptians the vital point is not the outward similarity between the king and a particular deity which might be suggested, for example, by statues of the god Amun with the individual features of the youthful Tutankhamun. There is similarity of deed as well as similarity of appearance; the king acts "like Mont (the god of war)" or "like his father Amon-Re." All the similarities point toward a comprehensive and fundamental kinship that links the king with all deities, so that he can be called simply "image (*tjt*) of the gods" (*Urk*. IV, 276, 15; 2045, 2); so Egyptians are not disturbed when Queen Hatshepsut says that she is the "likeness" of the male god Amon-Re.[103]

The king, like the cult image of a god, is normally hidden, being separated from the people in his palace. But when he steps outside and "is manifest" to his subjects, surrounded by symbols of power and protection, he becomes the *deus praesens* for the adulating and rejoicing people, allowing them to feel the presence of the creator god, whose deeds he accomplishes again. What he does is "not the work of men"; his words are "the utterances of god himself."[104]

The god who is chiefly recognized in the appearance of the king is Re, the creator and preserver of the world. "You are Re," high officials of the New Kingdom cry out to the king;[105] earlier, in the Middle Kingdom, Amenemhat III (1844–1797 B.C.) is said to be "Re . . . who is seen in his rays."[106] A century later the king is said to be "Re of foreign lands,"[107] and in the

[102]Hornung, "Mensch als Bild Gottes"; cf. also Blumenthal, *Untersuchungen* 98–99. For the pictorial identification of the king with gods see Ali Radwan, *MDAIK* 31 (1975) 99–108.

[103]*Urk*. IV, 244, 14 (the word for image [*snnt*] is in the feminine).

[104]*Urk*. IV, 1236, 2 (the action is attributed to the power of Amun); 165, 13—both statements are about Tuthmosis III.

[105]Usersatet to Amenophis II: R. A. Caminos, *The Shrines and Rock Inscriptions of Ibrim* (ASE 32, 1968) 70 with pl. 28 l. 9; Haremhab to Tutankhamun: Hari, *Horemheb* pl. 19 l. 4 (tomb relief from Saqqara in Leiden).

[106]Blumenthal, *Untersuchungen* 100; examples with other gods pp. 99–103.

[107]On Thirteenth Dynasty seals from Byblos: H. Goedicke, *MDAIK* 19 (1963) 1–6; W. F. Albright, *BASOR* 176 (1964) 44–45.

New Kingdom "Re of the kings" and "Re of the rulers."[108] Ramesses II is "likeness of Re, illuminating this world like the sun
disk,"[109] and his successor Merneptah is "sun disk of mankind,
who drives darkness from Egypt."[110] The boundaries between
likeness, comparison, and identification seem blurred to us,
and a manifestation "like Re" becomes imperceptibly a manifestation "as Re."[111] It is said of Amenophis III that "every one of
his statues correspond[s] to a manifestation of the person of
Re" (*Urk*. IV, 1724, 14). There is a whole series of statues of
this king in particular—and later of Ramesses II—that were the
objects of cults during the ruler's own lifetime.[112] Some of the
statues of Ramesses II have the name "Ramesses—Meryamun
the god," which seems to refer to a deification of the living
ruler, as does the entire phenomenon of statue cult. But in
contrast with his statues, the king himself is not a "manifestation" (*ḫprw*) of the sun god, even though he may be an "image"
of him; during his lifetime he receives no cult, thus differing
from a true cult image or a sacred animal.

We come now unavoidably to the question of the king's divinity—a question that has been answered in many different
ways, from the work of Alexandre Moret, *Du caractère religieux
de la royauté pharaonique* (Paris 1902) to Georges Posener's *De la
divinité du pharaon* (Cahiers de la Société Asiatique 15, Paris
1960). Is the king himself a god, is he only metaphorically a
"sun king," or does he have a dual nature, half man and half
god? It would be foolhardy, and beyond the scope of this book,
to analyze here the complex and involved problems of Egyp-

---

[108]I gave examples of this and other "solar" epithets in *StG* 18 (1965) 76 with n.
42; add the king as "Re of the nine bows" (i.e. all peoples) from the reign of
Haremhab on (Hari, *Horemheb* pl. 51, 53) and Tuthmosis III as "sun disk of all
lands" (*Urk*. IV, 887, 16).

[109]G. Legrain, *Statues et statuettes de rois et de particuliers* II (CGC, Cairo 1909) 9.
See also D. Wildung, "Ramses, die grosse Sonne Ägyptens," *ZÄS* 99
(1973) 33–41.

[110]A. H. Gardiner, *Late-Egyptian Miscellanies* (BiAe 7, 1937) 15, 10–11.

[111]Cf. M. T. Derchain-Urtel, "Gott oder Mensch?" *SAK* 3 (1975) 25–41.

[112]Detailed presentation by Labib Habachi, *Features of the Deification of Ramesses
II* (ADIK 4, 1969); see the review article by D. Wildung, "Göttlichkeitsstufen
des Pharao," *OLZ* 68 (1973) 549–65.

tian royal ideology. Our concern is the nature and manifestation of Egyptian gods, and I shall restrict myself to this aspect of kingship. Nor shall I discuss the deification of nonroyal individuals, which is for the most part a late phenomenon.[113]

The king's titles and epithets appear to show that he is in fullest measure a god. In his official titulary he is called "perfect god" (*ntr nfr*), in the early Old Kingdom even "greatest god,"[114] and in the third intermediate period once, most anachronistically for the time, "greater than the gods."[115] There are also the specific acclamations as the sun god which I have referred to above, and comparable phrases that call the king Horus, Mont, Khnum, Sakhmet, and so on. The gods are his "brothers,"[116] and one is often uncertain whether the word *ntr* in a text refers to the king or to a "genuine" deity. It is understandable, therefore, that the king continues to be viewed as a god or "god king," or at least as the "incarnation" of a deity.

But despite all this, the Egyptian king is not a deity. In the book referred to above, Georges Posener showed how greatly the king's qualities and capacities differ from, and are inferior to, those of the gods—even if one concedes both that the very human traits of Posener's "roi des contes" can also be found in the gods in myths and that Posener measures the king against a view of the gods which is perhaps too idealized.[117] Siegfried Morenz presented the subordination of the king to the gods as a logical process that lasted millennia, which he saw as the *Rise of the Transcendent God* (the title of one of his books, discussed in Chapter 5). It has also been possible to add to the picture by identifying subtle features of the terminology that defines the

[113]Cf. D. Wildung, *Egyptian Saints: Deification in Pharaonic Egypt* (New York 1977).

[114]Snofru and some of his successors in Sinai inscriptions, possibly a forerunner of the later *ntr nfr*: D. Wildung, *Die Rolle ägyptischer Könige im Bewusstsein ihrer Nachwelt* I (MÄS 17, 1969) 112. For the king as *ntr* in private names see H. G. Fischer, *ZÄS* 105 (1978) 42–43.

[115]E. Otto, *Die biographischen Inschriften der ägyptischen Spätzeit* (PÄ 2, 1954) 135 (inscription 4, Twenty-second Dynasty).

[116]*Pyr.* §28c and *passim*, but probably always used of the deceased king.

[117]Cf. the reviews of H. Kees, *OLZ* 57 (1962) 476–78; J. G. Griffiths, *JEA* 49 (1963) 189–92.

king's divinity and its limits.[118] Even for the Egyptians this divinity of the king was a problem, which they tried to solve with ever more formulas and definitions. They knew that there was no simple identity between the king and the god Horus or between king and sun god. As early as the Fourth Dynasty the famous diorite-gneiss statue of Khephren shows the king, whose titulary states that he is "Horus in the palace," under the protection of the sky god Horus, while the same king is the "son of Re," and so subordinate to the sun god.

The larger numbers of texts that begin to become available with the first intermediate period give firmer outlines to the king's divinity. The king is destined to rule "in the egg," that is, from birth, but he is not divine from birth on.[119] He acquires his divinity only during the rituals of accession to the throne; from then on it is his ex officio. "Appear as a god," Amenemhat I (1991–1962 B.C.) encourages his successor Sesostris I in his posthumous Instruction, and Sesostris says in a building inscription, "I arrived as Horus after I had grown mature."[120]

So the king clothes himself with the insignia that he acquires at his accession and places himself in the role of the creator god, securing for himself, by means of rites and symbols of might, the power of the gods. In this role all the terms and epithets that are fitting for the gods are his due also. The king is not a god, but so long as there remained anything of the original reality of Egyptian kingship, he was a token of the efficacious power of the creator god in this world.

[118]H. Goedicke, *Die Stellung des Königs im Alten Reich* (ÄgAbh 2, 1960); E. Hornung, *Geschichte als Fest* (Darmstadt 1966) 23ff.; Otto, *Gott und Mensch* 63–83.

[119]The myth of the divine birth of the king (nn. 74–75 above) does not contradict this, because only the birth of kings who are already reigning is depicted.

[120]A. de Buck in *Studia Aegyptiaca* I (AnOr 17, 1938) 50 (1, 14). In the same Berlin leather roll the courtiers reply to "their god," i.e. the king (2, 1) (translation: Lichtheim, *Literature* I, 116–17). For further examples of the king as a "god" or "divine" see Blumenthal, *Untersuchungen* 94ff.

5 ↘ Characteristics of the Gods

For the believer, every deity is a separate figure with unmistakable features, among which are certain characteristics that are shared with no other deity. In our study of the Egyptian conception of god these individual qualities of particular gods are less important than those that are common to all gods and that provide evidence for what, in Egyptian eyes, a god was.

Among the characteristics common to all gods there stands out a group that renders the deities disconcertingly transitory and subject to the march of time. Egyptian gods have a beginning and an end in time. They are born or created, they change with time, they grow old and die, and one day they will exist no more. These characteristics contrast sharply with our accepted notions of what and how a god should be, and need to be studied in detail.

Origins

The idea that gods are born is perfectly consistent with our normal conceptions. The myths of all peoples tell of the natural or supernatural origins of the gods. The great gods of Greece are immortal but they are not unbegotten, even though their birth may be accomplished in some supernatural way. Magic surrounds the emergence of Aphrodite Anadyomene, who is born of the foam of the sea; Athene comes forth from the head of Zeus; while the newborn Hermes steals the cattle of his brother Apollo.

The finest and richest Egyptian myth of the birth and youth

143

of a god concerns the child Horus. It associates Horus with Osiris; since it subordinates the older sky god in hawk form to the later anthropomorphic Osiris, the myth cannot be among the oldest in the Nile valley, but it is recognizable from many allusions as early as the Pyramid Texts.[1] Harsiese "Horus-son-of-Isis" and Harpokrates "Horus-the-child" become separate, specific forms for the youthful Horus whom Isis has born and reared. In the Graeco-Roman period there is an equation of Harpokrates and Eros, in which the feature that is common to the two gods is not their function, but the fact that they are children. In the myth we hear of a time "when Horus was a child"; then his meat offering still consisted of pigs, which were later taboo.[2] So Horus is not eternally a child, but ages with time.

Isis conceives Horus after the death of her brother and husband Osiris, hovering over the corpse of the murdered god in the form of a kite.[3] Horus is protected by the gods while he is still in his mother's womb (CT spell 148), until he comes into the world in Chemmis in the delta (Pyr. §1703) and is brought up "in solitude, one knows not where he was,"[4] well hidden in the marshy thickets of the Nile delta (Figure 15). The magical prowess of his mother Isis protects him from the persecution of his opponent Seth and saves him from wild animals; Nephthys and the crown goddesses Wadjet and Nekhbet care for him as nurses and servants. When he has grown up he goes out into the world in order to wage the struggle for his father's inheritance, until, after many battles, he finally triumphs over Seth,

[1]On the childhood of Horus see Münster, Isis 5–12, who bases her exposition primarily on spell 148 of the Coffin Texts (CT II, 209c–226a); for bibliography see R. O. Faulkner, The Ancient Egyptian Coffin Texts I (Warminster 1973) 126 n. 1.

[2]Münster, Isis 11–12 with n. 164.

[3]Depicted frequently from the New Kingdom on; examples in Otto, Osiris und Amun, pls. 17–20. See also id., "Eine Darstellung der 'Osiris-Mysterien' in Theben," in W. Helck, ed., Festschrift für Siegfried Schott (Wiesbaden 1968) 99–105 with pl. 4. The posthumous conception is implied already in Pyr. §§632, 1635, while CT IV, 37g states that "Buto" (in the delta) is the place of delivery.

[4]Louvre C 286: A. Moret, BIFAO 30 (1930) 743; Assmann, ÄHG 441; Lichtheim, Literature II, 83.

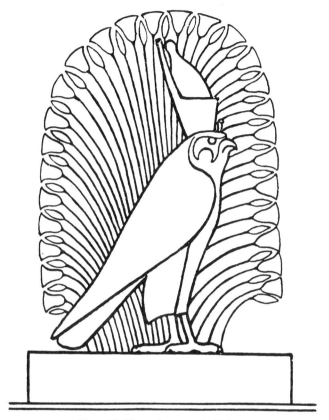

Figure 15. Horus in a marsh thicket.

his eternal adversary, and is ceremonially established in the inheritance of his father by the court of gods in Heliopolis.

There is no other Egyptian narrative of the birth, growth, and youth of a deity which is as extensive or dwells with such delight on concrete details. There are, however, numerous allusions to the fact that all gods, or particular gods, are "born" (*msj*), and in Egyptian iconography there are other child gods or youthful gods in addition to Horus: the moon god Khons with the "lock of youth," the sun god as the "child on the flower" (Figure 16), as well as Horus' own "children."

145

Figure 16. The sun god as a child on
the primeval lotus.

In the system of the Heliopolitan ennead five successive generations of deities can be distinguished: the primeval deity Atum creates the first couple Shu and Tefnut, who are not born in the usual way; their offspring Geb, the god of the earth, and Nut, the goddess of the sky, in turn produce four children—Osiris, Seth, Isis, and Nephthys. With Horus, the son of Osiris and Isis, who does not in fact belong to the earlier, schematic ennead, we reach the fifth generation, and the four "sons of Horus" could even be counted as a sixth. But for the Egyptians the precise order of generations is not the decisive point; it can even be changed, so that Shu and Tefnut may appear as the parents of Osiris, and Seth as the brother of Osiris or of Horus. What is important is the principle that the pantheon is ordered genealogically (see Chapter 7).

Apart from the goddesses who "bore" other specific deities in myth, there is the idea of a "mother of the gods" who bears all the gods. In the New Kingdom and late period the sky goddess Nut, who bore the sun according to the Pyramid

Texts and the moon according to the Coffin Texts,[5] often has the epithet "she who bore the gods." This epithet refers to the heavenly bodies, whom the sky goddess daily "bears" and again "swallows"—an idea that leads to the depiction of Nut as a sow.[6] But when in late texts the goddess Neith is called "mother of the gods," the reference is to her long-established role as mother of Sobek and of Re, just as Isis, the mother of Horus, is called simply "mother of the god."[7] The example of Isis also shows how this role of mother may be extended, for she is already called "mother of all gods" in the New Kingdom.[8] In this case the "gods" are not just the heavenly bodies, as Nut is mother of the stars, but literally all deities.

Corresponding to the idea of a universal "mother of the gods" is that of a "father of the gods," to whom all other deities owe their origin. At first Amun and only a little later other gods such as Ptah and Horus acquire an epithet in common which seems to have been coined in the New Kingdom: "father of the fathers of all gods." It is first attested before the Amarna period, in the Cairo hymn to Amun, and is used as late as the early centuries A.D.; the Egyptians also applied a somewhat modified form of it to the chief gods of their Asiatic neighbors.[9] Still more widespread than this intensified form is the epithet "father of the gods," which is applied to Atum, Geb, and Shu in addition to the gods just mentioned—that is, to deities who have an essential role in the process of creation.[10] From the Middle Kingdom on it is associated especially with the god Nun,[11] who is the primeval waters, from which all the

[5]Sun: *Pyr.* §§1688b, 1835; *CT* II, 38c; 398a; VI, 270a. Moon: *CT* III, 397b.

[6]H. Grapow, "Die Himmelsgöttin Nut als Mutterschwein," *ZÄS* 71 (1934) 45–47. The text from the Osireion is republished by Neugebauer-Parker, *EAT* I, 67ff.

[7]H. Ranke listed examples with Neith, Hathor, and Isis: *MDAIK* 12 (1943) 119 no. (6). On Isis called "mother" see Münster, *Isis* 205–6.

[8]A Ramessid example Münster, *Isis* 205; for later evidence (also with Mut and Hathor) cf. Bergman, *Ich bin Isis* 132–33.

[9]References in Zandee, *De hymnen aan Amon* 93; W. Helck, *"Vater der Väter"* (NAWG 1965, 9); Assmann, *Liturg. Lieder* 327 with n. 62.

[10]Zandee, *De hymnen aan Amon* 93–94; H. Altenmüller, *SAK* 2 (1975) 14–15.

[11]*CT* IV, 188/189c; additional examples in M. S. H. G. Heerma van Voss, *De oudste versie van Dodenboek 17a* (Leiden 1963) 51 n. 42. The epithet is borne quite frequently by Hapy, the god of the inundation.

gods indeed originated, in divine form. Akhenaten even calls his god Aten "mother and father of what you created"[12] in Aten's aspect as primeval and creator god—a logical description of the oldest god, who brings the first deities into being without female aid.

The reigning king addresses the gods as his "fathers" and the goddesses as his "mothers"; only after his death may he greet them as his "siblings." Over and above all of them there is a primeval, universal "father of the gods," who created all living beings. But even this primeval father has a genesis; he has not been present for all eternity but arose at creation, as the idea is formulated in a text in the Ptolemaic temple of Edfu.[13] According to other sources he is already present before creation in the primeval ocean,[14] and arose in it "of himself" in order to accomplish the work of creation and set in motion the origin of the world. The oldest god, with whom the deceased king identifies himself in the Pyramid Texts, was "formed by his father Atum," before earth and sky, human beings, or gods had come into being (*Pyr.* §1466); for the New Kingdom Berlin Ritual of Amun creation was a time "when no god had come into being and no name had been invented for anything."[15] The world before creation is therefore a world without gods. In it there arises mysteriously—"of himself, without being born"[16]—a first primeval god, who then calls the rest of the gods and the entire cosmos into being.

This is not the place for describing the process of the creation of the world and the origin of the gods in detail, a task that would require a long chapter on Egyptian creation myths.[17] But whether the creator brings the first divine couple into being from his own semen by masturbation or through his creative

[12]Sandman, *Texts* 12, 8–12; Twenty-sixth Dynasty parallel cited by H. Ranke, *MDAIK* 12 (1943) 126 no. (53).

[13]*Edfou* I, 498, 16.

[14]Especially clear in *Urk.* VIII, 117 no. 144g, of Ptah; I gave other examples in *StG* 18 (1965) 73.

[15]Moret, *Rituel* 129.

[16]Ceiling inscription in Theban Tomb 59 (referring to Re-Harakhte; my own copy).

[17]The best survey is by S. Sauneron and J. Yoyotte in *La naissance du monde* (Sources Orientales 1, Paris 1959) 17–91.

word from a conception in his mind, or whether he "forms" them (*msj*) in a way that is not specified any more closely, it is characteristic of the Egyptian conception of god that god created the gods. This statement is found so frequently from the Pyramid Texts on that we can confine ourselves to a small selection of examples.

In New Kingdom hymns the creator god is praised again and again as "he who created the gods" (*jrjw-nṯrw*),[18] an epithet that retains the same form as late as the native temple texts of the Graeco-Roman period.[19] There is a related statement in the daily temple ritual of the New Kingdom, according to which Amun "formed all the gods."[20] In earlier periods only gods are found in these formulas; not until relatively late are gods and mankind placed in parallel, so that the creator is praised as "he who created everything that exists, who built (*qd*) men and created the gods,"[21] or for "bringing mankind into being, forming the gods and creating all that exists."[22] But as early as the Coffin Texts all living beings have their origin in the creator god, as is proclaimed in the "monologue of the creator god" in spell 1130: "I brought the gods into being from my sweat; men are from the tears of my eye."[23] Here the origin of the types of being is differentiated—the "sweat" of god is a term for the fragrance that emanates from him, and which we have already encountered as betokening the presence of a god; incense, the per-

[18]Cairo hymn to Amun 2, 7: Grébaut, *Hymne 7*; J. Zandee, *JEOL* 16 (1964) 61 l. 6; 18 (1965) 258.

[19]Junker-Winter, *Geburtshaus* 37, 16, about Khnum; for a similar late period formula with *qmˀw-nṯrw* cf. H. de Meulenaere, *JEOL* 20 (1968) 3 n. 12.

[20]Moret, *Rituel* 127 l. 5, and similarly 133 l. 2. The same is said of Ptah in the "Memphite Theology" (l. 59: Junker, *Götterlehre* 65). E. A. E. Reymond, *CdE* 40/79 (1965) 64–65, gives examples of the "forming" of the gods from the temple of Edfu.

[21]J. Spiegel, *ASAE* 40 (1940) 258 l. 5 (Twentieth Dynasty); similar example E. Drioton, *ASAE* 44 (1944) 118 (Ptolemaic).

[22]*Edfou* VI, 16, 4.

[23]*CT* VII, 464g–465a. According to the Cairo hymn to Amun 6, 3 (Grébaut, *Hymne* 16) the gods arose from the utterance and men from the eye of the creator (cf. also 4, 2, Grébaut p. 11: he "commanded, and the gods came into being"). For the survival of this distinction cf. Otto, *Gott und Mensch* 58; on the later extension to the gods of the origin from tears see H. H. Nelson, *JNES* 8 (1949) 342 fig. 40 ll. 14–15.

fume used in the cult of the gods, is also called the "sweat of god" (*Wb.* I, 582, 8–9). Humanity's origin from "tears" and hence from the eye of the creator is based on a play between the words for "human being" and "tear." Like every Egyptian wordplay, this one reveals a deep affinity between the entities that are associated, showing the "harmony" of the world which is reflected in language. The dichotomy in our origin is illuminated as if by lightning—"we all came from his eye,"[24] from the weeping eye of god which was afflicted by temporary blindness. "The weeping I did was because of the uproar against me; mankind belongs to the blindness that is behind me," says Nun as the creator god in the Coffin Texts (*CT* VI, 344f–g). God overcame the affliction of his eye, but man's origin means that he is destined never to partake in the clear sight of god; affliction blights everything he sees, thinks and does. How painfully this image from an early civilization and from the depths of man's soul brings home to us the inadequacy of even the most exact theory of origin!

Again and again the statement that a god created the gods has been cited, with the arguments I reviewed in chapters 1 and 2, as proof of an alleged Egyptian monotheism. But it is wrong to cite them thus, because this god, who created the gods and to whom the whole cosmos owes its existence, is not a specific god behind and above all gods, but simply the particular creator god in question. He may be Ptah, Re, Amun, or Atum—in principle any god who is worshiped as a creator. A superficial analysis of the many and various examples, as in the monotheistic interpretation, would lead logically to the conclusion that the gods created one another reciprocally: Ptah created all the gods, thus including Re; Re created all the gods, thus including Ptah; and so on. It is clear that the Egyptians did not think so narrowly. Their conviction was that it was in the nature of a creator god, whoever he might be, to have created everything that exists; Tuthmosis IV dedicated his monuments to "the lord who created everything that exists" (*Urk.* IV, 1540, 16). The creator god must therefore also have created the gods, who are in Egyptian ontology powers of the existent

[24]From a Ramessid hymn: A. Erman, *ZÄS* 38 (1900) 28 l. 2; Assmann, *ÄHG* no. 193.

world only (see Excursus below). That he should have created all the gods is fundamental to the nature of the creator god, and the statement that he did so also tells us something important about the ontology of the gods: they have a beginning that coincides with the beginning of the ordered world.

Only for the primeval gods and for the creator god himself is this beginning not precisely fixed. Their roots are in timelessness before creation and so pose problems, both for the Egyptians and for us, which we shall have to tackle below. The Egyptian solution is a paradox: in the Coffin Texts, for example, Horus was born of Isis "before Isis came into being";[25] or Isis herself is said to be "older than her mother."[26]

But all other gods are defined clearly: their existence has a beginning—they were born or created. Does death correspond to this birth, does an end in time correspond to a beginning in it? I consider these questions in the next section.

Old age and death

The example of the murder of Osiris taught earlier students of religion that Egyptian gods can be mortal. This phenomenon fitted badly with ideas about the nature of gods which were then current—gods simply had to be immortal. For Victor von Strauss und Torney:

> The death of Usiri is an enigma, not because of the events surrounding it, about which I have already said all that is needed, but because it is the death of a god, which does not otherwise occur in Egyptian legends of the gods . . . one must ask what are the characteristics of a god who can die . . . and be buried.[27]

Only a year later, in 1890, Alfred Wiedemann proposed an explanation that was still being championed by S. A. B. Mercer thirty years ago: the gods were formed in the image of man,

[25]CT IV, 76c; cf. Münster, *Isis* 10.
[26]Bergman, *Ich bin Isis* 280. In the "Memphite Theology" the creator god Atum, who elsewhere has no origin, is credited with Ptah-Nun and Ptah-Naunet as parents (ll. 50–51: Junker, *Götterlehre* 16).
[27]*Götterglaube* I (1889) 91.

and are therefore both mortal and subject to other constraints: "But even the gods are no different from man. True, their lives were longer, but they too ended in death; their power was greater, but still limited. For the Egyptians man and man alone was in all spheres the measure of things."[28] This all-too-human explanation, which was familiar already in antiquity, is not satisfactory; but unlike von Strauss und Torney, Wiedemann realized that the mortality of Egyptian gods was not confined to Osiris and thus confronted the issue in its full breadth. In this he was followed by Gerardus van der Leeuw, but the latter took the analysis further, to the ontological foundation of things: "Everything, including the divine, has an end, insofar as it dies, but is also endless, insofar as it is reborn."[29]

According to van der Leeuw, existence, whether divine or not, has an ineluctable limit that is not final but is constantly being passed in the return to life. I shall consider below whether this view of Egyptian ontology is correct, or whether, at least in eschatology, we meet a boundary that cannot be transgressed—a final, definitive horizon to existence. But our immediate question is whether this mortality does apply in principle to all Egyptian gods, as it would appear to do—I say "in principle" because we cannot expect to find evidence for the death of each of the many deities.

The violent death of Osiris at the hands of Seth is so well known that we may happily omit to document it in detail. But references to it are characteristic of the restraint with which the Egyptians report the death of their gods. Texts speak of the tomb and the resurrection of Osiris, and both are even depicted pictorially; there are allusions to what his enemies "did" to him, his "deathly tiredness," and the laments of his sisters, Isis and Nephthys, are mentioned—but Egyptian texts of the pharaonic period never say that Osiris died. In the cult celebration of the Osiris myth at the festival at Abydos this detail—the god's violent death—remains unmentioned. Again and again we find this avoidance of explicit statements that a god died, whoever the god may be; for the text, and still more the image, would fix the event and even render it eternal. In the Egyptian

---

[28]*Religion* 91 = 173; retranslated here. Cf. S. A. B. Mercer, *The Religion of Ancient Egypt* (London 1948) 302.

[29]*Godsvoorstellingen* 124.

view it is unthinkable that the death of Osiris or his dismemberment by Seth should be represented pictorially and thus be given a heightened, more intense reality. So we must content ourselves with allusions—which are, however, clear enough. Plutarch's *De Iside et Osiride*, which is free from Egyptian restraint, informs us even about the gory details of the story;[30] a century before him Diodorus (I, 22) mentioned the burial of Isis.

From the Nineteenth Dynasty onward the sun god's "old age" in the evening after his long, exhausting journey through the day is part of a common formula, in which the "old man" in the evening is contrasted with the newborn "child" in the morning.[31] At the same time—in the late New Kingdom—the Egyptians were not afraid to incorporate this motif in iconography and to depict the sun god in reliefs and paintings as a "tired old man" leaning heavily on his stick, either in the sun disk or in his bark;[32] this image contrasts sharply with earlier pictures, which show the evening or night manifestation of the sun god as an erect man with a ram's head.

Apart from this daily aging, the sun god grows definitively older through the eons, a process that is described in somewhat drastic terms in two Egyptian myths. The Book of the Divine Cow, which asssumed its canonical form during the Amarna period,[33] describes the old and weary sun god whose condition provokes an evil mankind to rebel. "His Person (the sun god Re) had become old, his bones being of silver, his flesh gold, and his hair true lapis lazuli"—a description of an image of a god in precious materials, but at the same time an

[30]J. G. Griffiths, *Plutarch's De Iside et Osiride* (University of Wales 1970) 134–47; Otto, *Osiris und Amun* 58–60 = 61–63.

[31]*Wb.* II, 313, 12; add *Medinet Habu* VI pl. 424 B, 4 (Atum as the "old man who is in the Nun"); see also A. W. Shorter, *Catalogue of Egyptian Religious Papyri in the British Museum, Copies of the Book pr(t)-m-hrw from the XVIIIth to the XXIInd Dynasty* I (London 1938) pl. 5, fourth col. from right; W. Wolf, *ZÄS* 64 (1929) 34–35 (Berlin hymn to Ptah).

[32]Two references cited *Amduat* II, 21; add A. Piankoff and N. Rambova, *Mythological Papyri* (ERT 3, 1957) no. 24, and some very clear Graeco-Roman examples I owe to J. Assmann: H. Brugsch, *Thesaurus inscriptionum aegyptiacarum* I (Leipzig 1883) 57; *id., ZÄS* 5 (1867) 24–25; *Edfou* I pl. 33c; J. Baines, *JEA* 58 (1972) 304–5.

[33]C. Maystre, *BIFAO* 40 (1941) 58–59; the earliest copy is on one of the gilded shrines of Tutankhamun.

elegant metaphor for the complete ossification of the aged deity. The aging of the creator threatens the order of the world and leaves the way open for hostile powers to do harm and cause confusion and collapse. The problem that this threat poses is solved in the myth. The fiery solar eye, which is seen as a goddess, goes out to protect the divine order against its opponents, but is finally stilled in its rage by an intoxicating drink. The sun god retreats from his rule to the farthest regions of the sky and installs the moon god Thoth as his representative. Even when he abdicates, he provides for a legal transfer of power so that order can become firmly established—a model of political conduct which is seldom emulated.

In the mythical story of Isis and Re, which I have already used in Chapter 3 as evidence for a hierarchy among names, the aged, feeble condition of the sun god is described with a Ramessid exaggeration and lack of respect. The saliva he dribbles from his trembling mouth drops to the ground and gives the cunning Isis the material from which she forms a torturing snake. By means of the snake's bite she forces the aged ruler of the world to surrender knowledge of his most secret name. Here, as in the Book of the Divine Cow, the aging happens in a mythical "once upon a time," and may serve as a precedent to explain imperfections in the present order of things. As early as the Coffin Texts the present is felt to be both an evil time and a time full of promise, when Osiris is buried but his son Horus takes over the reins of world government; in his role as the sun god Re, Horus is "tomorrow," whereas Osiris is "yesterday" (CT IV, 192/23b–c). In the Nineteenth Dynasty Turin Canon of Kings the restricted and defined time that is assigned even to divine rule is removed from the vagueness of myth and placed in the temporally fixed world of history. At the beginning of the papyrus, before the lengths of reign of earthly kings, are placed those of various gods, all precisely defined: Ptah, Re, Shu, Geb, Osiris and so forth. The papyrus attributes to each a long but limited stretch of time, after which the throne passes to another god.[34]

[34]A. H. Gardiner, *The Royal Canon of Turin* (Oxford 1959) pl. 1. col. 1. Manetho also gives "lengths of reign" for gods: W. G. Waddell, *Manetho* (Loeb Classical Library, Cambridge, Mass. and London 1956) 2–27.

We do not know whether the Egyptians believed from the beginning that the gods were subject to time and hence to death and that their existence had a limit. The image of the divine but aging and dying king, which was an analogy before their eyes, may make such an assumption likely; but the evidence that has been cited so far all dates from the end of the Amarna period (c. 1340 B.C.) and later. A related idea, which also cannot be documented before the New Kingdom, is that the god Thoth, the scribe and archivist of the gods and reckoner of time who "reckons years, months, days, hours, and moments,"[35] assigns a fixed lifespan not only to people but also to the gods.[36] However, a magical spell from the Middle Kingdom Book of the Two Ways uses as a threat the possibility that the sun god Re might die,[37] while Nepri is referred to in the Coffin Texts as one "who lives after his death" (CT II, 95e).

In the New Kingdom underworld books the sun god's daily death and rebirth is a dominant motif and also a promise that all the blessed dead will enter through death into a new, rejuvenated life. The Amduat, which was the chief religious text in royal tombs from the time of Tuthmosis I to the Amarna period, describes the sun god's nightly meeting with his corpse. The vignettes to the sixth hour of the night show three tombs in which the parts of the solar scarab are buried; fire-spitting snakes guard them, and the god's creative word wakes the divided corpse from its sleep of death.[38] In the register below a five-headed snake encircles the "corpse of Khepry," which is at the same time that of Osiris.[39] Like everything that is mortal, the dead sun god who has sunk into the underworld becomes an

[35]G. Posener, Catalogue des ostraca hiératiques littéraires de Deir el Médineh I (IFAO DF 1, 1938) no. 1080 ll. 1–2.

[36]Many examples listed by P. Boylan, Thoth the Hermes of Egypt (London etc. 1922) 84, 193 (mainly Ptolemaic); G. Posener, Annuaire du Collège de France 63 (1962–63) 301–2; see also n. 35 above. As a moon god Khons acquires the same role: Bonnet, Reallexikon 141.

[37]CT VII, 419b, cf. H. Kees, Totenglauben und Jenseitsvorstellungen der alten Ägypter (2d ed., Berlin 1956) 299; L. H. Lesko, The Ancient Egyptian Book of Two Ways (Berkeley etc. 1972) 109.

[38]Amduat II, 115–16. The goddess no. 430 is probably Isis; cf. the "castle of the divine adoratrice (= Isis)" in J. Vandier, Le papyrus Jumilhac ([Paris 1961]) 76–78.

[39]Amduat II, 119, 123–24. Cf. also Chapter 3 n. 111.

"Osiris," entering into the role, nature, and form of the god whose death was archetypal. Like deceased human beings, Re acquires the quality of *jm'ḥ* "reverence" in the underworld.[40]

Apart from the tombs of the solar corpse, the Amduat shows those of many other deities, especially in the seventh and eighth hours of the night. In the late period tombs of gods are also depicted and mentioned in texts as being on earth—in Thebes even the tombs of the eight primeval gods,[41] who were not created and should therefore reach back into the deathless world before creation, but who fall prey to the consistent extension of the idea of mortality which encompasses all deities. The best-known tombs are those of Osiris at Philae,[42] Dendara,[43] and Abydos[44] (among many other places). A text from the eighteenth nome of Upper Egypt also speaks of an entire necropolis of tombs of gods,[45] and the sites of tombs of gods are known from Edfu and Hermopolis.[46]

Facts such as these reinforce the superficial impression of an Egyptian fixation with death; in the words of Thomas Mann, Egypt seems to be the country where "'your dead are gods and your gods dead.'"[47] From an early period "gods" was a common word for the inhabitants of the other world, and from the Eleventh Dynasty the necropolis is called the place where the gods are.[48] Chapter 17 of the Book of the Dead states that every

[40]*Amduat* I, 195–96; II, 187.

[41]Sethe, *Amun* §§102–4.

[42]H. Junker, *Das Götterdekret über das Abaton* (Denkschriften der Kais. Akad. der Wissenschaften, Phil.-hist. Klasse 56, Vienna 1913).

[43]F. Daumas, *Dendara et le temple d'Hathor* (IFAO RAPH 29, 1969) 67–69.

[44]Otto, *Osiris und Amun* 44–45 = 47–48.

[45]J. Vandier, *Le papyrus Jumilhac* ([Paris 1961]) 126, 139.

[46]Edfu: Derchain, *Le papyrus Salt 825* 102. Hermopolis, tomb of Thoth: F. Zimmermann, *Die ägyptische Religion nach der Darstellung der Kirchenschriftsteller* (Paderborn 1912) 61, who contents himself with a "euhemeristic" explanation. See also T. Hopfner, *Plutarch über Isis und Osiris* I (Monographien des *Archiv Orientální* 9, Prague 1940) 161–62; M. Alliot, *Le culte d'Horus à Edfou* II (IFAO BE 20, 1954) 513–27; S. Sauneron, *Les fêtes religieuses d'Esna* (Esna 5, Publications de l'IFAO 1962) 329–30.

[47]*Joseph und seine Brüder* (in *Gesammelte Werke* V [Frankfurt a.M.: S. Fischer Verlag 1960]) 1085, end of the chapter "Dreifacher Austausch."

[48]For references see *Amduat* II, 7; III, 59. The stela from Ballas is republished by H. G. Fischer, *Inscriptions from the Coptite Nome* (AnOr 40, 1964) no. 45.

god must go down into the west, the realm of the dead, on the orders of Re—who is himself mortal (*Urk.* V, 14). New Kingdom texts, which place gods and men on a par by stating that both must go down into the realm of Osiris,[49] show that the "gods" in such statements are not just the blessed dead. In chapter 154 of the Book of the Dead the fate of death, which is referred to as "decay" and "disappearance," is claimed to await "every god, every goddess, all animals, and all insects,"[50] and there is a similar statement at the beginning of the Book of Gates, in which the sun god "assigned (mankind) to the hidden place, to which men and gods, all animals and all insects whom this great god created, betook themselves" (*Bpf* 1–2). As in Book of the Dead 17, so here the creator of the world is responsible not only for the existence of all living beings but also for their end, without himself being imperishable; the Book of Gates in particular contains impressive images of his nightly sojourn in the realm of the dead.

Are there any exceptions to this general rule; are any gods immortal? Hans Bonnet claimed that Seth—the murderer of Osiris—was immortal.[51] He cited in support a passage in the Pyramid Texts in which the king wishes to evade his day of death as Seth did: "The King has evaded his day of death like Seth's evasion of his day of death; the King has evaded his half-months of death like Seth's evasion of his half-months of death; the King has evaded his months of death like Seth's evasion of his months of death; the King has evaded his year of death like Seth's evasion of his year of death" (*Pyr.* §1453). Bonnet related this unambiguous example to the gods' prophecy to Queen Hatshepsut that in addition to the "share of Horus" she would receive the "years of Seth"—which are therefore an especially long stretch of time.[52] Finally, he cited Seth's invinci-

---

[49]A. H. Gardiner, *Late-Egyptian Stories* (BiAe 1, 1932) 58, 11–12.

[50]Naville, *Todtenbuch* I, 179; Allen, *Book of the Dead* 154; Hornung, *Totenbuch* 332. Cf. also C. E. Sander-Hansen, *Der Begriff des Todes bei den Ägyptern* (DVSM 29, 2, 1942) 8; Morenz, *Religion* 25 = 24. The deceased is not striving for "permanence," as Morenz suggests, but for freedom from bodily decay.

[51]*Reallexikon* 714.

[52]*Urk.* IV, 244, 16–17; Middle Kingdom parallel in H. Schäfer, in *Studies Presented to F. Ll. Griffith* (London 1932) 428.

bility, which serves, together with his violent nature, as a welcome coercive force for magicians who wish to achieve illegitimate ends.[53]

Only the passage in the Pyramid Texts can really be taken as evidence of a search for immortality. The "years of Seth," on the other hand, are "a reign full of power and fruitfulness, which may last 'millions of years' but is in the last analysis contained within time," as Wolfhart Westendorf put it.[54] Herman te Velde has pointed out mummiform representations of Seth,[55] of which there are several dating to the Nineteenth Dynasty and later, which show that even this ambivalent god shares the mortality of all living beings. As a corollary he has a beginning, although his birth is irregular and displays his twilight nature, which partakes of the existent and of the nonexistent: he erupts violently from his mother's womb, spreading disorder from the day of his birth.[56]

Seth, whose realm is the desert and other marginal areas of the world, exists on the boundary between the transitory and the everlasting. The same boundary separates order and chaos, the existent and nonexistent. Apopis, the eternal enemy of the gods (Figure 17), does not belong with the existent,[57] and has no beginning or end. Only the latest temple in Egypt, the temple of Esna, contains a reference to the origin of Apopis; he is interpreted etymologically as the "one who was spat out," the product of the goddess Neith's saliva in the primeval water.[58] In earlier periods his existence seems to know no beginning or

[53]T. Hopfner gave numerous examples of evocation of Seth from the Graeco-Roman period: *ArOr* 3 (1931) 131–38. For Seth in general te Velde, *Seth*; E. Hornung, *Symbolon* n.s. 2 (1974) 49–63.

[54]*ZÄS* 92 (1966) 141.

[55]*Seth* 104 n. 6.

[56]*Seth* 27–28. In the New Kingdom his day of birth was called the "beginning of strife."

[57]His "destruction" is mentioned in the Amduat and the Book of Gates (see also *BPf* 346), and elaborated upon in the later Book of Apopis (R. O. Faulkner, *The Papyrus Bremner-Rhind* [BiAe 3, 1933]). According to the curse formula on a Ptolemaic stela in Leiden, the violator of a tomb will, like Apopis, "not exist": H. de Meulenaere, *Orientalia Gandensia* 3 (1966) 101ff. l. 15.

[58]S. Sauneron in *Mélanges Mariette* (IFAO BE 32, 1961) 235–36; *id., Les fêtes religieuses* (n. 46 above) 265.

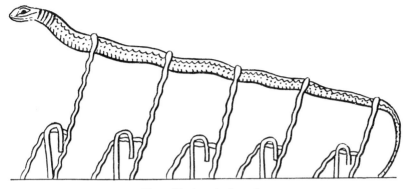

Figure 17. Apopis, bound.

end. He is already there at the creation of the world and must be defeated for the first time by the creator god and driven out of the ordered world of existence.[59] From then on he continually opposes the sun god in his path and threatens the deceased in the underworld. Every day and every night powerful magic is necessary to repel him from the solar bark; he is burned up and "destroyed"—he is called quite simply "the destroyed one" (*BPf* 346)—but he is always there again. His existence cannot be extinguished, as is shown most impressively in a scene in the Book of Gates, where he appears, as always, as a snake, but twelve human heads emerge from his coils; the accompanying text says that these are the heads of the people he has swallowed (*BPf* 210–15). As the sun god travels past, the situation is reversed at his behest: the heads come out of the coils and "consume" the snake's body so that "it perishes" and Apopis is "destroyed." But as soon as the sun god has passed "the heads enter their coils (again)"—which they have only just "consumed." The enemy's snake body is indestructible; only for a moment can his threat be countered. The sun god and the other gods are indeed there all the time, but in a different way, in the alternation of death and resurrection, not in the unchanging endlessness that is the lot of Apopis as a power of chaos.

[59]Inferred indirectly from *Urk.* V, 7, 1–3, where the *msw-bdšt,* who are closely related to Apopis, are destroyed on the primeval "hill."

Like men, the gods die, but they are not dead. Their existence—and all existence—is not an unchanging endlessness, but rather constant renewal. From an early period the "dead" are only the damned, that is, those who are condemned in the judgment after death, or hostile powers;[60] to be dead is not the same as not to exist. Siegfried Morenz emphasized that "for the Egyptians constant regeneration was part of duration."[61] The blessed dead and the gods are rejuvenated in death and regenerate themselves at the wellsprings of their existence.

Many passages in texts and, from the New Kingdom on, pictures show that from a very early period the Egyptians saw rejuvenation and regeneration as the true meaning of death.[62] "You sleep that you may wake; you die that you may live," as the Pyramid Texts formulate the hope with archaic brevity (*Pyr.* §1975b), and in this early collection of spells the deceased also becomes a small "young child with his finger in his mouth" (§665a). In the Coffin Texts the deceased is "a rejuvenated god whom the perfect West (the realm of the dead) bore" (*CT* I, 88b), and he renews ("repeats") "life after death, like Atum, daily" (V, 291k). By providing burial equipment for his officials the king enables them to "rejuvenate" themselves as "revered (deceased) ones" (a hymn to Sesostris III[63]), while the weak, aged Sinuhe hopes that through his "departure" to the next world his body will be "rejuvenated."[64]

At the beginning of the New Kingdom the Amduat presented this old and well-known idea in a striking new image.[65] In the last hour of the night the sun god and his innumerable retinue of gods and blessed dead enter as "old one," "old man," "weak with age," and "gray-haired one" into the body of a giant snake, 1,300 cubits long, in order to leave it rejuvenated as "young children." The snake, through which they

[60]Hornung, *Höllenvorstellungen* 35.

[61]*Religion und Geschichte* 222 (reprinted from *Asiatica. Festschrift für Friedrich Weller zum 65. Geburtstag* [Leipzig 1954] 420).

[62]For a selection, which could easily be expanded, see *Amduat* II, 193–95.

[63]H. Grapow, *MIO* 1 (1953) 198 l. 8.

[64] *MES* 30 (B167–68).

[65]*Amduat* II, 188–91, with the names nos. 857–68.

walk from tail to mouth, is called "world-encircler";[66] made visible, it is the world-encompassing boundary between world and nonworld, the existent and the nonexistent. Regeneration is impossible in the ordered and defined world. It can happen only if what is old and worn becomes immersed in the boundless regions that surround creation—in the healing and dissolving powers of the primeval ocean Nun. The sun god in his bark is raised from Nun every morning, as is shown in the concluding picture in the Book of Gates. Those who sleep are rejuvenated in Nun, and in a Ramessid hymn the deceased cry out to the sun god that they too are rejuvenated through entry into Nun, "slough off" their previous existence, and "put on" another,[67] as a snake does its skin. It is not surprising that the encircling and rejuvenating element is seen as a snake in the Amduat. But this mysterious process is depicted in many images, which are not mutually exclusive: the sun's rejuvenating journey through the night can take place within the body of the sky goddess[68] or in the body of a gigantic crocodile.[69] The "awakening" of the gods and sacred objects in the morning is described in many texts;[70] the entire world emerges rejuvenated from the chaos of night.

In temporal terms, too, regeneration is possible only outside the ordered world of creation. In order to be rejuvenated, that is, to reverse the course of time, one must step for a little outside time and see oneself at the beginning of the temporal world, at creation or even in the world before creation, which knows no time. Rebirth in the morning is therefore a renewal of creation, and is achieved with the help of the primeval gods, who sent the sun forth from their midst on the "first occasion" at the beginning of creation;[71] like the creation of the world,

[66]Following L. Kákosy, *OrAnt* 3 (1964) 19 n. 26, a better rendering than that given in *Amduat* II, 178.

[67]Gardiner, *Chester Beatty* I, 34, II pl. 17 (11, 8–9).

[68]A. Piankoff, *Le livre du jour et de la nuit* (IFAO BE 13, 1942); *id., Ramesses VI* pls. 149–59, 186–96; and frequently elsewhere.

[69]E. Brunner-Traut in W. Helck, ed., *Festschrift für Siegfried Schott* (Wiesbaden 1968) 32ff.

[70]See Assmann, *Liturg. Lieder* 183 with n. 76.

[71]*Amduat* II, 191, and often in later compositions.

sunrise can thus be called the "first occasion."[72] In the Book of Caverns the sun god announces to the underworld dwellers, "I enter into the world from which I came forth, I rest on (the place of my) first birth."[73] He therefore returns to the world before creation, from which he went forth on the "first occasion" and ever again goes forth. According to a late libation text, the aging gods return to their place of origin, the primeval world of creation "where they lived, were small, and became youths."[74]

The idea that the gods must be renewed each day is not abandoned even at Amarna; the Aten, the sole god of Akhenaten, is "born in the sky daily (anew),"[75] and thus experiences the same cycle of death and rebirth as the traditional gods. Seen from this point of view, according to which rejuvenation and renewal are possible only through death, the mortality of Egyptian gods is less surprising. It enables them to become young again and again, and to escape from the disintegration that is the inevitable product of time. It might seem that the gods of Egypt, although mortal and, as Plutarch says, "not imperishable,"[76] were in the last analysis eternal, ever-growing through their cyclical renewal: the sun god himself is called "the one who rejuvenates daily, without reaching his end."[77] The difficulty we experience in conceiving of perishable gods would then seem to be eliminated. But the solution is not so simple, for there are passages in texts of various periods which speak of a final, definitive end to the time of the gods, a sort of "twilight of the gods" which sets a limit to their "eternal" renewal.

We should not expect this removal of the gods at the end of time to be well documented. The Egyptians were not given to eschatological utterances, which place a question mark over

[72]Neugebauer-Parker, *EAT* I text H.

[73]A. Piankoff, *Le livre des Quererts* (Cairo 1946) pl. 15, 3.

[74]H. Junker, *Die Stundenwachen in den Osirismysterien* (Denkschriften der Kais. Akad. der Wissenschaften, Phil.-hist. Klasse 54, Vienna 1910) 87.

[75]Sandman, *Texts* 14—but in only one copy of the text. For this idea at Amarna see also G. Fecht, *ZÄS* 94 (1967) 42 with n. 30.

[76]J. G. Griffiths, *Plutarch's De Iside et Osiride* (University of Wales 1970) 150–51, chap. 21.

[77]Pap. Berlin 3049, 9, 3: *Hieratische Papyrus aus den königlichen Museen zu Berlin* II (Leipzig 1905) 74; Assmann, *ÄHG* 282.

the existing order, and so are themselves not "in order" and better avoided; otherwise chaos, which has been successfully banished, might be conjured up again. We can therefore assume that the possibility of a time without gods was much more firmly grounded in the Egyptians' awareness than the few clear allusions to it would suggest. A phrase such as *m ḏrw nṯrw* "in the realm of the gods," in the sense of "so long as the gods are there," is found first in Graeco-Roman temple texts (*Wb.* V, 586, 4); otherwise eschatology is for the most part the domain of magical spells.

The Coffin Texts, from which I have already mentioned a magical spell that implies the death of the sun god, also include a famous spell in the Book of Two Ways which contains the first clear statement about the end of all time (spell 1130). The anonymous "lord of all," by which is meant Atum, speaks to the crew of the solar bark: "I made millions of years into something between me and that weary-hearted one, the son of Geb (that is, Osiris). Then I shall dwell with him in one place. Mounds will become cities and cities mounds, and estate will destroy estate" (*CT* VII, 467e–468b). After the "millions of years" of differentiated creation the mayhem before creation will return; only the primeval god (Atum) and Osiris will remain "in one place"—no longer separated in space and time.

The later Book of the Dead, chapter 175, describes this final state of affairs still more clearly: "This earth will return to the primeval water (Nun), to endless (flood) as in its first state. I shall remain with Osiris after I have transformed myself into another snake which men do not know and the gods do not see."[78] At the end of the world there will no longer be men and gods, as is clear from a Ptolemaic parallel text in the temple of Opet at Karnak, which was identified by Eberhard Otto: "There is no god, there is no goddess, who will make himself/herself into another snake"[79]—or, as Otto paraphrased: "The transformed primeval god is alone and no longer has any witnesses

---

[78] E. A. W. Budge, *The Book of the Dead* III (Books on Egypt and Chaldaea 30, London 1910) 74; Allen, *Book of the Dead* 184; Hornung, *Totenbuch* 367.

[79] C. de Wit, *Les inscriptions du temple d'Opet, à Karnak* I (BiAe 11, 1958) 112–13 col. 13; III (BiAe 13, 1968) 59.

Figure 18. The sun god as a child within the Ouroboros.

to his existence."[80] Only he and Osiris can change back into the enduring, original form of a snake, that is, into the same form—or rather formlessness—which the eternal enemy of the gods, Apopis, possesses as a power of chaos. It is also visible in the *Ouroboros,* the snake biting its own tail (Figure 18), as the regenerating nonexistence that encircles the world. The snake remains, but the world it encloses sinks away into the primeval water and vanishes with the gods and all living beings; the state of things before creation returns.

In magical texts there are a number of allusions to the cessation of creation and the return to the chaos of the beginning. As a last resort magicians threaten to bring about the end

[80]*CdE* 37/74 (1962) 251–55; quotation from p. 253.

of the world, no doubt in the hope that they will never have to put their threats into effect, and in the process provide macabre parallels with the nuclear age:

> If the one on the water (the crocodile) opens his mouth,
> if he shakes with his two arms,
> I shall cause the earth to go down into the primeval water,
> and the south will be the north
> and the earth will turn round.[81]

There can be a time without gods not only at the end of the world but also, as an interregnum, in the midst of historical time. According to Queen Hatshepsut, the hated Hyksos ruled "without Re" and hence illegally;[82] and Tutankhamun saw the time before his accession as one when the gods and goddesses of Egypt remained aloof, did not respond to any prayer, and "destroyed what was created" (*Urk.* IV, 2027, 15–20). The Israel stela of Merneptah speaks of how the sun god "turned back to Egypt" after the horrors of the Libyan invasion had been overcome.[83] This, however, is a temporary absence of the gods from this world which is overcome with the accession of a new king; only in the forms of expression employed is it comparable with the "twilight of the gods" at the end of all time.

It has become clear that the Egyptian gods are indeed, as Plutarch maintained, "neither unbegotten nor imperishable."[84] They begin with time, are born or created, are subject to continuous change, age, die, and at the end of time sink back into the chaotic primal state of the world. The nature of the Egyptian gods, whose temporal limitations we have just learned, is finite in other respects too.

---

[81]H. O. Lange, *Der magische Papyrus Harris* (DVSM 14, 2, 1927) 57. For further threats of this sort see especially S. Schott, "Altägyptische Vorstellungen vom Weltende," *Analecta Biblica* 12 (1959) 319–30; L. Kákosy, "Schöpfung und Weltuntergang in der ägyptischen Religion," *Acta Antiqua Academiae Scientiarum Hungaricae* 11 (1963) 17–30.

[82]*Urk.* IV, 390, 9 = *JEA* 32 (1946) pl. 6 col. 38.

[83]Line 25: KRI IV, 18–19. There are similar phrases at the beginning of the inscription.

[84]Cf. n. 76 above.

165

The limits of divine power and efficacy

Only a few Egyptian gods had any power outside a closely circumscribed geographical area. For the most part they were "responsible" only for a town, a nome, or a region of the world, and their efficacy decreased in proportion to the distance from their cult centers. As a result, travelers prayed to the deities of the areas in which they were at the time,[85] so that, for example, expedition leaders placed themselves under the protection of the deities responsible for desert tracks and mines or quarries where they worked; the gods of their home towns could help them little when they were far away. This is why Nubian, Asiatic, and Libyan gods acquired such importance for Egyptians who crossed the boundaries of their own country. In the Nubian and Asiatic provinces of their empires the pharaohs of the Middle and New Kingdoms worshiped the deities who had power there—in Nubia, for example, Dedwen, who was of virtually no significance north of Aswan.[86] Doubts could arise as to which god was responsible for a particular area or sphere of action; at such times people often fell back on the most general term for god, *ntr*, as is shown by the example of Sinuhe in Asia.

Portable statues enabled the gods to be effective at great distances, as for example, when King Tushratta of Mitanni sent a figure of Ishtar of Niniveh to the sick Amenophis III. Statues of Egyptian gods can scarcely have gone on such long journeys; the only attested case is that of the image of Amun-of-the-way, which was taken to Byblos around 1070 by the Theban official Wenamun.[87] Images of gods could, however, travel a certain distance in festival processions, and reciprocal "visits" of gods to one another are well documented.[88]

[85]T. E. Peet, *University of Liverpool, Annals of Archaeology and Anthropology* 17 (1930) 89–90.

[86]P. Derchain, *CdE* 37/74 (1964) 266. See also E. Otto, "Anerkennung und Ablehnung fremder Kulte in der ägyptischen Welt," *Saeculum* 19 (1968) 330–43.

[87]A. H. Gardiner, *Late-Egyptian Stories* (BiAe 1, 1932) 64 (1, 34), 72 (2, 55); translations: Simpson, *Literature* 145, 152; Lichtheim, *Literature* II, 225, 228.

[88]A. H. Gardiner, *JEA* 39 (1953) 22 with n. 1.

In the New Kingdom, when Egypt was a world power, the sun god acquired more universal pretensions that went beyond his previous narrow spatial limits. Foreign peoples were drawn into the Egyptian creator god's sphere of influence: like the whole world, he created them and keeps them alive. Akhenaten describes in the great hymn to the Aten how his god separated their languages, distinguished their characters, and cares for their sustenance.[89] In the Book of Gates, which was composed at the end of the Amarna period, these "cosmopolitan" ideas continue to have an impact. All of humanity—represented by the four "races": "mankind" (that is, Egyptians), Asiatics, Nubians, and Libyans—is represented in the underworld. Horus greets them collectively as the "cattle of Re," and promises them a blessed existence in the afterlife.[90] Here the creator is a shepherd who tends all of humanity as his "flock."[91] It is only logical that his power extends far beyond Egypt, so that at the battle of Qadesh in Syria he hurries to the aid of the hard-pressed Ramesses II and brings him victory:

> I pray from the ends of the foreign lands
> and my voice resounds in Southern Heliopolis (= Thebes).
> I found Amun had come when I cried out to him.
> He gave me his hand, and I rejoiced.[92]

There is a suggestion here that space and time have been overcome and that the deity has become transcendent. Other evidence from the late New Kingdom points in the same direction: Amun "hears the prayer of the one who calls to him; in a moment ('t) he comes from afar to the one who cries out to him";[93] of the same god it is said that "every day is for you a moment; it perishes when you set (as the sun)."[94] Siegfried Morenz interpreted these three passages as evi-

---

[89]Sandman, Texts 94–95; Assmann, ÄHG 219; Lichtheim, Literature II, 98.

[90]BPf 176–81; Hornung, Unterweltsbücher 21, 233–35; Piankoff, Ramesses VI 169.

[91]F. Hintze, ZÄS 78 (1942) 55–56; D. Müller, "Der gute Hirte," ZÄS 86 (1961) 126–44.

[92]C. Kuentz, La bataille de Qadech (MIFAO 55, 1928) 252–53 = KRI II, 42–43.

[93]Zandee, De hymnen aan Amon pl. 3, 17.

[94]Hymn of Suty and Hor, Urk. IV, 1944, 13; Assmann, ÄHG no. 89.

dence for transcendence "in the traditional, general sense . . . of aiming to . . . transcend space and time."[95] But I believe that they attest to no more than a relativization of space and time: the gods are thinking and acting on a grander scale. Their rule before the beginning of history, whose precise length in years is recorded in the Turin Canon of Kings and in Manetho,[96] is vastly longer than that of any historical king—but it is a limited, measurable span. In the next world time is also measured on a different scale, so that the judges of the dead "regard a lifetime as an hour"[97] but without stepping outside the categories of time and space. The Book of Gates shows in visible form how beings in the next world are assigned a lifetime (ʿḥʿw) from an inexhaustible store, which is envisaged as a snake (BPf 181–85).

I shall consider Morenz's view of the "transcendence" of Egyptian gods in more detail in a later section of this chapter. Here I am concerned only with establishing that in Egyptian thought there was no "true" transcendence of space and time, and shall cite only two additional pieces of evidence, one concerning this world and one the next. A New Kingdom cosmological text that is very close in time to the Qadesh poem of Ramesses II states: "The distant region of the sky is in total darkness. Its limits (ḏr) to south, north, west and east are not known. These (cardinal points) are fixed in the primeval waters as 'weary ones.' . . . Its land is not known . . . by the gods and spirits. There is no light there at all, (and) it stretches under every place. . . ."[98]

So the dark, watery world before creation lies outside the path of the sun god, and is characterized by the primeval ocean and primeval darkness. In it the cardinal points are abrogated ("weary"); it knows no boundaries and cannot be penetrated by the rays of the sun or reached by any of the gods. The boundary of the created world, which the cosmological text describes as enclosing the sky, also includes the underworld, where the damned must dwell in realms that the sun god does

[95]Heraufkunft 6–7 = 78.
[96]Cf. n. 34 above.
[97]Volten, Politische Schriften 26 l. 155.
[98]Pap. Carlsberg I, 2, 20–31: Neugebauer-Parker, EAT I, 52–54.

not approach during his nightly journey, and which are never illuminated by a ray of light nor penetrated even by the voice of the creator god. Darkness—conceived mostly as the "primeval darkness" before creation and encircling it—is thus quite generally the boundary of the ordered world and the limit of the king's rule.[99]

Even the creator of all cannot pass this farthest boundary. From the Coffin Texts on he is often called *nb-r-ḏr*,[100] which we normally translate "lord of all" but which means literally "lord to the end (or limit)," and thus includes the idea of a boundary, like the one in the underworld that cannot be passed by his creative word.

Nor is the power and knowledge of the gods boundless; strictly speaking, even the most powerful creator god is not "omnipotent." In the story of Isis and Re the god fails to perceive Isis' stratagem and appears to be powerless against the snake she has created to torture him (Chapter 3, n. 91). But even she, the cleverest of all the gods and the greatest magician,[101] does not know the creator's most secret name, although "god knows every name," as the Instruction for Merikare puts it.[102] The boundary is always there, but in the world of the gods it is thought to be very, very distant. The gods live on a different scale and have a vastly increased but not endless existence. Countless eyes and ears intensify the power of their senses[103] and enhance their ability to combat the enemy Apopis, who is deprived of his sense organs and cannot see or hear.[104] In the late period the solar ram has not only four heads but also "777 ears, millions and millions of eyes, and hundreds of thousands of horns" (*Urk.* VI, 75, 18–21)—immeasurably increased faculties.

---

[99]For references see E. Hornung, *StG* 18 (1965) 78; *Amduat* II, 7–8.

[100]*CT* VI, 131j–k, in parallel with *nb–tm* "lord of all"; see also *CT* I, 251a.

[101]Cf. Münster, *Isis* 196.

[102]Volten, *Politische Schriften* 75 l. 138.

[103]Late period examples of this idea were given by S. Sauneron, *BIFAO* 62 (1962) 31. As early as the New Kingdom the sun god sees and hears all: J. Zandee, *JEOL* 18 (1965) 264.

[104]Hornung, *Höllenvorstellungen* 14 with n. 12.

Conceptions of God in Ancient Egypt

Diversity

The limits to the gods' nature in time, space, power, and knowledge, which we have seen in a number of texts, are part of the
more general phenomenon of their diversity (*Differenziertheit*).
This fundamental characteristic of everything that exists—this
diversity—renders it impossible to credit the gods with absolute qualities or absolute existence. When we turn to Egyptian
ontology in the next section we will be able to gain a deeper
understanding of this phenomenon; here I present evidence for
it from a number of different contexts.

The large number of the gods is itself an aspect of their
diversity. The essence of the primeval god is that at first he is
one and then, with creation and the diversity it brings, he is
many. In the New Kingdom "the one, who made himself into
millions" is a common epithet of the creator which renders this
characteristic explicit.[105] "Millions"—enormous and unfathom-
able but not infinite multiplicity—are the reality of the world of
creation, of all that exists. This insight is preserved as late as
the temple texts of the Graeco-Roman period, which apply new
formulations of the old epithet to Amun; he is "a million millions in his name" (*Urk.* VIII no. 138b), and his city, Thebes,
can be called the "container (*hn*) of a million," that is, the
vessel of the richly diverse Amun.[106] In the temple of Edfu it is
stated explicitly that "he made himself into millions *of gods*,"
and what is meant is really gods, not just beings of various
types, or manifestations.[107] When, at Philae, Amun and Ptah are
separately given the ancient epithet "he who made (himself
into) millions"[108] in the same building (the birth house) in the
temple complex of Isis, we see again how this quality belongs

---

[105]For Ramessid examples see G. Fecht, *ZÄS* 94 (1967) 33 n. 7; J. Zandee,
JEOL 18 (1965) 255–56; J. Assmann, *Saeculum* 23 (1972) 125 with n. 62; for late
period and Graeco-Roman examples see Sethe, *Amun* §200.

[106]Sethe, *Amun* §§200–1; E. Drioton, *ASAE* 44 (1944) 127(c); in the latter the
primary reference is to the god Heh, but "million" is at least implied.

[107]*Edfou* III, 34, 10.

[108]Junker-Winter, *Geburtshaus* 49, 47 (Amun: *ntr wʿtj jrj ḥḥ*); 29, 8 (Ptah-Tenen: *jrj
sw m ḥḥw*).

170

quite generally to the creator god, whatever name he may bear. Evidently the Egyptians felt there was no contradiction in logic when in one case Amun and in another Ptah manifested himself in the "millions." Nor is "pantheism" at work here, but rather the insight that the world is necessarily diverse and multiform and owes this state to the creator god.

In addition to diversity in time, space, and form, there is the difference of sex. Like all beings, a deity is male or female; fusion of the two sexes is largely restricted to the primeval god, the one, and is thus characteristic of the undifferentiated unity before creation. The creator is androgynous,[109] male-female, "father of the fathers and mother of the mothers."[110] Akhenaten called his god Aten mother-father and, according to the illuminating interpretation of Maurice Pillet[111] and Wolfhart Westendorf,[112] envisaged himself in the same way, in his role as representative of the creator god; the nude but sexless colossi from Karnak are evidence of this. The process of creation is precisely the emergence from the single creator god, whose sex is not differentiated, of a sexually differentiated divine couple, Shu and Tefnut, who in their turn conceive other couples of both sexes and thus initiate procreation and birth. One of the characteristics of the world before creation is therefore that "birth had not come into being" in it,[113] and the oldest god had to arise "of himself." As early as the Coffin Texts the deceased in his role as creator god considers himself not to have been born (*CT* I, 344c).

The origin of the created world in a process of diversification, of the separation of elements that were previously united, dominates Egyptian ideas of creation. Earth and sky, which were originally united, are separated by Shu; light comes forth from darkness; land emerges from the primeval water; the cre-

[109]S. Sauneron in *Mélanges Mariette* (IFAO BE 32, 1961) 244 n. 1. J. Leclant gave many references to androgyny in Egypt in *Syria* 37 (1960) 7–8.

[110]As with Ptah-Tenen at Philae (n. 108 above).

[111] *Mélanges Mariette* (IFAO BE 32, 1961) 91.

[112] *Pantheon* 21 (1963) 269–77. For a different view and recent bibliography see Baines, *Fecundity Figures* §2.2.3.1.

[113]Inscription of Udjahorresnet: G. Posener, *La première domination perse* (IFAO BE 11, 1936) 6–7 with n. s.

ator god "divided (*wpj*) the nature of the one from that of the other,"[114] thus endowing every being with its unmistakable individuality. This is the background to the surprising statement in spell 261 of the Coffin Texts that Hike, the god of magic, was created by the "sole lord before two things had come into being in this world" (*CT* III, 382e, 383a).

If we are to understand the nature, origin and death of Egyptian gods, their characteristically limited nature, and the diversity of the pantheon, we must study Egyptian ontology. I turn to this in the following excursus, which is based on my unpublished inaugural lecture in Basel, "Ägyptens Auseinandersetzung mit dem Nichtsein" (February 18, 1969).

Excursus: The challenge of the nonexistent

When an Egyptian had to answer for his deeds on earth at the judgment after death, he cast his self-justification in the form of denials, which make up the celebrated "negative confession" in chapter 125 of the Book of the Dead. One of these denials is "I do not know the nonexistent."[115]

When the deceased is accepted at the judgment as one of the justified and blessed, and is allowed to proceed to the pastures of the hereafter, his way passes by many dangerous places, among which is a gate called "swallower of those who do not exist" (*BPf* 45).

Finally he reaches Osiris, the ruler of the dead; he is then before a god who is characterized by one among many epithets as one "to whom comes that which is and that which is not (*ntt jwtt*)."[116]

---

[114]Cairo hymn to Amun 4, 3: Grébaut, *Hymne* 11. The mountains are already "divided" in *Pyr.* §2064.

[115]C. Maystre, *Les déclarations d'innocence* (IFAO RAPH 8, 1937) 26.

[116]K. Sethe, *Aegyptische Lesestücke* (2d ed., Leipzig 1928) 63, 5; Assmann, *Liturg. Lieder* 240 with n. 163. For the same phrase used of the holy city of Abydos cf. J. Spiegel, *Die Welt des Orients* 2 (1955) 401. Both Amun and Osiris are "lord of the existent, to whom belongs the nonexistent": Abd el-Mohsen Bakir, *ASAE* 42 (1943) 86 l. 4 with pl. 4 (= Assmann, *ÄHG* no. 88); The Epigraphic Survey, *The Tomb of Kheruef* (OIP 102, 1980) pl. 21, right column, text p. 39 with 40 n. w. Both these texts are of the New Kingdom, whereas the first formula goes back to the Middle Kingdom.

These are three examples chosen almost at random from the large number of passages in which the Egyptians speak of non-existent entities. What do they mean? Up till now the problems in interpreting these statements have been avoided by translating as simply "nonexistence" (or "the nonexistent"), and then at most remarking in a footnote that what is meant is that which does not yet exist, which could potentially exist—and that is the end of the matter. But the "nonexistent ones" mentioned above, who are to be swallowed by the gate in the hereafter, are deprived of all potential to exist; they constitute something that is definitively and irrevocably nonexistent. In many other cases, as, for example, when the king renders his enemies "nonexistent," the interpretation as not yet existing is not appropriate, even though it may be valid for one of the many aspects of Egyptian nonexistence.

So the problem remains unsolved, the more so since the only attempt to deal with it thus far reaches the paradoxical conclusion that "being and nothingness [are] identical."[117] In tackling the question afresh I am well aware of the conceptual difficulties involved: in the background of any study of nonexistence stands the entire field of modern ontology. Here there is a risk of writing no more than amateur philosophy. Only when the sources have been identified and analyzed, and their content has been clarified, can philosophy elucidate the concepts implied by our topic. Only then will it be possible to examine the conceptual framework of Egyptian ontology and perhaps to fit it into the historical perspective of what Martin Heidegger calls the "contemplation of the existent as existent"—into the history of philosophy. I shall therefore leave open the question of whether we should properly speak of "nonexistence" or of "the nonexistent," and beg indulgence over inconsistencies. We should certainly not speak of the "being of the existent" or of the "noth-ing of the nonexistent";[118] these terms are inappropriate for ancient Egypt. Philologically we are on firm ground, for such Egyptian terms as *tm wnn* and *nn wn* are clear negations

---

[117]P. Derchain, "Zijn en niet-zijn volgens de Egyptische filosofie" [in Dutch and French], *dialoog* 2 (1962) 171–89.

[118]["Das Nichten des Nichts," an allusion to Martin Heidegger, *Was ist Metaphysik?* (1929, collected edition Frankfurt a.M., forthcoming).—tr.]

of the verb "to be"—the former containing a negative verb and the latter a particle. There is also the negative relative adjective (*jwtj/jwtt*) and a substantive derived from it; literally translated, these can only mean "that which is not" or "that which does not exist." The Egyptians also distinguished clearly between verbs such as "to be," "to become," and "to live." But what do they mean when they speak of "that which does not exist"?

The nonexistent, which by its nature cannot be seen or comprehended, may be sought wherever the existent is lacking; in temporal terms this means before creation. Egyptian texts of all periods state that the existent—anything that exists—was created, and so has a beginning. Even the creator god, who created everything that exists and hence—for the Egyptians as well as for us—cannot himself have been created, is not without an origin; as it is often phrased in epithets of gods who created the world, in particular the sun god, he "came into being by himself" (*ḫpr-ḏs.f*) or "began (the process of) coming into being." He has a beginning; outside that beginning there is nothing that exists or came into being, but only a state of nonexistence, which is described by using negations. Obvious parallels for this are the Babylonian *Enuma eliš* or Epic of Creation, the Indian Rig-Veda, and many creation myths of other cultures; here, however, I shall concentrate on the Egyptian ideas.

The Egyptian language possesses a special negative verb form, one use of which is to describe how things were before creation: the *n sḏmt.f* form, which is translated "when . . . had not yet. . . ." In an important article on "The World before Creation," published in 1931,[119] Hermann Grapow listed the features of the created world which are negated in this way; his catalogue, which can now be somewhat extended, makes a good starting point for an attempt to define Egyptian "nonexistence."

The spatial nature of the world is negated: earth and sky have not yet come into being, and the "raising of Shu" has not yet taken place—that is, the air god Shu has not yet separated

---

[119]"Die Welt vor der Schöpfung," *ZÄS* 67 (1931) 34–38, with parallels from non-Egyptian creation myths. Cf. also H. Donner, *ZÄS* 82 (1957) 9, on *Proverbs* 8.

earth and sky by his raising of the sky above the earth, which is part of the process of creation. The primeval elements lie together, unseparated, leaving no space free in which the creator god could stand and creation could emerge.[120] A later variant of these statements adds the underworld to earth and sky (Urk. VIII, 34 no. 42)—the realm of the dead does not yet exist either. According to another relatively late text the creator god has not yet found a place on which he could stand[121]—a strikingly terse denial of the existence of space.

There is no space, nor are there living beings who might inhabit it; both gods and men have yet to come into being—another idea that is found in the earliest relevant texts.[122] Later allusions to creation assume that it was preceded by a state of affairs in which "there was not announced the name of anything,"[123] referring thus to the work of the creator god, in which he calls all creatures and things into being. This is an indirect statement, confirmed by other sources, that before creation there is "no thing," that is, no matter, whether animate or not, for that which is nameless does not exist.[124]

There is no death[125]—how could there be, when life is completely absent?—but it is still characteristic of the Egyptian etiology of the existent that as early as the Pyramid Texts of the third millennium B.C. the phenomenon of death is seen as a necessary concomitant of creation; here is the context for the idea that even the gods are mortal. Before creation there is also no birth; the first gods do not come into being through sexual procreation. The rhythmical alternation of day and night is

[120]References for all these statements are in the article by Grapow, n. 119 above.

[121]R. O. Faulkner, The Papyrus Bremner-Rhind (BiAe 3, 1933) 60, 6 (26, 23); 70, 9 (28, 24).

[122]Pyr. §1466d; tomb of Paser: Grapow, ZÄS 67 (1931) 36. Cf. also CT IV, 101h: "when the nature (shrw) of the gods had not yet been made" and, for specific deities, CT VI, 281a–c.

[123]Pap. Berlin 3055, 16, 3–4: Moret, Rituel 129.

[124]Grapow, ZÄS 67 (1931) 36–37 (Philae). According to Pap. Bremner-Rhind 28, 23 (n. 121 above) there were "no forms (ḫprw)".

[125]Pyr. §1466d. According to a later text there is no death in the primeval ocean Nun: S. Schott, Die Reinigung Pharaos in einem memphitischen Tempel (NAWG 1957, 3) 55.

lacking, as is time itself, which the Egyptians categorize unambiguously with the existent.

The negations I have mentioned so far, which characterize the state of nonexistence before creation, are of a type familiar to us from other cultures. The ancient statement that in this state "conflict had not yet come into being" may seem more bizarre (*Pyr.* §1040c; 1463d). This is a specific allusion to the conflict of Horus and Seth, that is, to the figures and situations of myth, but at the same time it is far more generally a negation of all positive struggle, as can be seen from the affirmative description of this state as being "weary" or "inert": there is nothing that could move or begin to struggle—there is total repose.

Then comes the surprising observation that there were "not yet two things" (*CT* II, 396b; III, 383a), an apparently unnecessary repetition, since there was in any case "no thing at all." But this statement is an explicit expression of the Egyptian view that before creation there was a unity, which could not be divided into two things, just as the creator god is often called the "one, who made himself into millions" (n. 105 above). "Two things" and "millions" are here the opposite poles of a single phenomenon—the diversity of the existent—which is denied in the case of the nonexistent. Nonexistence is one and undifferentiated. The creator god mediates between it and the existent and separates them. He is the original one, who emerges from the nonexistent and marks the "beginning" of the process of coming into being by differentiating himself into the plurality of "millions"—the multiplicity of the existent and of the gods.

This is the intellectual foundation of Egyptian polytheism: insofar as it exists, the divine must be differentiated. In order to refer to a unity in the realm of the existent the Egyptians use the dual or juxtapose two complementary concepts: Egypt is the "Two Lands" or "Upper and Lower Egypt"; space is "sky and earth"; time is *nḥḥ* and *ḏt*; the totality of what is conceivable is "the existent and the nonexistent."

I have now cited enough negative definitions of nonexistence. There are also a few very distinctive positive definitions of the situation before creation. The most important elements that constitute the state of nonexistence are two: limitless waters or the primeval flood (Nun in Egyptian), and completely opaque, total darkness (*kkw zm'w* in Egyptian). Additional features are the weariness or inertia, abysmal depth, and boundlessness of the primeval state, but these are really no more than peripheral definitions that are the logical concomitants of the two primeval elements.[126] The belief that primeval flood and darkness constitute the state before creation is among the oldest known Egyptian ideas about creation; in the ancient world the conception seemed so natural that it was adopted even by Christian Gnostics, who combined it with the Greek notion of chaos.[127]

So far almost all the evidence I have cited has consisted of mythical images of a type familiar in other cultures. Egyptian ontology is based on the insight that the nonexistent is not simply transformed into the existent and thus eliminated. Creation does not remove what was there before it; as well as the sum total of existence there is a remainder which is endless and which is never transformed into existence. For the world of creation the elements from which the state before creation is constituted—primeval flood, primeval darkness, weariness, and negation—are present in two ways. They are the final limit, or the realm beyond all boundaries, which is encountered when one reaches outside the limited world of being; and they are also present in our midst within the ordered world of creation. I have already discussed the nonexistent as the boundary that cannot be crossed, where the efficacy of the gods and of the king reaches its limit. In an astronomical text it is described as being in the sky, beyond the path of the sun; underworld books testify to its presence in the depths. In chapter 175 of the Book of the Dead the underworld is said to be "utterly

---

[126]For weariness or inertia see *CT* II, 33f; V, 166h (of the primeval god, as in Pap. Bremner-Rhind 28, 24 [n. 121 above]); V, 312f (of Nun, as frequently); on the remaining categories see E. Hornung, *ZÄS* 81 (1956) 29–32.

[127]See the references I gave in *StG* 18 (1965) 74. For the Gnostic text which states the chaos of the beginning was darkness and "bottomless water" see A. Böhlig and Pahor Labib, *Die koptisch-gnostische Schrift ohne Titel aus Codex II von Nag Hammadi* (Deutsche Akademie der Wissenschaften zu Berlin, Institut für Orientforschung, Veröffentlichung 58, 1962) 36ff. = *The Facsimile Edition of the Nag Hammadi Codices, Codex II* (Leiden 1974) II, <97>ff.

deep, utterly dark, utterly endless."[128] In it, a dark, watery abyss opens up and swallows sinners like the jaws of hell.[129] Whoever falls down there into the bottomless depths "does not exist," as it is stated in as many words; after the deceased has been assigned to destruction in the judgment of the dead he has become a "nonexistent one."

These limitless depths also house the enemies of the gods, in particular Apopis, who daily stretches out his snake's head to attack the sun god, and must forever be driven back into nonexistence. For the Egyptians the form of a snake, which is appropriate for this archenemy, has a particular affinity with nonexistence. The primeval god who outlives the existent world changes into a snake at the end of time, and after the Amarna period the Egyptians devised the image of the snake coiled back on itself, called "tail-in-mouth"; in the Roman period this image was called the Ouroboros, the "tail-swallower" (Figure 18).[130] The complete circle of the snake's body illustrates—so far as it is possible to depict it—the nonexistent, which encompasses the world continually on all sides. In late Antiquity this image remained so powerful as a symbol that Gnostic writings and magical gems influenced by Gnosticism used it freely; in them the Ouroboros still signifies the "outer darkness" that encircles the world, that is, ultimately, the nonexistent or the extreme circumference of the world—the two amount to the same.[131]

There is a similar image in the New Kingdom underworld books: a snake, out of which one hour after another is mysteriously "born," and then "swallowed" again when the hour is past—which thus embodies the limitless, vertiginous aspect of time.[132] This extreme circumference of the existent, to which the

[128]E. A. W. Budge, *The Book of the Dead* III (Books on Egypt and Chaldea 30, London 1910) 73; Allen, *Book of the Dead* 184; Hornung, *Totenbuch* 366.

[129]On this and what follows see Hornung, *Höllenvorstellungen* 31–34.

[130]Earliest example on the second gilded shrine of Tutankhamun: A. Piankoff, *The Shrines of Tut-Ankh-Amon* (ERT 2, 1955) pl. 48.

[131]C. Schmidt and V. MacDermot, *Pistis Sophia* (Nag Hammadi Studies 9, Leiden 1978) bk. III, chap. 126. Compare also the snake that "encircles the cave of Aion," Claudian, *De consulatu Stilichonis* II, 424–36 (cf. P. Derchain, "A propos de Claudien, Eloge de Stilichon, II 424–436," *ZÄS* 81 [1956] 4–6).

[132]Earliest representation *Amduat* II, 175–76 (translate *dt* "time"), in the eleventh hour of the night; there are also several examples in the Book of Gates (*BPf*). In

Egyptians give the visual form of the "curled snake (*mḥn*),"[133] is both spatial and temporal. The snake curled back on itself encompasses a four-dimensional world that has an end—which the spherical models of modern physics also present as turned back on itself; the Ouroboros seems to be the only visual symbol that shows this turning back on itself.

To repeat and to amplify: for the Egyptians the entire extent of the existent, both in space and in time, is embedded in the limitless expanses of the nonexistent. The nonexistent does not even stop short at the boundaries of the existent, but penetrates all of creation. The astronomical and cosmological text I cited earlier states that "the distant region of the sky is in total darkness" and that this world, "in which darkness (that is, the nonexistent) is present," "stretches under every place"—is omnipresent (n. 98 above). No wonder, then, that Egyptians encounter the nonexistent wherever they go. If they dig a foundation trench, the ground water in it reminds them of the state before creation, and they pour sand to make a new "primeval hill" so that the existent may emerge from the primeval water, which is present in the ground water.[134] The yearly inundation brings the timeless nonexistent back into the world of creation and "the earth is Nun," as a text of the Twenty-fifth Dynasty phrases it.[135] Even the vivifying breath of the wind "goes forth from the Nun,"[136] and every night darkness returns, the state which for the Egyptians too was "in the beginning everything";[137] it "obliterates faces (that is, makes them unrecognizable)"[138] and extinguishes all forms, temporarily dissolving the outlines of

the earliest representation of the Ouroboros (n. 130 above) he is called *jmn-wnwt* "he who hides the hours," that is, the time snake.

[133]This is the oldest name of the Ouroboros, later replaced with "tail-in-mouth" (*sd-m-r*').

[134]A. Moret, *Du caractère religieux de la royauté pharaonique* (Université de Paris, Faculté des lettres, Paris 1902) 134; *Edfou* VIII, 237 (scene titles); P. Barguet et al., *Karnak Nord* IV (FIFAO 25, 1954) 11 with n. 7.

[135]M. F. L. Macadam, *The Temples of Kawa* I (London 1949) 25, fourth line. The idea is attested earlier, in the New Kingdom: Zandee, *De hymnen aan Amon*, stanza "600", pl. 5, 21; A. Erman, *ZÄS* 38 (1900) 24 = Assmann, *ÄHG* 394.

[136]Nina de G. Davies and A. H. Gardiner, *The Tomb of Huy* (Theban Tombs Series 4, London 1926) pl. 38C l. 3.

[137]Goethe, *Faust* Part I, l. 1349.

[138]A. Erman, *ZÄS* 38 (1900) 27 = Assmann, *ÄHG* 395.

the existent. Sleepers, who lie there "as if dead," dwell in Nun, the primeval ocean, as Adriaan de Buck showed in his study of the Egyptian conception of sleep;[139] dreams well up from this abysmal depth. If mere sleep betokens a temporary submersion in the depths of the cosmos, the same is more true of death, which reminds one of the final limit of the existent in the most brutal fashion, even if it does not itself constitute that limit.

This excursion through the landscape of the existent in Egypt could be extended; everywhere in the landscape we would come across the nonexistent, especially in the desert, which contains fabulous animals that do not exist. But let us move on to our chief concern. Where the nonexistent is present, if at all, only on the remotest horizons of the existent, as when it is presupposed before creation and may one day return at the end of time, it is scarcely more than an abstract problem, material for speculation in a vacuum. If astronomy tells us that the world will no longer exist in four thousand million years' time, the news leaves us cold and will not make us change our lives—the prospect is too distant. But where, as in Egypt, the nonexistent is felt to be present everywhere and all the time, it is not confronted in an intellectual, abstract fashion, but engages man entirely.

The challenge presented to the Egyptians by the constantly present reality of the nonexistent has two main aspects, one hostile, the other fruitful and regenerative.

The hostile confrontation is with the powers that belong to the nonexistent outside creation but invade creation and must be driven out of it. It is the task of the king and the gods to do this. Ramesses II is said, among other epithets, to be "he who makes rebellious foreign lands nonexistent,"[140] and similarly it is said of many other kings that they render "rebellious," that is, disloyal foreign peoples "nonexistent" or "uncreated." It is not enough to kill them, for the Egyptians believe that new life emerges from death; they must be driven out of the existent world. This expulsion is necessary not only for political enemies of Egypt and of its king; everyone who transgresses the fixed limits of order distances himself from the existent

[139]*De godsdienstige opvatting van den slaap* (MVEOL 4, 1939) 6–13.
[140]J. Yoyotte, *Kêmi* 10 (1949) pl. 7, 2; 11 (1950) pl. 7, 4; similar phrase K. A. Kitchen, *JEA* 50 (1964) 52 fig. 3.

and, if he continues to transgress, falls into the abyss of non-existence. So in the regions of the damned in the Egyptian underworld the aim is not to torture the condemned sinners, but to extinguish their existence at the sinisterly named "places of annihilation."

We can now understand rather better the "negative confession" at the judgment after death, which I quoted at the beginning. The deceased, who is being cross-examined, says, "I do not know the nonexistent," thus showing that he is someone who has stayed within the boundaries of order and hence of the existent and has not overstepped the limits that have been laid down; he therefore arrives in the expectation that he will continue to be alive and existent after crossing the threshold of death with its associated dangers. There is a similar statement about the blessed deceased in the Coffin Texts: "His abomination is the nonexistent (*jwtt*); he has not seen that which is disordered (*jsft*)" (*CT* VI, 136k).[141] Here "abomination" also means that which is ritually prohibited or taboo. And since, as ruler of the dead, Osiris is lord of the blessed and of the damned, he is praised as a god "to whom comes the existent and the nonexistent."

But there is also the other side of nonexistence, its potential for fertility, renewal, and rejuvenation. Daily the sun dips into the primeval ocean, which daily enfolds all living beings in sleep. It purifies and vivifies, and the sun's re-emergence from the Nun at dawn is a rebirth in the fullest sense, in which the world momentarily attains again its state of perfection at the time of creation. In the natural cycle of the year the fertile land of the Nile Valley is also submerged in the primeval flood in the form of the inundation of the Nile, which "forms (*msj*) that which exists,"[142] bringing to it new strength and fertility. Anything that exists becomes exhausted and needs regeneration, which can be achieved only through the temporary removal and negation of existence; this necessity is the basis

<hr/>

[141]Cf. G. Kadish, "The Scatophagous Egyptian," *Journal of the Society for the Study of Egyptian Antiquities* 9 (1979) 203–17, who interprets the numerous passages in the Coffin Texts about "not eating excrement" and "not going upside-down" in much the same way, as assertions of a moral commitment to the correct order of things.

[142]Zandee, *De hymnen aan Amon* pl. V, 21–22 (stanza "600").

of the positive, indeed absolutely essential, significance of what the Egyptians call the nonexistent, which is anything but negative.

For the Egyptians even death itself cannot call into question or abrogate living existence more than temporarily. It always brings with it a very great danger that existence may be extinguished, and this danger must be countered with extraordinary precautions; in this light Egyptian expenditure on mummification, burial, and grave goods becomes comprehensible. But from another point of view, as we have already seen in some detail, death means rejuvenation, renewal of all that exists, and the gateway to an enhanced life in the next world. So death in particular reveals the ambivalence of the nonexistent, which for Egyptians can be not just a reality but a positive and absolutely essential reality. Only through the nonexistent does creation become possible, so that the gods and the king are especially dependent on it for the perpetual renewal of their work of creation and for the avoidance of lifeless finality.

In the Egyptian view the existent is in need of constant regeneration from the depths of the nonexistent; only then can it maintain its living existence. It is, however, lost if it overlooks the negative, corrosive, deadly side of the nonexistent. The Egyptians are aware that every personal being, including the gods, must die; but they state specifically that only the nonexistent is dead in the sense of being in an enduring state. The Egyptians remain detached and balanced, and avoid falling into nihilism or abrogating the self by surrendering to an unlimited state of nonexistence in which everything is possible; both these attitudes would constitute a devaluation of the existent and a fixation with the nonexistent. Several writers have stressed quite correctly that no trace of mysticism can be found in ancient Egypt. The Egyptians never succumbed to the temptation to find in the transcendence of the existent release from all imperfection, dissolution of the self, or immersion in and union with the universe. They remained active and often, to us, startlingly matter-of-fact; any sort of ecstasy appears quite alien to their attitudes. For them the nonexistent is the inexhaustible, unrealized primal matter, the *pleroma* from which they take strength and which challenges them to create something that exists without qualification or hindrance.

Characteristics of the Gods

This was the task entrusted by Egyptian society to its supreme representative, the king: to complete what was unfinished, to re-form creatively what was finished, and to preserve the existent, not as a status quo but in a continuing, dynamic, even revolutionary process of remodeling and improvement. The idea of perpetual revolution is not so new as it appears and proclaims itself to be; it is a fundamental notion of humanity, and, at least in Egypt, it has its roots in ontology, in the perception that finality, that is, fixity is appropriate only to the nonexistent. Anything that exists is always on the move.

The Egyptian concept of the nonexistent includes aspects that we consider to belong with the unconscious, such as the sleeper who dwells in the Nun; the fact that wine comes from the Nun and is thus a portent of the nonexistent;[143] and every state that is anarchical or inchoate. One could say that in Egypt "the nonexistent" signified quite generally that which is inchoate, undifferentiated, unarticulated, and unlimited; or, in affirmative form, the entirety of what is possible, the absolute, the definitive. In comparison with the nonexistent, the existent is clearly defined, and articulated by boundaries and discriminations. It can be set in order and experienced: there are didactic works (the "onomastica") which teach one to know "everything (or better: every category) that exists"—in fact, of course, only a selection of it.[144]

Since the created world is bounded and ordered in time and space, it follows that it has an end and must disappear; it is an island or an "episode" (Thomas Mann) "between nothingness and nothingness."[145] It has duration, but there is no such thing as eternal existence, which would be a contradiction in terms. The pair of Egyptian words we translate "eternity" (nḥḥ and ḏt) in fact means "time"; for this reason the only preserved explicit statement about the existent defines it as nḥḥ and ḏt.[146]

[143]H. P. Blok, Acta Orientalia 8 (1930) 200 (libation vessel in the Louvre).
[144]Gardiner, Onomastica.
[145]"Lob der Vergänglichkeit" (1952, in Gesammelte Werke X [Frankfurt a.M.: S. Fischer Verlag 1960] 383ff.); Bekenntnisse des Hochstaplers Felix Krull (1954), bk. 3, chap. 5 (Gesammelte Werke VII, 546–47).
[146]CT IV, 198–203b; see further E. Hornung, "Zum ägyptischen Ewigkeitsbegriff," FuF 39 (1965) 334–36. The entirety of this "time"—not "eternity"—is the "lifetime" of the gods. See now also J. Assmann, Zeit und Ewigkeit im alten Ägypten (AHAW 1975, 1); p. 8 n. 1 above.

The significance of the Egyptian ordering of the existent is not only that it was the earliest attempt in human history—as early as the third millennium B.C.—to work out the intellectual basis of an ontology, but still more that the basis which was established had a practical utility. The Egyptians did not create an abstract intellectual structure, but retained a pragmatic attitude to their ontology, using concepts they were able to live with, which sustained their own lives. Scarcely any other civilization has integrated the nonexistent and its creative potential so perfectly into its way of life, acknowledging the nonexistent without falling prey to it. Perhaps this is the source of Egyptian creativity, of the balance and sense of the measure of things which we encounter in all manifestations of Egyptian culture, and which are striking especially in comparison with other Near Eastern cultures of the time. The seriousness of the "brothers in Egypt" which Hölderlin praised,[147] and the rigidity that seems to characterize all Egyptian artistic forms, cannot disguise the fact that the Egyptians lived a full life whose energies overflowed at festivals, even though (or precisely because) they remained constantly aware of the horizon that limits this earthly existence. They were aware of the rule that a living, humane order can be maintained only if it includes within itself an appropriate component of disorder and acknowledges the nonexistent within and around us.

This long excursus has been necessary in order to provide the background against which those characteristics of the Egyptian gods which at first seem most alien can be comprehended. We can now see better why the Egyptians never constructed a closed theological system or produced a normative definition of the nature of a deity—except in the Amarna period. Anything that is dogmatically fixed becomes estranged from the existent and must end by conflicting with reality.

For the Egyptians the fact that their gods exist means that they are subject to the limitations and diversity that characterize all existence. The undifferentiated one of the beginning differentiated himself through his work of creation, he "made

---

[147]F. Hölderlin, *Der Tod des Empedokles,* 3d version ll. 325–30 (*Sämtliche Werke,* Grosse Stuttgarter Ausgabe IV [1961] 133).

himself into millions"; mankind can experience him only in the multiplicity of the created, mortal, and changing gods. In them the Egyptians encounter an existent reality that does not need to be transcendent in order to be the greatest and the most perfect, unique and incomparable.

The uniqueness of god

"Unique god, without equal"; this common invocation of Egyptian gods sounds as monotheistic as anything can be. But just as almost any Egyptian god can be the "greatest" (see below), he can also be "unique"; even the dom palm and the Asiatic goddess Qudshu are addressed as "unique god"[148] and "without equal"[149] respectively. The epithet "unique" is attested as an independent appellation of a god in the early dynastic period,[150] and in the Pyramid Texts the god Nefertem is "without equal" (Pyr. §483b–c).[151]

The apparent contradiction in logic between the epithet "unique" and the many deities to whom it is applied is easily explained. Extended and more precise forms of the epithet make clear its true referent, which is the unique character of the divine in general. Every Egyptian god is "unique in his fashion (w' hr $hw.f$)":[152] there is no other who is the same as him. In the daily cult service the priest must declare before the god who is being worshiped, "I have not equated your nature with that of another god."[153] Despite the multiplicity of the names and forms of gods and despite the phenomenon of syncretism, the Egyptians attach great importance to maintaining the uniqueness of each of their deities. This emphasis has nothing to do with monotheistic conceptions or "tendencies," but prevents the gods from being equated indiscriminately with one another.

[148]I. Wallert, *Die Palmen im alten Ägypten* (MÄS 1, 1962) 134.

[149]M. Tosi and A. Roccati, *Stele e altre epigrafi di Deir el Medina* (Catalogo del Museo egizio di Torino 2, 1, Turin 1972) 103 no. 50066.

[150]Kaplony, *Inschriften* I, 431–32.

[151]L. A. Christophe, *ASAE* 51 (1951) 349 with n. 1, gives examples of this epithet with the goddesses Mut, Maat, and Sakhmet.

[152]J. Sainte Fare Garnot in *Les sagesses* 189–90, referring to *Wb.* III, 216, 4ff.; for additional examples see E. Edel, *ZÄS* 79 (1954) 76.

[153]Moret, *Rituel* 59.

Not until the radical change in thought under Akhenaten does the epithet "unique" acquire the meaning with which we are familiar; the truly unique God Aten does not tolerate the existence of gods other than himself. Outside this brief episode we should take the word "unique" literally only when reference is being made to the creator god, who was unique in the beginning and "made himself into millions (through his work of creation)."

Only outside the world of creation, in the fleeting transition from nonexistence to existence, do the Egyptians encounter the absolute oneness of god. In his creative labors the first and initially unique god dissolves oneness into the diverse multiplicity that makes every deity unique and incomparable, despite the many characteristics they share in common.

The greatness and transcendence of god

The Islamic motto *Allahu akbar* "God is the greatest" applies also to ancient Egypt, and a whole series of epithets of Egyptian gods alludes to this quality of greatness. Because the Egyptian language possesses no separate form for the superlative, the adjective "great" probably corresponds in many instances to our superlative "greatest"; the "Great House" (*pr* ⸱⸱)—the royal title which is familiar to us in the form "pharaoh"— should be understood as the "greatest house," and similarly "great god" (*nṯr* ⸱⸱) in the texts should be taken as "greatest" god."

A number of extended forms express the superlative unambiguously—for example, the formula "greatest god of the great gods," which is attested for Khons in the Twenty-first Dynasty.[154] In the course of the late period Thoth is elevated from being "twice great"[155] to "thrice great," the Greek Hermes Trismegistos.[156]

---

[154]Edwards, *Decrees* pl. 29 ll. 111–12. In the Eighteenth Dynasty Amun is stated to be "greater than any god": S. Sauneron, *ASAE* 52 (1952) 146 l. 2.

[155]From the Twenty-sixth Dynasty on: G. R. Hughes, *JNES* 17 (1958) 8.

[156]At Dendara (*Dendara* I, 30, 13; II, 104, 4) and Tuna el-Gebel (V. Girgis, *MDAIK* 20 [1965] 121). The oldest certain examples of the equivalence Thoth = Hermes Trismegistos date to about 165 B.C. and are in Greek and demotic

It is characteristic of the Egyptian conception of god that the epithet "greatest god" can be given to the most varied deities, often in a single text. In the Pyramid Texts the sun god is often the "greatest god," as is the blessed deceased in two passages,[157] while in the underworld books of the New Kingdom "greatest god" and "this great god" are the normal designations of the sun god Re. But in this latter group of texts Osiris, Atum, Anubis, Horus Mekhentienirti, and winged snakes also receive the epithet "greatest god."[158] The genuinely "great" gods of Egypt all have this epithet: as well as to Re and his various manifestations (Harakhte, Atum, Khepry, and so forth), Osiris, and Amun, it is applied to Anubis,[159] Ptah,[160] Thoth,[161] and a number of others.[162] Even gods whose importance is purely local acquire the epithet: the lion god Mahes,[163] Soknopaios[164] in the Faiyum, and local manifestations of Horus,[165] as well as the deities who

texts from Saqqara: T. C. Skeat and E. G. Turner, *JEA* 54 (1968) 207–8; J. D. Ray, *The Archive of Hor* (Egypt Exploration Society, Texts from Excavations 2, London 1976) 20 n. t. See also M.-T. and P. Derchain, *Göttinger Miszellen* 15 (1975) 7–10. For Thoth "five times great" see R. K. Ritner, *Göttinger Miszellen* 49 (1981) 73–75; 50 (1981) 67–68.

[157]Examples in J. C. Goyon, *Le papyrus du Louvre N.3279* (IFAO BE 42, 1966) 61–62 n. 8.

[158]*Amduat* I, 67 no. 285; 94 no. 394; the rest of the examples are in the Book of Caverns: A. Piankoff, *Le Livre des Quererts* (Cairo 1946) = *id.*, *Ramesses VI* 45–135, pl. 7–34.

[159]Several examples in the tomb of Haremhab in the Valley of the Kings: E. Hornung, *Das Grab des Haremhab im Tal der Könige* (Bern 1971); also at Abydos: Edouard B. Ghazouli, *ASAE* 58 (1964) 130 fig. 17; in the Book of Caverns (see n. 158 above); and elsewhere.

[160]Case of Ptah-Sokar-Osiris already in the Twelfth Dynasty: Ahmed Fakhry, *Monuments of Sneferu at Dahshur* II, 2 (Cairo 1961) 67 fig. 388.

[161]Hari, *Horemheb* 373 (Abahuda near Gebel Adda in Nubia).

[162]Geb: A. Piankoff, *ASAE* 49 (1949) 135 (Twenty-first Dynasty) = A. Piankoff and N. Rambova, *Mythological Papyri* (ERT 3, 1957) no. 1, p. 74; Seth: W. Barta, *MDAIK* 20 (1965) 100 (Nineteenth Dynasty); Khnum: Hari, *Horemheb* 372 (Eighteenth Dynasty); Nefertem: pl. 58; Harsiese: pl. 59; Reshef: Labib Habachi, *ASAE* 52 (1954) 541, and J. M. A. Janssen, *CdE* 25/50 (1950) 210 fig. 18 (both Ramessid); Amset: W. F. Reineke, *Forschungen und Berichte* 8 (1967) 62–63 (Twentieth/Twenty-first Dynasty).

[163]Edwards, *Decrees* pl. 19 l. 59 (Twenty-first Dynasty).

[164]E. Winter, *Der Entwurf für eine Türinschrift auf einem ägyptischen Papyrus* (NAWG 1967, 3) 68 (Ptolemaic).

[165]Horus of Baki, a local form in Nubia: J. Černý, *JEA* 33 (1947) 55 no. 38.

appear at the king's jubilee or *sed* festival,[166] and deified kings.[167] There is no corresponding epithet for goddesses, but "the great one" (or again "the greatest one"?)[168] is attested for Isis,[169] Sakhmet (*Urk.* IV, 1763, 12–13), and the cataract goddess Satis.[170] There must be many more examples: both for gods and for goddesses, the material I cite in the footnotes here is taken from recent publications and could undoubtedly be increased and extended to deities not mentioned here.

The fact that literally any god can be the "greatest" of all the gods should warn us against isolating the "greatest god" as a figure separate from the other deities. The same is also true of the statement that one god created all the others and of the use of *nṯr* for a god in the instruction texts. In each case we find that the specific, well-known deities of the Egyptian pantheon were meant, never a supergod behind the gods.

Yet Hermann Junker, one of the most important and wideranging egyptologists of his generation, attempted for decades to isolate the "greatest one" (*Wr*) as a separate deity who was the original, universal god of world and sky. In 1934 he gave a detailed exposition of his theory in the second volume of his immense work, *Gîza*,[171] and in his later books he repeatedly propounded the same hypothesis, although in a markedly weaker form.[172] In his last publication on the subject he no longer considered the "greatest one" to be any more than the "original term" for the later Atum,[173] thus acknowledging that it is impos-

[166]E. Uphill, *JNES* 24 (1965) 375.

[167]See Chap. 4 n. 114 above.

[168]*wrt*. In Egyptian there are two words for "great," ʿȝ and *wr*, whose meaning and usage are not fully distinct from each other. Here it is noteworthy that ʿȝ is normally used for "great(est)" gods, whereas *wr* is normally applied to goddesses.

[169]Münster, *Isis* 203 (from the Pyramid Texts on).

[170]D. Dunham and J. M. A. Janssen, *Semna Kumma* (Second Cataract Forts 1, Boston, Mass. 1960) 27.

[171]*Gîza* II, 47–57; earlier brief presentation in H. Finke, H. Junker, and G. Schnürer, eds., *Geschichte der führenden Völker* 3 *Völker des antiken Orients* (Freiburg 1933) 31.

[172]*Götterlehre* 25–37; *Pyramidenzeit* (Einsiedeln etc. 1949) 15–25; "Die Religion der Ägypter," in F. König, ed., *Christus und die Religionen der Erde* II (Vienna 1951) 570–88; *Gîza* XII, 97–109; *Geisteshaltung* 134–37.

[173]*Geisteshaltung* 134.

sible to prove that the "greatest one," or the "god" of the instruction texts, had an independent cult. In the case of Atum, however, we know that he displays special characteristics as the creator of the world and a primeval god, and partakes in the nonexistent, but he is in no way a god above and behind the rest of the gods.

"The greatest one" is indeed an ancient and important epithet of Atum, but as early as the Old Kingdom other gods are also claimed to be the "greatest," and the pattern of use of the adjective does not support the assumption that it refers to a particular deity who is otherwise anonymous.[174] There is little point in speculating about the original names, characteristics, or localizations of gods, for the beginnings of Egyptian belief in gods are earlier than the invention of writing, or at the very least earlier than the oldest religious texts. The "Memphite theology," which was for Junker one of the most important pieces of evidence for the belief in a High God, has now been dated not to the early Old Kingdom, where he placed it, but to the Ramessid[175] or perhaps the late period;[176] it certainly does not reflect the Old Kingdom conception of god.

We must limit our study of the Egyptian pantheon to the developed form that we find in the historical period. There is simply no evidence for its earlier origins. Nor is there any indication that its origins are of a uniform character, as our habits of thought predispose us to expect. Experience consistently teaches us that the causes both of historical and of religious phenomena are complex, and that our simplifications do violence to the material.

This is not to condemn all simplification or generalization,

---

[174]See especially the critique of Zandee, *De hymnen aan Amon* 120–27. Cf. also R. Anthes, *OLZ* 40 (1937) 222–23; Kees, *Götterglaube* 270–78; Gardiner, *Onomastica* II, 267*–69*; H. Stock, *Saeculum* 1 (1950) 631–35; H. Frankfort, *Kingship and the Gods* (Chicago 1948) 356; Morenz, *Religion* 156–57 = 149–50; J. G. Griffiths, *CdE* 33/66 (1958) 188–89.

[175]Dating of H. Schlögl, *Der Gott Tatenen* (Orbis Biblicus et Orientalis 29, Fribourg and Göttingen 1980) 110–17. L. Holden compares some features of the text with Coffin Texts spell 647 (*CT* VI, 267–69), *American Research Center in Egypt, Annual Meeting* (Boston 1981) 36.

[176]F. Junge, "Zur Fehldatierung des sog. Denkmals memphitischer Theologie," *MDAIK* 29 (1973) 195–204.

for it is often a valuable aid to the elucidation of developments and may be necessary for their identification in a mass of material. For example, Siegfried Morenz, in *The Rise of the Transcendent God in Egypt* (1964),[177] traced very clearly a consistent tendency of Egyptian religion through almost three millennia. Compression of this sort clarifies much that would otherwise be obscured by the enormous quantity of data. But we must constantly bear in mind that general developments in history—including those in the history of religion—are only approximately and discontinuously rectilinear; rather, they meander or spiral. The small selection of phenomena cited by Jan Zandee in his review of Morenz's work, in which he deliberately played the "devil's advocate,"[178] renders the "rise" much more diffuse and reverses its direction at some points.

But there is a simplification of a different type, whose method is comparable to that of Junker, which is much more dangerous. It is the assertion that a "transcendent god" exists as a separate entity; this assertion is based not on an epithet but on other features of Egyptian gods. If simplification is taken too far, the "star of the first magnitude," whose path is to be studied, could easily become an artificial satellite, a product of the modern scholar's mind. Morenz was aware of these dangers. He stated explicitly that his term "transcendent god" "does not [refer to] a particular deity, but [characterizes] the Egyptian conception of god as such, and in all its manifestations" (p. 8 = 79); he also pointed out that the characteristics he was concerned with are found in the most various deities, among whom the "great gods," Re, Amun, and Ptah "lead the way" (*ibid.*). So we have on the one hand a unitary conception of god and on the other many gods of different types—the same problem that is alluded to in the title of this book. It is clear from many statements by Morenz that he saw "the great and single reality of God behind his many manifestations"; in other words, he considered that the one, transcendent God of the later history of religions "shines through" again and again in the religious world of the Egyptians. This is a declaration of faith that

[177]Morenz, *Heraufkunft.*

[178]*ThLZ* 91 (1966) 261–65; cf. also *id.*, *Het ongedifferentieerde denken der oude Egyptenaren* (Leiden 1966) 13–14.

cannot be tested critically. But it is necessary to test whether characteristics of this God, for example, transcendence, can be discovered in ancient Egyptian belief.[179]

Every god is "transcendent" in the sense that his being reaches beyond that of this world and its norms; in the richness of his nature and in his range of activity he is always vastly superior to human beings. Simply because the locus of being and action of Egyptian gods is not on earth, they must be "transcendent." But in Egypt one cannot speak of a true transcendence that would raise a deity above space, time, and fate and extend his being into the realms of the absolute and limitless. We have seen earlier in this chapter that all the passages in texts which might be taken to point in this direction tend to relativize, rather than abrogate, the categories of space and time which apply to the world of creation. Morenz does not, therefore, pursue this line of thought but takes as his starting point "that in the early dynastic period in Egypt the highest god was embodied in the ruler and hence (from the point of view of Egyptian society) immanent" (p. 6 = 78); in this perspective transcendence is "the increasing withdrawal of god from this immanence and accessibility" (*ibid.*).

It is quite clear that throughout Egyptian history royal power becomes continually weaker; the king submits himself more and more profoundly to the might and will of the gods, and his dependence on other human and earthly possessors of power increases. The development of royal tombs, from the gigantic pyramids on the plateau of Giza, through the modest brick pyramids of the Middle Kingdom and the concealed rock tombs of the New Kingdom, to the relatively very small tomb chambers of the third intermediate period in Tanis, is probably the most striking illustration of the king's diminishing prestige.[180]

In the early dynastic period the king is like a terrestrial polar star, around which revolve all the constellations of civil, and to a considerable extent of religious, life. During the time of the

[179]The evidence mentioned in the rest of this chapter is presented in Morenz, *Heraufkunft,* to which reference should be made for documentation.

[180]Even here the development is not linear; rather, there is a recurring tendency to elaborate a hierarchy, in which the king and his tomb have clearly defined privileges, as I have shown in *ZÄS* 105 (1978) 59–66.

pyramid builders in the central Old Kingdom the deceased king ascends to the polar star in the sky, but his living successor is from now on the "son of Re." This definition of the king's relationship with the sun god, which was formulated in the Fourth Dynasty, has always been seen as a diminution of status, and it has been noted that at the beginning of the Fifth Dynasty the royal funerary monument takes second place in size and importance to the solar temples. Proponents of this view have always assumed that in the early dynastic period the king had been, as "Horus," entirely a god, so that in the Fourth and Fifth dynasties he subordinated himself as the "son" of the highest god. But I have shown at the end of Chapter 4 that it is quite uncertain that as "Horus" the king was identical with or an "incarnation" of Horus. All we can safely say is that from the beginning of Egyptian history the king was termed Horus, just as from the Fifth Dynasty on the deceased king was termed Osiris; for the early dynastic period and Old Kingdom we do not know precisely in what form the relationship between Horus and the king was envisaged. The extensive textual evidence of the Middle and New kingdoms suggests that at his accession Pharaoh took on the role of Horus, and at his death he took on the role of Osiris, adopting the attributes of these gods without being identical with them. This form of divinity does not relate to him as an individual but to his office.

In assuming that god was originally immanent and "accessible" in the king, Morenz projected backward in time a developmental tendency that cannot be documented before a later period, and thus started from a hypothetical, and questionable, point of departure. It is equally questionable to interpret the formula that the king is the "son" of the sun god as indicating a withdrawal from an earlier immanence (for which we have no evidence at all). It seems rather that in the early Old Kingdom—for whatever reasons—there was a "rise" of the sun god which in the end forced the king to define his previously vague relationship with that god. The formula of sonship does not necessarily signify a reduction in status; rather it is a kind of bracketing, which henceforth connects the lord of the gods very closely with his likeness on earth, or a collective program of rule, which requires the kings of Egypt to repeat on earth the deeds of the sun god at creation.

In the Fifth Dynasty there is a similar development in the king's relationship with Osiris. The "rise" of this new ruler of the realm of the dead results in the deceased king's being defined as "Osiris," which does not mean that the two are equated, but that the king acquires a further divine role.

Later developments follow very closely the direction indicated by Morenz—if one disregards some short periods of reversal, such as are found in all history. At the end of the Old Kingdom the kingship is brought to the verge of insignificance and has to bow before the might of the gods and of the great feudal lords. Phiops I (c. 2292–2260 B.C.) is the first king to be depicted kneeling while offering to the gods, and in his inscriptions he displays a hitherto unknown regard for deities whose sphere of influence is far away in the provinces. As the king's power on earth continues to decline, men turn more and more to the gods as the ultimate cause and sanction of events; in the turmoil of the first intermediate period (c. 2140–2040 B.C.) the gods are credited for the first time with responsibility for political affairs (p. 211, below).

When, at the beginning of the Middle Kingdom, Egyptian kingship is reformulated and meditates upon its ideological foundations, divine authority continues to take precedence over it; from now on the king makes reference to his "election" by a god and acts according to the "commands" of the god. Even the most important ruler of the New Kingdom, Tuthmosis III (1490–1436 B.C.), bases his claim to the throne on an oracular pronouncement of the god Amun and ascribes his victories to the god's agency. This development culminates in the "theocracy" of the Twenty-first Dynasty, in which the oracular decisions of Amun regulate everything that happens down to relatively insignificant administrative and political matters; even the installation of an official and the solution of a case of theft are governed by divine oracle. "Amun is King," the name of one of the kings of the Twenty-first Dynasty who resided in Tanis, marks the culmination of a development in which the king becomes ever more dependent on the power and decisions of the gods.

But historical space is spherical; however straight the line of any development may seem to us, ultimately it comes full circle; the end may be displaced a little by the force of events, but nevertheless it lies close to the point of departure. The same is true here, too, for the slogan "Amun is King" heralds a greater immanence of god in the historical, terrestrial world, a descent from his assumed transcendence. In terms of the Egyptian conception of history the beginning and the end of the process are still closer together; the Royal Canon of Turin, which records an early Ramessid systematization (thirteenth century B.C.) of earlier ideas about the succession of kings, places the rule of gods on earth at the beginning of the list, before all the kings.

This idea was influenced by a revival of the tendency to situate the gods more firmly within history, but it may also reflect unintentionally the true situation at the beginning of history, when the gods were associated more closely with events on earth. The inanimate and animal forms of the gods suggest that they were originally immanent, and the cloth fetish used as the hieroglyph for god is particularly strong evidence for an immanent, "accessible" god. Here Morenz's projection backward in time from later developments seems justified, even if one disputes an original divine immanence in the king or in the predynastic chief.

In *The Rise of the Transcendent God* Morenz identified correctly and presented in a concentrated and stimulating form an important tendency in the development of Egyptian religion. But the title he gave to his work can easily lead the historian of religion astray. In Egypt it is possible to observe the historical "rise" of various major gods, such as Re, Osiris, Ptah, and Amun. Shifts from immanence to transcendence—and the other way round—can be seen in the most various deities. But at no time was there a transcendent God in Egypt, and a fortiori no *Rise of the Transcendent God*, which was indeed for Morenz the "History of God in Ancient Egypt."[181] With the sole exception of

[181]"Die Geschichte Gottes im alten Ägypten," title of a summary of his work in the *Neue Zürcher Zeitung*, Oct. 18, 1964, 6. [The German *Heraufkunft des transzendenten Gottes* is ambiguous in that it may allude to the single God in a way in which the English rendering does not; an alternative form that brings out the ambiguity is *The Rise of God's Transcendence.*—tr.]

Akhenaten, the "waning" king of Egypt does not confront a single "waxing" god who becomes ever more transcendent, but a multiplicity of gods who buttress his authority. Among them the sun god in his various forms and names sets the tone, for he is the original creator whose deeds every king must repeat.

In Egypt gods and human beings together inhabit the existent, that is, the ordered world of creation. The truly transcendent realms of the universe are godless, being reserved for the "enemies," the powers of chaos. The nonexistent, in which the primeval deities are in some sense "transcendent," as is the creator god at the beginning of creation, begins where boundaries and diversity end. We must accustom ourselves to the fact that by their nature Egyptian gods are neither transcendent nor eternal, unconditional, absolute. The "anonymous" god of the instruction texts is no exception, even though he is often cited as the chief evidence for transcendent features or "monotheistic tendencies" in the Egyptian conception of god.

The lecture given by Jozef Vergote at Strasbourg ("La notion de Dieu"), which I have already used in the discussion of terminology in Chapter 2, also contains a list of the most important characteristics that are ascribed to the anonymous *nṯr* of the instruction texts (pp. 168–70), characteristics that constitute for Drioton and Vergote a further confirmation of their monotheistic interpretation. But if one reviews the phrases cited, one discovers no attributes of a different order from what I have cited so far, nothing that might point to a single, transcendent God. The headings "The Unique God" and "The Omnipotent God" (both p. 168) are misleading, for they do not accord at all with the content of their respective sections. A god who created the world is not "omnipotent" because he is a creator god, and the arguments for a "unique" god are still weaker: "The uniqueness of the transcendent God can thus be deduced only from the monotheistic character of the maxims as a whole" (p. 168).

The reasoning has become circular—the conclusion that is to be proved is assumed in advance. A monotheistic, transcendent God who stands high above all gods should show himself to be what he is through his nature and his actions. But the instruction texts do not say any more than that he intervenes in the affairs of the world and brings his "orders" to fruition, that he judges, rewards, and punishes, that nothing can succeed without or against him; all these are qualities and modes of action which are also attributed to various specific deities. Even in the "Song of Praise for the Transcendent God" (Morenz p. 47 = 111) in chapter 18 of the Instruction of Amenemope, where the superiority of god over man is indeed strongly emphasized, the famous concluding lines with their striking images depict both god and man as being in the same boat: "Man's tongue is the ship's rudder, and the Lord of All is its pilot."[182] Continuing the same metaphor, one may say that this ship is the coracle of the existent on the ocean of the nonexistent, across which both god and man must navigate together.

In the course of Egyptian history the authors of the instruction texts, like the king, submit more and more completely to the will, action, and percipience of the deity; in the "age of personal piety," to which Amenemope (c. 1200 B.C.) also belongs, man surrenders himself entirely into god's hands, and scarcely even hopes for solace from human actions. But down to the very end both belong to the same existent world and rely upon each other as partners. I consider their partnership in the next chapter.

[182]Lange, *Amenemope* 98.

6 ◟ Divine Action and Human Response

Human beings live in a world in which the gods are invisibly but powerfully active. Every morning, when an Egyptian priest opens the sealed shrines in a temple sanctuary, the god's awesomeness and majesty take possession of him; in the daily ritual for Amon-Re, the king of the gods, he says, "Your awesomeness is in my body and your majesty pervades my limbs."[1] "Awesomeness" and "majesty" represent attempts to render the Egyptian terms *snḏt* and *šfšft* in a modern language; *snḏt* can also mean "fear" of someone, and *šfšft* the commanding "authority" that surrounds a dignitary.

When the priest sees the image of the god, he feels the power that emanates from the divine being; when the god himself appears, he manifests the same power in radiance, aroma, and fire (see Chapter 4). The first emotion that grips an Egyptian who encounters a deity or the image of a god is fear, mixed with wonder and exultation. At a theophany earth and sky rejoice, the entire world jubilates, and laughter and festivity abound.[2] But in order to make any kind of meeting possible an Egyptian deity must also say "fear not," as is recorded in the story of the Shipwrecked Sailor—for the gods are superior, unpredictable, sometimes uncanny powers. As well as love and kindness, their faces project terror.

But the gods are not there in the world in order to spread

[1]Moret, *Rituel* 66.
[2]Assmann, *Liturg. Lieder* 250–60, cites a wealth of examples.

197

fear and terror and to turn their human partners into timid slaves—only man is capable of such inhuman conduct, when he exercises power over other men. The gods created the world and ensure that not only mankind but all beings can live and grow in it. But to what end? What made the creator god call the world and all its creatures into being and keep them in being? No Egyptian text is known which gives direct, unambiguous answers to questions of this sort: the Egyptians evidently did not consider these to be serious issues. The gods can create only that which is perfectly formed, and the first state of the world is one of perfection and balance. The state before creation is not worth striving after, even for the creator god—since he is alone in it, all that there is for him is a dialogue with that which does not answer and which does not indeed exist. By differentiating himself and coming into existence he initiates the dialogue and give-and-take from which gods and mankind live.

Expressed in our terms, an Egyptian justification of the creation of the world might have resembled the one I have just sketched, but no such statement is preserved. There is, however, in the Coffin Texts (c. 2000 B.C.) the famous "monologue of the creator god," which is an enumeration of the four most important deeds of creation:

> I did four good deeds
>   within the portal of the horizon.[3]
> I made the four winds
>   so that every man might breathe in his surroundings.[4]
> That is one of the deeds.
> I made the great flood
>   so that poor and rich might have power.[5]
> That is one of the deeds.
> I made every man like his fellow.
>   I did not ordain that they do wrong (*jzft*);
>   their hearts disobeyed what I had said.

[3]I.e. even before he stepped out of the horizon and was manifest in the terrestrial world.

[4]Because the "surroundings" (*h'w*) can be understood spatially or temporally, I have rendered the word in this general way.

[5]I.e. share in the fecundity of the Nile's inundation.

198

That is one of the deeds
I caused that their hearts should not forget the west,
    so that offerings be presented to the gods of the nomes.
That is one of the deeds. (*CT* VII, 462d–464f)

This passage is almost an Egyptian program of "Liberty, Equality, Fraternity," proclaimed as the foundation of a new order after the collapse of the Old Kingdom. The creation of air, nourishment, equality of opportunity, and constant involvement with the realm of the dead and the gods are the four outstanding deeds of the creator god, and also the material and spiritual basis of human existence.

Through the initial separation of earth and sky, space comes into being, and with it the breath of life—the most important gift of the gods to mankind. From the late New Kingdom on there are scenes of protective goddesses wafting breath to the deceased with their wings, for air is life; in the arid desert climate of Egypt every "breath of the north wind" vivifies and refreshes. The hieroglyph for life, which is the commonest attribute held in the hands of gods, signifies that they possess and dispense life. Countless scenes on the walls of temples and tombs show them holding this hieroglyph to the nose of the king, who represents all of humanity, and through whose nose the breath of life enters human beings (Plate II).

We, who belong to a breathless age, should be able to appreciate the deep and timeless significance of these scenes. Is not the creative breath of life, which dilates and liberates the soul, the most precious attribute of a worthwhile human existence? Is there not a risk that in our time humanity will be suffocated by inhuman systematization or by the waste products of technology? Are there not many who risk their lives in order to be able once more to breathe freely? The Egyptians could be confident that their gods would always give them "a new space to breathe in," as Rilke hoped the gods would return to do for his generation.[6] Within this "space for breath" and for freedom, a great and creative culture arose.

Life and freedom are visibly held in the hands of Egyptian gods and are destined for all living beings, not just for human-

[6]R. M. Rilke, *Sämtliche Werke* II (Wiesbaden: Insel Verlag 1956) 185.

ity. As early as the Old Kingdom tomb reliefs show how the creator's loving care affects all of nature and provides nourishment even for the hedgehog in its nest. In New Kingdom solar hymns there is the image of the chick in the egg which the sun god enables to breathe and keeps alive. This image, which the Egyptians used in their script as a sign for the preposition or adverb "within,"[7] is the most absolute expression of the "inwardness" of the gods' constant care for the world. Like the rays of the sun, it penetrates all the world of creation; in the great hymn to the Aten Akhenaten proclaims, "Your rays envelop all lands as far as the end of everything you created."[8]

At the same time Akhenaten's artists devised the image of the sun disk with rays (Figure 20), the most impressive of all symbols of the loving care of the sun god, whose light signifies life, as he sustains the world. The far-reaching rays of the sun disk terminate in human hands that hold the sign of life out to the noses of the royal family. With abundant clarity this image depicts light as the bearer of the breath of life. Light is life, even in the dark realm of the dead through which the sun god passes. The New Kingdom underworld books describe how, wherever the sun god's rays and his creative word reach, sealed doors spring open, the crippling darkness is banished, and the dead rise up to renewed life.

Before the time of Akhenaten the Cairo hymn to Amun praised the rich blessings the sun god bestows on all creatures:

> He who makes fodder that nourishes cattle,
> and "wood of life" (food plants?) for mankind;
> who makes what the fish in the river live upon,
> and the birds in the air.
>
> He who gives breath to the one in the egg,
> and causes the young of the salamander to live,
> who makes what mosquitoes live on,
> and worms and fleas likewise. . . .[9]

---

[7]A. Hermann, "Rilkes ägyptische Gesichte," *Symposion* 4 (1955) 440–41 with pl. 2 (reprinted Darmstadt 1966).

[8]Sandman, *Texts* 93, 14–15; Assmann, *ÄHG* 216.

[9]Grébaut, *Hymne* 17.

Akhenaten uses images that were already familiar in the great hymn to the Aten, in which the creator dispenses the breath of life to all his creatures—most notably when he speaks of the "chick in the egg." This motif continues to be used in later times, in texts ranging from Ramessid hymns to the temple texts of the Graeco-Roman period.[10] The function of sustaining life is not exclusive to the sun god; every god who is worshiped as a creator also sustains life—if he did not take lasting responsibility, his work of creation would be meaningless. Thus it is said of Ptah that he "created everything that exists . . . (and) keeps everyone alive with his (craftsman's) fingers."[11]

This truly inexhaustible provision for all—the sun god is often said to be the one who "does not sleep" on his way[12]—expresses not only the god's responsibility but also his love of all that he created. From the beginning of the historical period names in the form "the one whom god loves"[13] provide evidence for divine "love" of humanity, while a form of royal epithet which states that the king is "beloved" of a god is first attested in the mid-Fifth Dynasty under Neferirkare (c. 2446–2427 B.C.) and later becomes extremely common.[14]

In the Eighteenth Dynasty this formula occurs in an intensified form, in which the king is said to be loved by the deity "more than all other kings," or, better expressed, has been "selected" from among all kings.[15] This "love," in the sense of selection, is graded into hierarchies; it is destined especially for the king, and almost always emanates from the superior being,[16] from god to king, from king to his subjects, from parents to child, husband to wife, mankind to things. Even in the highly

[10]Examples are cited by Otto, *Gott und Mensch* 144–45.

[11]J. Spiegel, *ASAE* 40 (1940) 258 ll. 5–6 (Twentieth Dynasty).

[12]Assmann, *ÄHG* 87 l. 123; 133 ll. 8–9.

[13]Kaplony, *Inschriften* I, 491–506; H. Ranke, *Die ägyptischen Personennamen* I (Glückstadt 1935) 155–61.

[14]P. Kaplony, *MDAIK* 20 (1965) 33.

[15]S. Morenz, "Die Erwählung zwischen Gott und König in Ägypten," in *Religion und Geschichte* 120–38 (reprinted from *Sino-Japonica. Festschrift André Wedemeyer zum 80. Geburtstag* [Leipzig 1956] 118–37). See also Blumenthal, *Untersuchungen* 75 (earlier example with Sesostris I); W. K. Simpson, "Amor Dei . . . ," in *Fragen* 493–99.

[16]J. Omlin, "Amenemhet I und Sesostris I" (Dissertation, Heidelberg 1962) 20.

emotional Amarna period the Aten's "love" appears to have been destined only for Akhenaten. In earlier periods the only statement that a god loves "mankind" is in the story of the Shipwrecked Sailor,[17] and the converse, that human beings "love" a god, is not found before the Ramessid period. In the "personal piety" of this period, in which all trust and all hopes for succor depend on the grace of god, the reciprocal love of god and man comes to the fore as a "free act of grace on the part of the god, unrelated to human actions."[18] In the Ramessid period there are formulas on scarabs such as "god loves the one who loves him" or "Ptah loves those who love him,"[19] and in a hymn Thoth is even loved by "everyone."[20] Thoth also "gives an office to the one he loves,"[21] so that his "act of grace" acquires a material significance.

But this phraseology is part of a late and separate development within Egyptian religion, in which man's status as a child and likeness of god is strongly emphasized along with "love" between god and man.[22] In earlier times it would probably have been thought unseemly to stress the subject's "love" of the king or of a deity; a more appropriate demeanor would be awe, reverential wonder, or joyous acclamation at the direct revelation of a higher being. In this rejoicing all of creation—"to the height of heaven, to the breadth of the sky, to the depth of the sea"[23]—unites in order to praise the creator and sustainer of the world. "All those whom you created dance before you"[24]—wild

[17]MES 46, 4–5 (ll. 147–48); cf. Simpson (n. 15 above).

[18]H. Brunner in Les sagesses 108.

[19]E. Drioton, "Maximes relatives à l'amour pour les dieux," Analecta Biblica 12 (1959) 57–68; id., Kêmi 14 (1957) 21–23. For additional examples and bibliography see Brunner in Les sagesses 108.

[20]A. H. Gardiner, Late-Egyptian Miscellanies (BiAe 7, 1938) 25, 10.

[21]P. Boylan, Thoth the Hermes of Egypt (London etc. 1922) 200; G. Posener, RdE 7 (1950) 72.

[22]Cf. Hornung, "Mensch als Bild Gottes" 150–51.

[23]Cairo hymn to Amun 7, 4: Grébaut, Hymne 19. The same emphasis on joy is found in Graeco-Roman temple texts; see Wb. VI, 55 and passim, where many new words for such ideas are noted; see also e.g. the texts collected by F. Daumas, Les mammisis des temples égyptiens (Annales de l'Université de Lyon 3d series 32, Paris 1958) pt. 2 chap. 3.

[24]Sandman, Texts 14, 5.

animals jump up, birds flutter their wings, fish leap in the water, and even the king joins, with the divine baboons, in the general jubilation.[25]

This joyous adoration is the strongest response that there is to divine involvement in earthly affairs. Any return on the part of mankind seems paltry when measured against what the gods grant. What are all material gifts, such as bread, beer, meat, and wine, in comparison with freedom, the breath of the creator, with protection, succor, and rescue from all distress? The gods, who dispense everything, themselves possess a superabundance of everything. In the story of the Shipwrecked Sailor "there was nothing which was not within" the distant island of the gods,[26] and the snake god of the island laughs when, in his simplicity, the stranded Egyptian promises him all the treasures of Egypt, despite the fact that the snake's realm already has an abundance of everything. The one thing that the snake god asks of the man as he returns home sounds modest enough: that he should "give (the god) a good name" in Egypt.[27]

The Egyptian gods desire that mankind should respond to their presence and their actions. They do not require to receive a cult and do not have to have material offerings, but they rejoice over the echoes that their creative word produces, and they are happy to receive both tangible and intangible gifts from mankind. The most important thing is the dialogue that is manifest in this form. To "enter" into a god's presence is to "make direct contact,"[28] and the king, as the representative of mankind, does not wish to come empty-handed into the god's presence. The offering he brings is not a tribute demanded from him and he does not seek to compel a return; it is a *gift*,[29] and contains something of the freedom that the gods dispense to mankind with the creator's breath.

In describing the cult of the gods I have deliberately emphasized a side of it that is very different from the common

[25]*Medinet Habu* VI pl. 421, 424 (reign of Ramesses III); cf. J. Assmann, *Der König als Sonnenpriester* (ADIK 7, 1970) 7–8.

[26]*MES* 43, 4.

[27]*MES* 46, 14.

[28]Winter, *Untersuchungen* 55.

[29]*Ibid.*

catch-phrase *do ut des* (I give so that you may give), which is used in the explanation of any sort of cult. The phrase seems to apply well to some areas of Egyptian cult, but it explains little and should certainly not be used as the only approach. Before mankind gives anything, the gods have already given everything.[30]

Here, as so often, it is the poet whose sensitivity enables him to perceive what really takes place when offerings are presented, and his intuition is confirmed by the primary sources. Faced with the countless offering scenes that cover the walls of the temple of Karnak and the other temples in Egypt, Rilke senses how what is immeasurable in the relationship between god and man acquires the "measure of offering," which allows man, who in the last analysis always offers himself, "always" to be "the giver."[31] Everything tends toward

> the place where the king's likeness
> —the god—like a child at the breast, is suckled,
>
> takes the milk and smiles. His sanctuary
> never ceases to breathe. He takes and takes,
> . . . .

Here too a creative breath is present, "never ceasing to breathe," and bringing constant increase. The gods, who already possess everything, can always accept more, and the extent of their being, which is great but not limitless, can always be increased. We have seen this constant tendency to extension in the names and forms of the gods; it is also present in the cult. Corresponding to the epithets "rich in names" and "rich in manifestations" there is the—much rarer—epithet "rich in festivals."[32]

Like all epithets, this one is not an ornament without significance, but reflects reality on earth. The large number of festivals referred to betokens the intensity of human response

[30]The *sḏmn.f* that accompanies speeches by gods in offering scenes is therefore a true past, not a "simultaneous present."

[31]All these quotations are from the poem about Karnak in the cycle "Aus dem Nachlass des Grafen C.W.," *Sämtliche Werke* II (Wiesbaden: Insel Verlag 1956) 120; for an interpretation cf. A. Hermann in *Symposion* (n. 7 above).

[32]Junker-Winter, *Geburtshaus* 35, 20 (relating to Nehemetawai).

whose climax comes in festal rejoicing and an increased echo from the world of creation, and thus signifies an enhanced existence for the gods. Again and again in royal inscriptions festivals of the gods are said to be extended and enriched, new festivals are established, and the temples, which house the cult, are indefatigably cared for. New and more costly cult images are made, and the number of carrying poles on which they are supported in processions is continually increased. This provision for the cult of the gods is an essential part of the king's role in history; it is also an important element in the economy and remains significant in our modern view of Egyptian history.

The Egyptians believed that by performing the cult and presenting themselves before the god they were at least increasing his existence and presence, while also keeping his negative, dangerous side at a distance. Cult actions do not coerce but they do encourage the gods to show their gracious side—for the converse of a god's love of mankind is his violent aspect, which is always present beneath the surface and must be assuaged by means of appropriate cult services. In the myth of the Destruction of Mankind the violent goddess whom the sun god sends out against an insubordinate humanity is mollified by an intoxicating drink that calms her ire and turns her from a raging lioness into a friendly cat. In the cult wine is used for the ritual assuaging of deities, especially goddesses in lioness form. It neutralizes their dangerous, unpredictable side—which is also an aspect of the divine king's makeup—and demonstrates the "theological significance of drunkenness," about which Hellmut Brunner has written.[33]

Thus the cult is not only mankind's response to the god but also protection against the god's threatening side. The *Conceptions of Hell* in the Egyptian underworld books, which I have studied in another book,[34] are emphatic and impressive evidence of how terrifying the gods can be. The entire, uncontrollable rage of the deity is directed against those who have been condemned in the judgment after death, who fall from the ordered,

---

[33]"Die theologische Bedeutung der Trunkenheit," *ZÄS* 79 (1954) 81–83. Cf. also *id.*, "Das Besänftigungslied in Sinuhe," *ZÄS* 80 (1955) 5–11; Kees, *Götterglaube* 8–11.

[34]Hornung, *Höllenvorstellungen.*

existent world and then, tortured in every imaginable way and "destroyed," are consigned to nonexistence. They are deprived of their sense organs, must walk on their heads and eat their own excrement; they are burned in ovens and cauldrons and swim in their own blood, which Shezmu, the god of the wine press, has squeezed out of them.

Against the terrifying cruelty of the gods, which in earlier mortuary texts does not just threaten sinners but is taken to be a general danger of the hereafter, man protects himself with rituals whose correct performance neutralizes the dangerous aspect of the deity and guarantees that the world will continue in the proper, ordered fashion.[35] From the time of the Pyramid Texts, the earliest collection of spells for the afterlife, we also find appeals of the deceased to various gods to protect him from all the dangers and obstacles of the next world and to stop other gods or the dead men from harming him. Invocations of this sort can be raised to the level of a threat against the gods[36]—a new and surprising variant in the relationship between god and man.

What we have learned so far about the actions of Egyptian gods cannot be better summarized than in Goethe's timeless lines from "Limits of Humanity":[37]

> What separates
> gods from men?
> Many waves roll forth
> before the gods,
> an endless stream;
> a wave lifts us,
> a wave swallows us,
> and we sink.

[35]For this aspect of the cult, which I do not here consider any further, see Derchain, Le papyrus Salt 825; S. Sauneron, in Le monde du sorcier (Sources Orientales 7, Paris 1966) 40–42; J. F. Borghouts, OMRO 51 (1970) 30–31.

[36]H. Grapow, "Bedrohungen der Götter durch den Verstorbenen," ZÄS 49 (1911) 48–54; Erman, Religion, 3d ed. 300–1; Morenz, Religion 27–28 = 26–27; S. Sauneron, BSFE 8 (1951) 11–21. On the strongest form of these threats, that of the destruction of the world, see Chapter 5, at n. 81; below, n. 50.

[37]"Grenzen der Menschheit" (c. 1775–80).

The waves of power go forth from the gods of Egypt, and mankind tosses among them. The gods are the great and powerful ones who make a mockery of human pretensions. The deity is "the efficacious one, who cannot be repelled in the sky or on earth,"[38] the great builder in whose hands mankind is "mud and straw."[39] The Egyptians evidently never experience a longing for union with the deity. They keep their distance from the gods, whom no one can approach too closely without being punished; but their hopes for the next world are based on becoming "like a god,"[40] on assuming the role of one of the great gods and thus themselves affecting the course of the world.

It is worth considering a little further the way in which the gods affect the world. Here our theme is power, energy, and efficacy, and my exposition may aptly be couched in the terminology of physics. I have already spoken of a "field" of force which should be imagined as surrounding every deity and producing on mankind an effect of a specific intensity. In this field, which is envisaged as limited and having an end (see Chapter 5), the "hidden" gods manifest themselves through their effect on human beings and on other objects of their attention. The force that operates in this field is called in Egyptian $ḥk'$, which is generally translated "magic"; I put the word in quotes in order to avoid misleading associations with what is normally understood by magic.

In every presentation of Egyptian religion some space must be devoted to the role of magic. This consideration traditionally carries a pejorative undertone, so that magic becomes identical with superstition and is seen as a cancerous growth on the pure, sublime body of belief. According to the widely quoted formulation of Adolf Erman, "Magic is a wild offshoot of religion; it attempts to coerce the forces that govern the fate of mankind . . . beside the noble plant of religion flourishes the rampant weed of magic."[41]

As with the problem of monotheism or polytheism, here too

[38]E. Otto, _Das ägyptische Mundöffnungsritual_ (ÄgAbh 3, 1960) I, 128, II, 117: "Wadjet, mistress of flame."

[39]Lange, _Amenemope_ 120.

[40]Merikare l. 56: Volten, _Politische Schriften_ 26.

[41]_Religion_ (1st ed., 1905) 148.

value judgments obstruct a clear, objective picture of the phenomenon. Physical rather than horticultural metaphors are appropriate to it—magic is not a plant, but a force. Every force is value-free, so long as the way in which it is used and the ends it is made to serve are not the main considerations.

Egyptian texts make it plain that ḥkꜣ "'magic'" is a force. In the Pyramid Texts (*Pyr.* §940b–c) and Coffin Texts (*CT* IV, 98j) it is used in parallel with ꜣt, another term for "power." In the tenth hour of the Book of Gates anthropomorphic deities and baboons are shown holding nets in their hands and using the "'magic'" that is on and in the nets to protect the sun god and render harmless his enemy Apopis (*BPf* 341–45). Here too there is a true field of force which is made visible in the form of the nets and is filled with the invisible but potent energy of "'magic.'" In Egyptian physics energy of this sort can also be envisaged as a substance; it is commonly said that "'magic'" is "swallowed" or "eaten," or that it is "in the body."[42]

Egyptian "magic" is an energy that works automatically and instantly and requires no particular medium for its transmission. When the god's creative word has been pronounced, "magic" ensures that it becomes reality. In the Cairo hymn to Amun it is said of the sun god Re that he "commanded, and the gods came into being."[43] For this reason "magic," personified as Hike (ḥkꜣ), is one of the three helping powers that stand by the sun god and always accompany him on his course (see Chapter 3). The instant formation of things according to the creative word of god is accomplished by means of this "magical" energy; without it the creation of the world would not be possible. Jan Zandee has amassed an extensive collection of text passages referring to the creative word of god and its effect;[44] here I mention only one example in the Coffin Texts, where the idea is present in its very strangest form: the creator god is said to have brought his own body into being by means of his magical power (*CT* VI, 344b).[45] And hence a text in the

[42]For the last of these formulations see the examples cited by Assmann, *Liturg. Lieder* 196 n. 22; for swallowing and eating cf. e.g. *CT* V, 391j, VII, 238e.

[43]Grébaut, *Hymne* 11 (4, 2).

[44]"Das Schöpferwort im alten Ägypten," in *Verbum* (Festschrift H. W. Obbink, Studia Theologica Rheno-Traiectina 6, Utrecht 1964) 33–66.

[45]The largely synonymous word ꜣḥw is used here. The creator god is Nun.

same collection implies that "magic" preceded creation (*CT* III, 382e–383c).

This primeval force not only rendered creation possible but also, in the hands—or rather the mouths—of the most various deities, serves to maintain its existence. The underworld teems with beings who live from the "breath of their (own) mouths"[46] or through the repetition of the sun god's creative word; here again the "magic" of the creative utterance is realized instantly. With her "magic" Isis protects the growing Horus against his enemies, and, together with other deities, she takes part in the "bewitching" of Apopis. Standing forward in the solar bark (*Amduat,* seventh hour), she conjures him, and, like a flash of "lightning," "magic"[47] strikes the enemy of the gods and deprives him of his senses, so that he "cannot find himself" (*BPf* 75) and is "destroyed" without great difficulty.

Here "magic" is a weapon of the gods which strikes the enemy unawares, annihilates his attack, and thus grants protection, security, and freedom to the constantly threatened world of order. The powers of the chaos before creation are never conquered entirely, but provoke a continual struggle which is fought by the gods in the sky and in the underworld, and on earth primarily by the king. In strict terms the most powerful weapon, the creative energy of "magic," should be available only to the gods; a magician on earth must therefore take on the role of a deity in order to exploit this dangerous and potent force. The king, who plays the part of the creator god on earth ex officio, has the magical power of creative utterance automatically at his disposal. Through the magical force of his word in ritual he imposes his will on distant lands.[48]

In this way "magic"—which one might term the "nuclear energy of early civilizations" because of its dangerousness and its power to transform the world—comes to be used by mankind, and, as is bound to happen, men exploit it to do wrong, thus alienating it from its original purpose. The creator god gave "magic" to human beings as a "weapon" specifically for self-defense—as it is formulated in the Instruction for Merikare

[46]See esp. *Amduat* fourth and fifth hours (the snakes nos. 287, 394–95; living from other "voices": nos. 317, 323, 347, 391–92).

[47]Phrased thus in a different context: *Amduat* I, 81, 7.

[48]M. Alliot, *RdE* 5 (1946) 108–9.

209

around 2060 B.C.[49] But people are captivated by what one can do with "magic," and do not consider the consequences of their actions. They do not hesitate to turn defensive weapons into offensive ones and to use them against the gods—to whom they owe this gift of "magic." Threats against the gods occur as early as the Pyramid Texts. These threats are intended initially to defend the deceased against gods who might prevent his ascent to the heavenly hereafter: "Every god who does not take (the King) to the sky will not be respected, will not have a *ba*, will not taste a cake, will not go forth to the mansion of Horus which is in the sky. . ." (*Pyr.* §1027).

Soon the force of "magic" comes to serve highly egoistic and aggressive purposes, especially in love charms, and the magician thinks nothing of threatening the powers that are invoked with the ultimate and most dire of events, the destruction of the world.[50] In human hands the force of "magic," which had originally been value-free, becomes perverted. The conspirators against Ramesses II (c. 1184–1153 B.C.) attempted with some success to employ written "magic" against the legitimate king in order to achieve their own personal goals.[51]

Here the beneficial force seems to have become an instrument of arbitrary aggression, and in the late period the Egyptians felt that unfettered "magic" was the antithesis of "law" (*hp*).[52] So there can now be a "black" "magic" that serves evil and is far-removed from the will of the gods.

From an early period the Egyptians believed that mankind could act independently or even against the gods. But they were also convinced that only the will of the gods is finally realized and produces lasting achievements. The earliest completely preserved instruction text, that of Ptahhotpe, states that

[49]Volten, *Politische Schriften* 75 (ll. 136–37).
[50]Similar threats occur also in Greek love charms from Egypt, e.g. D. Wortmann, *Bonner Jahrbücher* 168 (1968) 92: "If you refuse to listen and do not swiftly do what I tell you, the sun will not set beneath the earth, neither will Hades nor the Cosmos (continue to) exist." [I am grateful to John Rea for the English translation.—tr.]
[51]H. Goedicke, "Was Magic Used in the Harim Conspiracy against Ramesses III?" *JEA* 49 (1963) 71–92.
[52]C. F. Nims, *JNES* 7 (1948) 245 (in a demotic text).

"Man's plans are never fulfilled; what happens is what god commands."[53] Later instructions repeatedly reformulate the same idea, as when Amenemope states, "The words that men say are one thing; what the god does is another."[54] The Egyptians sense the superior will and efficacy of the gods also in political life. The earliest clear evidence for this belief is in the inscriptions of the nomarch Ankhtifi, of the time following the first collapse of the state (c. 2120 B.C.).[55] After this the idea develops much as Morenz describes in his *Rise of the Transcendent God*.[56] From the Middle Kingdom on the "command of the god," which has the effect of the creative word and demands to be fulfilled at once, tends increasingly to be the exclusive arbiter of royal policy. I have referred in Chapter 5 to the high point and termination of this development in the Theban "theocracy," in which the god Amun ruled as king. The kings of the New Kingdom and late period require divine aid to lead their campaigns; Ramesses II, in danger from the enemy at the Battle of Qadesh (1285 B.C.), and his much later successor Ptolemy VIII Euergetes II (145–116 B.C.) rely on the helping deity, who is "more effective than a million soldiers."[57]

We know from the story of Sinuhe and other sources that private individuals also attribute their actions in critical situations to a divine, and often incomprehensible, will.[58] The more state authority fails, the more important is the gods' role as helpers of individuals in need; in the New Kingdom this side

[53]Z. Žába, *Les maximes de Ptahhotep* (Československá Akademie Věd, Prague 1956) 25 ll. 115–16. Cf. also p. 50 above.

[54]Lange, *Amenemope* 97 ll. 16–17 (chap. 18). Aksel Volten collected this and similar maxims in *Anii* 118, 124–25; add now Ankhsheshonq 22, x + 25: S. R. K. Glanville, *Catalogue of Demotic Papyri in the British Museum* II (London 1955) 50–51. See also H. Brunner, "Der freie Wille Gottes in der ägyptischen Weisheit," in *Les sagesses* 103–20.

[55]G. Fecht in W. Helck, ed., *Festschrift für Siegfried Schott* (Wiesbaden 1968) 54.

[56]Morenz, *Heraufkunft*; cf. Chapter 5, last section.

[57]C. Kuentz, *La bataille de Qadech* (MIFAO 55, 1928) 251 = KRI, II, 41 (Ramesses II); Winter, *Untersuchungen* 101 (Ptolemy VIII, unpublished inscription at Philae). Similar statement by Ramesses III: W. Helck, *ZÄS* 83 (1958) 35 ll. 10–11.

[58]From the first intermediate period to the Macedonian period: J. J. Clère, *RdE* 6 (1951) 153–54. These examples may be fictions intended to justify morally questionable actions, see J. Baines, *JEA* 68 (1982) 40–42; see also n. 55 above.

of the gods crystallizes into a separate deity, the god Shed, the "savior," who is addressed on countless stelae by people seeking help or praising him for his help.[59] On a chariot that is often drawn by griffons Shed pursues dangerous animals, keeping them away from mankind; he therefore takes over functions that in earlier periods belonged exclusively to the king, the great hunter and conqueror of threatening animals. Now people are entitled to hope for more from the divine sphere than the king could ever have provided; confidence in the divine rescuer is so great as to fuel the hope that he might increase the predetermined span of a lifetime and even "save the one he loves who is in the underworld and place someone else (there) in exchange for him."[60]

In extreme cases god the helper of those in need can bring human beings as near as possible to immortality, but here he meets the absolute limit of existence to which the Egyptian gods, as powers of the existent world, are subject. They are neither immortal nor omnipotent, and this remains so until the end of Egyptian religion. The development I have sketched never, therefore, leads to an absolute control of events by the will of god; there is always room for human initiative, which in ancient Egypt is never subject to anything like the Islamic *in shā allah* "God willing."[61]

Since the Egyptian gods are unable to transcend the boundary of the existent, the problem of theodicy does not arise.

[59]On Shed see G. Loukianoff, *BIE* 13 (1930) 67–84; B. Bruyère, *Rapport sur les fouilles de Deir el Médineh (1935–1940)* (FIFAO 20, 3, 1952) 138–70; Bonnet, *Reallexikon* 676–77; H. Brunner, *MDAIK* 16 (1958) 13–19; E. Otto, "Gott als Retter in Ägypten," in G. Jeremias et al., eds., *Tradition und Glaube. Das frühe Christentum in seiner Umwelt. Festgabe für K. G. Kuhn zum 65. Geburtstag* (Göttingen 1972) 9–22.

[60]Edwards, *Decrees* 5 n. 34 = E. Brugsch, *La tente funéraire de la Princesse Isimkheb* (Cairo 1889) pl. 5: funerary tent of the Twenty-first Dynasty. The same idea occurs earlier, without the "replacement" motif, in the Leiden hymn to Amun: Zandee, *De hymnen aan Amon* pl. 3, 16 (stanza "70"). According to a personal name of the fourth century B.C. the god Horus "killed death": K.-T. Zauzich, *MDAIK* 25 (1969) 226 n. (f). See also G. Posener, *Annuaire du Collège de France 70* (1970–71) 395.

[61]*Theōn thelontōn* and similar phrases are first found in Greek letters from Roman Egypt: H. I. Bell, *JEA* 34 (1948) 89–90.

There is no need to justify god in the face of the injustice and evil in the world. Evil is inherent in the nonexistent and hence is older than the gods and present in the world from the beginning. The gods cannot be made responsible for it, but are the very powers that combat evil and continually drive it out from the existent world. "I did not ordain that [mankind] do wrong (*jzft*); their hearts disobeyed what I had said," says the creator god in the Coffin Texts, in the celebrated justification of his work of creation.[62] It is the fault of human beings, but also the consequence of their origin in blindness, that they leave space for wrongdoing in their hearts (the organ that determines action).

The gods of Egypt can be terrifying, dangerous, and unpredictable, but they cannot be evil. Originally this was true even of Seth, the murderer of Osiris. Battle, constant confrontation, confusion, and questioning of the established order, in all of which Seth engages as a sort of "trickster,"[63] are all necessary features of the existent world and of the limited disorder that is essential to a living order. But gods and people must together ensure that disorder does not come to overpower justice and order; this is the meaning of their common obligation toward *maat*.

The concept of *maat*, which we have encountered so far only as a personification, the goddess Maat, has been very much discussed, but still awaits the thorough study necessary to do justice to its complexity and importance. Stated briefly, *maat* is the order, the just measure of things, that underlies the world; it is the perfect state of things toward which one should strive and which is in harmony with the creator god's intentions. This state is always being disturbed, and unremitting effort is necessary in order to recreate it in its original purity. Like the injured and perpetually healed "eye of Horus," *maat* therefore symbolizes this pristine state of the world.

So the Egyptians could view *maat* as a substance, a material element upon which the whole world lives, which is the nour-

[62]For the full text see pp. 198–99 above.
[63]Cf. the interpretation of te Velde, *Seth*; E. Hornung, *Symbolon* n.s. 2 (1974) 49–63.

ishment of the living and the dead,[64] of gods and of men. From the Coffin Texts on, the gods "live on maat,"[65] but according to texts of the same periods they also created *maat* and can dispense it—Amenemope even sees *maat* as the "great burden of god," which he may share out as he wishes.[66] According to texts of the Graeco-Roman period,[67] *maat* descended at creation from the sky to earth, and thus came also to be in the hands of mankind. From an early period the king of Egypt was very closely connected with *maat*,[68] and he too "lives on *maat*."

There is scarcely an Egyptian temple that does not include among its many representations of cult scenes the "offering of *maat*" (Figure 19). The king, who when in the presence of the gods is the representative of the entire world of humanity, holds up and presents a figure of *maat*, which is shown as a squatting goddess with the hieroglyph of an ostrich feather on her head. As is demonstrated by the daily temple ritual, every material thing that is presented in the cult, such as bread, beer, incense, and so forth, can be identified with *maat*.[69] The "offering of *maat*" therefore summarizes in a highly charged image everything that cult, offering, and response to the gods' actions signify. The officiant's restrained gesture of holding up *maat* in visible form to the gods constitutes a sign that the world of mankind, and all the constantly endangered and fragile relationships and connections on which it depends, are in order, just as they were at the time of creation.

This is the response the gods need, and it brings full circle our analysis, which took the gods' actions as its starting point. The gods do not need any material gifts, but they do need human response to their existence; they want to be experienced

[64]CT II, 35g, VII, 238d; A. H. Gardiner, *JEA* 32 (1946) 50 n. (h); L. A. Christophe, *BIFAO* 49 (1950) 133 no. 9, cf. 142 n. (h) = Moret, *Rituel* 142.

[65]E.g. *CT* VII, 468e, of the "lord of all"; *Urk.* IV, 384, 16, of Amun.

[66]Lange, *Amenemope* 104 l. 5 (chap. 20). On the passage cf. Bergman, *Ich bin Isis* 208.

[67]*Urk.* VIII, 76k = P. Clère, *La porte d'Evergète à Karnak* (MIFAO 84, 1961) pl. 67; *Edfou* V, 85, 13.

[68]L. A. Christophe collected a number of relevant titles and epithets: *BIFAO* 49 (1950) 138–46.

[69]Moret, *Rituel* 138–65.

Figure 19. King Ramesses II (1290–1224 B.C.) offers Maat to Ptah.

in the hearts of men, for only then does their work of creation acquire its lasting significance. Lack of response and silence are characteristics of the nonexistent; within the existent world there is the lively, uninterrupted dialogue between god and man, which is contained within the polarity of love and fear.

Maat, which came from the gods at creation, returns to them from the hands of men; it symbolizes the partnership of god and man which is brought to fruition in Egyptian religion. This partnership, this action and response, is the key to the otherwise inexplicable mixture we find of free will and pre-

215

destination.[70] Through creation gods and men acquire a common task: to maintain their existence, which has an end, against the unending nonexistent and together to build a living order that allows space for creative breath and does not become atrophied.

[70]On this question see G. Fecht, *Literarische Zeugnisse zur "persönlichen Frömmigkeit" in Ägypten* (AHAW 1965, 1) 123ff., and on the problem of "gods and fate," Morenz, *Religion* 69–78 = 66–74.

7 ↘ Classification and Articulation of the Pantheon

In his *Über den ersten ägyptischen Götterkreis* (*On the Earliest Group of Egyptian Gods*) of 1851 Carl Richard Lepsius identified "some closed groups" in the seemingly limitless and formless mass of Egyptian deities.[1] The Egyptians used various methods of ordering their endless pantheon; as elsewhere in their thought, these principles do not compete with one another, but coexist equally. In this chapter I follow the useful categorization of the methods of classification presented by Eberhard Otto in his survey of Egyptian polytheism.[2] The only term of his that I wish to avoid is "numerical schemata" (*Zahlenschemata*): I prefer to speak of a numerical and genealogical classification, which is to be distinguished from local and social classifications.

Numerical and genealogical classification

The simplest and smallest grouping of gods is the pair or couple. Very few pairs are of the same sex; exceptions are the sisters Isis and Nephthys and the hostile pair of brothers Horus and Seth, whose eternal conflict, which Thoth can settle only temporarily, reflects the complementary duality of the world and the necessity for constant confrontation.

As a rule, pairs or couples of gods are divided by sex into

---

[1] *Götterkreis* 167 = 11.
[2] *Saeculum* 14 (1963) 260ff. On numerical classification see especially Kees, *Götterglaube* 155–71.

god and goddess, as illustrated by the four pairs of deities who make up the ogdoad of Hermopolis: Nun and Naunet, Huh and Hauhet, Kuk and Kauket, Amun and Amaunet. Comparable female doublets of male divine names and deities are known as early as the Pyramid Texts, but can hardly have been a feature of Egyptian religion in its original form. In later times ever more doublets are found, such as the "female Re" (Raettawy) in the early Eighteenth Dynasty, and later the "female Anubis" and "female Sokar." I have shown in Chapter 3 that these are not bloodless abstractions.

When a son or daughter is added to a divine couple the result is a triad, the preferred and most frequently encountered grouping of Egyptian deities. Our sources are so inadequate that we must remain in doubt as to whether the third figure is an addition—that is, whether we should view triads historically as two plus one. In historical terms the gods Amun and Osiris are followed at once by the triads Amun / Mut / Khons or Osiris / Isis / Horus, without there being a discernible intervening stage with a couple Amun / Mut or Osiris / Isis. In the case of the triad of Elephantine the daughter Anukis is not attested until much later than the parents Khnum and Satis, who are very prominent in the early dynastic period (see Chapter 3), but it is by no means certain that at the beginning of history Khnum and Satis were seen as a divine couple. Ptah and the goddess Sakhmet, for example, were long worshiped side by side in Memphis before they joined with Nefertem to form a Memphite triad. This latter can first be documented in the New Kingdom and thus follows the pattern which is by then found in a number of other places in the country.

The genealogical classification of the pantheon, which can already be seen clearly in the Pyramid Texts, was very important from an early date;[3] but we should follow Eberhard Otto in assuming that the idiom of kinship in which triads are presented is secondary in comparison with the ancient and important symbolism of the number three.[4] "Three" is the simplest and hence the preferred way of expressing "many" or

[3]Cf. also H. te Velde, "Some Remarks on the Structure of Egyptian Divine Triads," *JEA* 57 (1971) 80–86.
[4]*Saeculum* 14 (1963) 267.

the plural, which is indicated in the Egyptian script by three strokes or by writing signs three times; there are also texts in which "three" is equated quite explicitly with the plural.[5]

The existence of a large number of deities and the preferred articulation of them into triads come together in the New Kingdom to form a trinity, or tri-unity[6]—not of God but of the gods and their cult places. The classical formulation of this specifically Egyptian trinity was achieved at the end of the Eighteenth Dynasty (late fourteenth century B.C.) in the Leiden hymn to Amun:

> All gods are three: Amun, Re, Ptah; they have no equal. His name is hidden as Amun, he is perceived as Re (literally, he is Re before (men)), and his body is Ptah. Their cities on earth remain forever: Thebes, Heliopolis, and Memphis, for all time.[7]

This trinity of Amun / Re / Ptah is also found elsewhere; its earliest attestation is not Ramessid, as Otto stated,[8] but dates to Tutankhamun (1347–1338 B.C.), the successor of Akhenaten. One of the trumpets from the burial treasure of the prematurely deceased king is decorated with a single scene showing the king before the new state triad.[9] Amun, who is still nominally the highest and most active of the three gods, holds out the sign of life to the king's nose; behind Amun stands Re (in the form of the hawk-headed Harakhte), and behind the king is Ptah (the silver trumpet from the tomb shows a similar grouping of the gods, but no figure of the king). On the "restoration stela" of the same king—with which he brought to an end,

[5]P. Kaplony, *MIO* 11 (1966) 161 n. 91.

[6]Cf. J. G. Griffiths, "Triune Conceptions of Deity in Ancient Egypt," *ZÄS* 100 (1973) 28–32.

[7]Zandee, *De hymnen aan Amon* pl. 4, 21–22 (stanza "300").

[8]*Saeculum* 14 (1963) 268.

[9]L. Manniche, *Musical Instruments from the Tomb of Tut'ankhamūn* (Tut'ankhamūn's Tomb Series 6, Oxford 1976) pls. 10 (silver trumpet), 11 (gilded trumpet). The gilded trumpet is much published: *Toutankhamon et son temps* (Le Petit Palais, Paris 1967) 183; [I. E. S. Edwards], *Treasures of Tutankhamun* (British Museum 1972) no. 45; *id.*, *Treasures of Tutankhamun* (USA exhibition catalogue, Metropolitan Museum of Art, New York 1976) 103; *Tutanchamun* (exhibition catalogue, Ägyptisches Museum, Berlin 1980) 78.

probably in 1345 B.C., the short period of transition during which Aten and Amun coexisted equally—he expresses his solicitude for all the gods and goddesses Akhenaten had persecuted, especially for Amun and Ptah.

A number of studies have shown that after the death of Akhenaten there was, contrary to earlier opinion, no "restoration" or instant return to the primacy of the state god Amun, nor did the capital revert to "Amun's city," Thebes. Rather, it is possible to observe as late as the reign of Haremhab (1333–1306 B.C.) a marked reserve in the attitude to Amun,[10] while the deities of Heliopolis and Memphis are given preference; the new capital city was Memphis, only a few kilometers from the cult center of the sun god in Heliopolis. After the failure of the religious revolution, Akhenaten's successors were evidently not prepared to return to the previous state of affairs and replace Amun in his old position of primacy as "king of the gods." As Hari has shown,[11] Haremhab avoids using the phrase Amonrasonther "Amon-Re, king of the gods," which had previously been much favored. Amun must now share with Re and Ptah his primacy among the other gods. The succeeding period, the Ramessid, brings a true renaissance of Amun as king of the gods, while the god Seth is added as a fourth to the triad Amun, Re, Ptah, although the triad survives as well.[12] The four main divisions of the Egyptian army, with which Sethos I (1304–1290 B.C.) and Ramesses II (1290–1244 B.C.) conduct their campaigns in the Near East, are now named after these four gods.

The dating of the celebrated stela of the year 400, which Ramesses II set up in his new capital city in honor of the god Seth, contains a striking and clearly intentional series of fours: "Year 400, month 4 of the *šmw* season, day 4."[13] Did his theologians mean to allude through this fictitious date to Seth as the fourth god alongside the state triad? The number four does occur elsewhere in the Egyptian pantheon as a classificatory

[10]See especially Hari, *Horemheb* 386ff.

[11]*Ibid.* 248.

[12]It is still prominent in the reign of Ramesses IV, cf. R. Anthes, *MDOG* 96 (1965) 16 (on the Great Harris Papyrus).

[13]P. Montet, *Kêmi* 4 (1933) 197, pl. 11, 15.

schema, evidently as a symbol of completeness or totality.[14] Four is the number of the cardinal points, of the winds, and of the supports of the sky, and, in myth, of the children of Nut and the sons of Horus; there are also several groups of four deities who protect the deceased.[15]

Four occurs doubled as the ogdoad of Hermopolis, and the name "eight-city" was given to their cult center Hermopolis as early as the Old Kingdom. Thus the ogdoad and related ideas about creation may be posited for the central Old Kingdom, even though the names of the four pairs of primeval deities are not attested until the late period. The names themselves vary, but always add up to eight, or rather to four couples of gods and goddesses.[16]

The most important classificatory schema is the ennead, an intensified form of the plural (three times three) first attested in the ennead of Heliopolis, which served as the model for further enneads in the pantheon; a complete listing of the nine gods occurs as early as the Pyramid Texts.[17] It is uncertain whether the figures of Geb and Seth on fragments in Turin from the time of Djoser (c. 2600 B.C.; Chapter 4 n. 20) form part of an "ennead," because there seems to have been an earlier grouping of gods which was called *ḥt* "corporation."[18] The Horus name

[14]C. de Wit, *CdE* 32/63 (1957) 35–39; G. Posener, *Sur l'orientation et l'ordre des points cardinaux chez les Egyptiens* (NAWG 1965, 2) 74.

[15]Cf. Kees, *Götterglaube* 167–71, where he also gave examples of the number four in the cult.

[16]Sethe, *Amun*, collected the evidence for them. His interpretation of the material, which remains fundamental to the topic, must be corrected with respect to the origins of Amun, cf. Chapter 3 n. 72; F. Daumas, "L'origine d'Amon de Karnak," *BIFAO* 65 (1967) 201–14.

[17]Pyr. §1655b. For detailed presentations of the evidence for the ennead and its problems see R. Weill, *RdE* 6 (1951) 49–79 (with history of research pp. 59–65); J. G. Griffiths, *Or* 28 (1959) 34–56. There are also several articles by R. Anthes (esp. *JNES* 18 [1959] 194–97; *MDOG* 96 [1965] 18–35), who believes that the ennead originally had nothing to do with Atum and his divine progeny. See also W. Barta, *Untersuchungen zum Götterkreis der Neunheit* (MÄS 28, 1973); id., *BiOr* 33 (1976) 131–34.

[18]Discernible as early as the First Dynasty in names of domains and in a king's name (*Smr-ḥt*); in the Pyramid Texts it is clear in *Pyr.* §§1041a (cf. K. Sethe, *Übersetzung und Kommentar zu den altägyptischen Pyramidentexten* IV [Glückstadt etc. n.d.] 318, 320–21), §1462d. See further R. Weill, *RdE* 6 (1951) 74–77.

of Djoser himself states that he is "the most divine one of the corporation," while his successor is "the most powerful one of the corporation," and the Horus name of Mycerinus "bull of the corporation"[19] is parallel to "bull (that is, lord) of the ennead" in the Pyramid Texts. It is tempting to suggest that the "corporation" was replaced by the "ennead" at the same time that the rise of the sun god was accomplished, and that both groupings originally referred to the indefinite plurality of all gods, just as at a later period "the entire ennead" can mean "the entirety of the gods."[20]

In the ennead the numerical and genealogical methods of classification are combined. The primeval being Atum engenders through self-impregnation the first sexually differentiated divine couple, Shu and Tefnut, and from them is born the next generation of gods, Geb and Nut; the union of this earth god and sky goddess produces the siblings Osiris, Seth, Isis, and Nephthys, who complete the ennead.

That is the usual composition of the ennead, but it is not canonical, nor, perhaps, is it the original one (see above). From the New Kingdom on, Seth is often banished from the ennead and replaced by Horus, while other manifestations of the sun god may substitute for Atum;[21] in the Amduat there is even a "male ennead" in which the four goddesses are replaced by four gods.[22]

Nor is the number of members of the "ennead" canonically fixed at nine, even though the genealogy ends with Osiris and Isis because of that number, omitting their son Horus and the four "sons of Horus." The later enneads, which were devised throughout the country on the model of the ennead of Heliopolis, sometimes have only seven members, as at Abydos, but in other cases fifteen, as in Thebes.[23] What was evidently most

---

[19]E. Drioton, *ASAE* 45 (1947) 53–54.

[20]E.g. M. A. Korostovtsev, *BIFAO* 45 (1947) 154 l. 4 = KRI VI, 22, 6 (inscription of Ramesses IV from Abydos).

[21]Early example of both these changes: *Amduat* II, 94–95.

[22]*Amduat* II, 122–23.

[23]Survey in Bonnet, *Reallexikon* 523–24; add an ennead of Harsaphes at Herakleopolis (late period: J. Vercoutter, *BIFAO* 49 [1950] 90); for the Theban ennead see M. T. Derchain-Urtel, *Synkretismus in ägyptischer Ikonographie. Die Göttin Tjenenet* (GOF 8, 1979) 13–23.

significant was the symbolism of the number nine. From the dual principle of Egyptian thought ("The Problem of Logic" below) there arose at an early date the curious idea of the "two enneads," which are often distinguished as the "great" one and the "small" one; in comparison with the "simple" ennead they together signify a more complete totality, as does the plural form "enneads," which is attested as early as the Pyramid Texts.[24]

The purpose of all these numerical principles, whether they use the number two or three as their base, is to create order in the pantheon; for the Egyptians this is always a diverse, plural order. Without abandoning the principle of plurality or excluding a single deity from the pantheon, its unmanageable multiplicity is condensed into a number that can be comprehended. Only under Akhenaten was an attempt made to reduce the large number of deities to fewer than three (which of course stands for "many").

Local classification

According to the principle of local classification, every deity acquires a fixed cult home, and the ranking of cult places more or less automatically results in a hierarchy of their deities, at the head of which stands the chief god of the capital city. Thus in the Eighteenth Dynasty Amun, who was worshiped as the highest god in the royal residence, Thebes, was the "state god." Amun, whose nature was extended to be the most universal and transcendent possible in Egyptian terms, is particularly closely linked with "his" city Thebes, which was known as the "city of Amun" from the late Eighteenth Dynasty on.[25] Universality and local connections do not have to be mutually exclusive, as is clear from the example of Amun, but often they are—as with Meresger, the goddess of the Theban peak,[26] whose

[24]*Pyr.* §§278c, 511c ("7 enneads" in one variant), 1064b (the great ennead is said to be "mistress of enneads").

[25]The designation survives in the Old Testament and Greek terminology for the city, see Sethe, *Amun* §1; for another Twenty-first Dynasty example see A. Piankoff, *ASAE* 49 (1949) 132 with pl. 2.

[26]B. Bruyère, *Mert-Seger à Deir el Médineh* (MIFAO 58, 1930), and, on the form of the name, L. Keimer, *BiOr* 5 (1948) 24. In the Wadi Hammamat even the

223

importance and influence do not extend beyond the narrow confines of the desert hills of western Thebes.

The way in which Egyptian deities are bound to their localities varies greatly, from their being fixed to a particular point in the landscape to their loose incorporation in a local "ennead" or "ogdoad," as is the case with cosmic and primeval deities. The local principle does not begin to be systematized until the late period; in early times cult topography is not central to the classification of the pantheon. A wag might say that this principle was never applied consistently or comprehensively by the Egyptians but only by a particular school of modern egyptologists. Hermann Kees[27] laid the intellectual foundations for this cult-topographical school, the influence of which has been felt until very recently. The value of research of this type is unquestionable; it has advanced considerably the analysis of local cults and the understanding of the religious landscape of Egypt, and it has cast light on the reality of the gods in the context of their cults.

But the method's "geographic atomizing," which Henri Frankfort criticized,[28] the dissection of religious life into minimal geographical units, does not contribute at all to understanding the nature of the gods. There is a great danger of being misled into thinking that if the original cult place of a god is identified, his origin and historical importance will be explained. All attempts to find an original home for Horus or Osiris have been quite fruitless. But it is impossible to halt modern scholars' search for the "home of the cult" or the "original nature" of a god, for we are too accustomed to looking for a single cause for everything. And there is still a seductive simplicity in view-

---

universal Amun can be worshiped in a mountainous peak: G. Goyon, *ASAE* 49 (1949) 357–58.

[27]"Grundsätzliches zur Aufgabenstellung der ägyptischen Religionsgeschichte," *Göttingische Gelehrte Anzeigen* 198 (1936) 49–61; *Götterglaube* chap. 2; a series of articles in the *ZÄS* entitled "Kulttopographische und mythologische Beiträge." On precursors of the method, such as Richard Pietschmann, and criticisms of them by Cornelio Pietro Tiele, cf. H. O. Lange, in P. D. Chantepie de la Saussaye, ed., *Lehrbuch der Religionsgeschichte* (4th ed., ed. A. Bertholet and E. Lehmann, Tübingen 1925) I, 443–44.

[28]*BiOr* 10 (1953) 159, 220–21. For criticism of the political interpretations often used as part of the method cf. H. Brunner, *MDAIK* 16 (1958) 12–13.

ing the history of religion as the religious politics of particular places and priesthoods.

In some cases it may be justifiable to assume that there were "local nature cults"[29] at the beginning of history, but there is no basis for generalizing the assumption. Whenever it is possible to see gods making their appearance in history, we find that their nature is complex from the beginning of their attestation and that the geography of their worship is correspondingly complex. The connection of all the important gods whose "rise" can be observed—Re, Osiris, Ptah, and Amun—with a particular cult place is clearly secondary.

We have seen in the introduction to Chapter 3 that at the beginning of history the cult of a number of deities was widespread throughout the country. We first encounter the ostensibly "local" gods of Elephantine, Sais, and Bubastis not as local but as universal deities. So it should not be surprising or disconcerting that Re, Osiris, Ptah, and Amun take on the role of universal gods from the beginning, without ever being restricted to a single place or to a single aspect of their nature. Osiris is not in origin the god of cattle nomads in the eastern delta, nor is Amun originally a wind god. The rich and complex nature of the gods cannot be accommodated to the excessively simple conceptual categories that we devise; no god can be caught in such a coarse-meshed net.

The fact that a god's cult becomes established in a place that feels a special affinity for him may tell us one thing—among many—about his nature, but it constitutes no more than a stage in his historical development. In the course of time his local connections become stronger. In the New Kingdom, and still more in the late period, there is a strong tendency to form fixed links between any deity, or manifestation of the great gods, and specific cult places; the most impressive evidence for this tendency is in long catalogues of gods which are similar to litanies. But Old Kingdom belief seems to have had a different structure, in which topography was not at all prominent. This apparent difference does not arise solely from the smaller amount of evidence we possess for beliefs of the earlier period.

---

[29]"Naturhafte Ortskulte": Kees, *Götterglaube* 2.

There are other significant indicators, such as the absence of any god of the royal residence or state god, and the lack of archeological evidence for major temples of the gods which could be compared to Middle and New Kingdom temples. There is also the evidence of inscriptions, which has not yet been analyzed in detail,[30] and the lack of a professional local priesthood before the Fifth Dynasty.

In Egypt the local principle of classification did not become widespread in religion until relatively late. From the Middle Kingdom on it leads to fixed combinations and even equations between gods and cult places and to a distinctly artificial division of deities between the two halves of the country, Upper and Lower Egypt. The fixing of Horus and Seth as the representatives of the two parts of the country has given rise to endless hypotheses about their "original" provenance and their role in prehistory. The distinction between an Upper and a Lower Egyptian Wepwawet is attested in the Middle Kingdom.[31] In the Book of Gates, that is, under the influence of the Amarna period, even the foreign Asiatic, Libyan, and Nubian peoples acquire their own protective deities, who are Egyptian deities (*BPf* 176–81). Finally, in the late period local classification envelops the entire Egyptian pantheon—and it was this late phase that egyptologists were first able to study. So it is a consequence of the way our subject has developed that it has been influenced so much by the idea of "local gods" and the local method of classifying gods; the application of that principle to earlier Egyptian religion can very easily lead to false conclusions.

Because every local system of classification must start from the presence of the gods in the cult, from their "availability" on earth, it contradicts to some extent their "hidden" nature, which is often emphasized in Egyptian texts. Here we encoun-

---

[30]The material is now collected in B. L. Begelsbacher-Fischer, *Untersuchungen zur Götterwelt des Alten Reiches* (Orbis Biblicus et Orientalis 37, Fribourg and Göttingen 1981).

[31]K. A. Kitchen, JEA 47 (1961) 10 with pl. 2; W. K. Simpson, *The Terrace of the Great God at Abydos* (Publications of the Pennsylvania–Yale Expedition to Egypt 5, New Haven and Philadelphia 1974) pls. 19 (10.2), 73 (66.1), 81 (59.1, Anubis, but identical figure and composition).

ter the problem, which I have already touched upon several times, of where the Egyptians considered their gods to reside.

Excursus: The abode of the gods

In the course of this book two observations have so far been made about the abode of the gods. First, statements about the gods' "true" appearance show that Egyptians saw countless images of the deities in their environment, but encountered the gods themselves only in exceptional circumstances (Chapter 4). Second, we know from a number of passages of texts, which I cited in the discussion of the mortality of the gods in Chapter 5, that the next world was the preferred sojourn of the gods. It remains here to enlarge upon these two points and to define their place in history.

The earliest home of the gods that we can discern is the sky. On the Narmer palette, at the beginning of history, two heads of the sky goddess, whose form is a cow, look down at events on earth (Figure 9); on the ivory comb of the early dynastic King Djet (c. 2840 B.C.) we have the first example of a deity traveling across the sky in a bark, a scene that is repeated countless times in later iconography.

In an Old Kingdom tomb inscription the deceased walks on the beautiful ways of the necropolis "to the gods,"[32] and the reference is probably to another world in the sky, which is described in more detail in the Pyramid Texts. In these spells the sky, in which the gods live and the domains of the blessed are situated, is evidently the goal of the king's journey into the next world. When Old Kingdom texts speak of a "god" on earth, they probably always refer to the reigning king in the role of the creator god.

In the intellectual ferment after the collapse of the Old Kingdom the question of the abode of the gods becomes an urgent issue for Egyptians, because the earthly "god," the king, is no longer the guarantor of an enduring order of society. When the Admonitions of Ipuwer say "If I knew where god is, I would serve him,"[33] they express a common sentiment, but they

---

[32]A. Mariette, *Les mastabas de l'Ancien Empire* (Paris 1884–85) 149.
[33]A. H. Gardiner, *The Admonitions of an Egyptian Sage* (Leipzig 1909) 41–42.

combine it with an explicit exhortation to tend the cult of the gods—and thus to anchor god more firmly to earthly reality. We can see the effects of this attitude in the Middle Kingdom, whose kings devote more attention to the cult of the gods than did their predecessors. This development provides the point of departure for an increased emphasis on the cult home of the gods and for the use of a local system of classification.

In the Middle Kingdom Coffin Texts the next world in the sky is complemented by the underworld, which is then minutely described in the New Kingdom underworld books. The dichotomy of sky and underworld for the afterlife, and also for the abode of the gods, is reflected endlessly in set phrases in New Kingdom texts. In the Cairo hymn to Amun the sun god is "the greatest one of the sky, the oldest one of the earth";[34] similarly, in the tomb of Khaemhat of the reign of Amenophis III the god is "the oldest one of sky and earth."[35] Other passages in texts make it clear that "earth" in this context means the underworld. In another hymn Amon-Re is "rich in manifestations in the sky and in the earth,"[36] and in the temple of Ramesses III at Medinet Habu "all gods who are in the sky" and "all gods who are in the earth" are represented side by side.[37] The Egyptians always distinguish carefully, by means of different prepositions, between beings that are *on* earth and beings that are *in* the earth, that is, in the underworld.

The Leiden hymn to Amun, which dates to the years following the reign of Akhenaten, systematizes divine presence more precisely.[38] In this scheme the *ba* of the creator god is in the sky, his corpse is in the underworld, and his image (*ḥntj*)[39] on earth.

---

[34]Grébaut, *Hymne* 4 (1, 4).

[35]J. Zandee, *JEOL* 16 (1964) 56 with pl. 1 = H. M. Stewart, *JEA* 46 (1960) 88–89.

[36]Abd el Mohsen Bakir, *ASAE* 42 (1943) 86 with pl. 4 l. 3; Assmann, *ÄHG* 207.

[37]W. Westendorf, *Das alte Ägypten* (Kunst im Bild, Baden-Baden 1968) = *Painting, Sculpture and Architecture of Ancient Egypt* (Panorama of World Art, New York etc. 1968) 193 (the translation there should be corrected as indicated in the text here); *Medinet Habu* VII pl. 506D–E. There is a better-preserved parallel set of figures, with several additional categories, on the pillars of the second hypostyle hall of the temple of Ramesses II at Abydos (unpublished).

[38]Zandee, *De hymnen aan Amon* pl. 4, 16–17.

[39]In the New Kingdom this word (*ḥntj*) is often used for the king as the "image" of the sun god, see Hornung, "Mensch als Bild Gottes" 134–35. In the

Thus the deity is thought to be present in the entire ordered world of creation, but in differing manner and differing forms. As in the Old Kingdom, so also now the preferred abode is the sky; perhaps for this reason certain liminal regions of the earthly world that are especially close to the sky are called "god's land."[40] The underworld is a secondary and temporary place of sojourn, in which the *ba* and the corpse are united every night. On earth, however, the gods live only in images, in the king as an image of god, in cult images in the temples, and in sacred animals, plants, and objects.

But for the Egyptians an image is not "merely" an image; it constitutes a reality and a physical presence. The temple is a "sky" on earth, which contains the efficacious image of the god and may serve as an abode for the god himself. When the priest opens the sealed doors of the shrine in the morning he is opening the "doors of the sky" so that he may see the image of god in the earthly "sky."[41] The exhortation to perform the cult regularly, which is heard in the text of Ipuwer, is also a promise of divine presence, one that is formulated more forcefully in the Instruction for Merikare (which also dates to the period of transition between the Old and Middle Kingdoms): "He (the creator) has built himself a chapel behind them (mankind). If they weep, he hears."[42] There, in his shrine on earth, the god can be reached and addressed at any time, even though his true abode may be far away in the sky. Therefore one, and by no means the least, of the aims of the cult is to make the earth an attractive place for the gods to live, to create in the temple a worthy residence for the god's image and a likeness of the sky, and to tend the cult image so well that it is happy to live among men.

It should also be mentioned that the Egyptians believed that a human being could take a god into his heart and provide

---

temple of Soleb the statue of the king, which is worshiped as a god, is the "living *ḥntj* on earth": Labib Habachi, *Features of the Deification of Ramesses II* (ADIK 5, 1969) 48 fig. 32 = LD 3, 85c.

[40]As pointed out to me by Jan Assmann.

[41]Assmann, *Liturg. Lieder* 260–61 with n. 59.

[42]Volten, *Politische Schriften* 75 ll. 134–35.

an abode for him there.[43] From the New Kingdom on there are occasional references to a "god who is in man," but this conception, which has been studied chiefly by Hans Bonnet,[44] combines elements of such varied origin that it would be impossible to utilize it within the present context without an extensive and detailed study.

In the tomb of Aya at el-Amarna the Aten is said to be "before us (literally in our face), but we do not know his body."[45] In this the god of Akhenaten follows the gods of earlier periods; despite his being revealed in the sun disk he is not visible to everyone. The earth is his field of action, but he himself is hidden in the heavenly beyond and requires an intermediary in order to come into contact with mankind, for he has no cult images on earth.

Many centuries after the Amarna period Egyptian religion came no longer to make a precise distinction between gods in the sky and in the underworld and images of the gods on earth. The first occurrence known to me of the blanket formula "every god and goddess of sky, earth and underworld" dates to the Twenty-first Dynasty;[46] it is then found in the Twenty-second Dynasty, on an arm band of Queen Karomama (c. 850 B.C.),[47] and continues to be used, with a number of variants, down to the Graeco-Roman period.[48] Now that primacy is given to the worship of visible images, the original ideas about the abode of the gods become greatly simplified; that abode is now identical with the ordered world in its threefold hierarchy of sky, earth, and underworld.

Social classification; henotheism

For the Egyptians deities were not all of equal rank. In iconography important gods are often singled out by being enthroned

[43]E. Drioton, *ASAE* 44 (1944) 20 (*dj sw m jb.f*).

[44]"Der Gott im Menschen," in *Studi in memoria di Ippolito Rosellini* I (Università degli Studi di Pisa, Pisa 1949) 237–52; summary in *Reallexikon* 225–28.

[45]Sandman, *Texts* 89, 14–15.

[46]Edwards, *Decrees* 104.

[47]P. Montet, *Kêmi* 9 (1942) 40 fig. 28.

[48]Junker-Winter, *Geburtshaus* 9, 13–15.

and holding the attributes of "life" and "power" in their hands, in contrast with the mass of other divine beings. According to the texts there are "great" (*wrw*) and "small" (*ndśw*) gods, and Ramesses IV states explicitly that he "studied" the great gods more than the small.[49] The demotic instruction text of Insinger papyrus, on the other hand, warns against despising a small god since he too has power.[50]

Both these texts are relatively late; we must now seek evidence for the ranking of gods in earlier periods. The title "king of the gods" (*njswt-ntrw*) is first attested, just once, in the ritual spells in the pyramid of Phiops I (c. 2292–2260 B.C.),[51] where it is given to the god Horus, who in the Pyramid Texts has long ceased to occupy the leading position that he may perhaps have held in the period of origin of the Egyptian pantheon. The title then becomes typical of Amun, who was the chief god throughout the Middle and New kingdoms, until he was displaced by Osiris at the beginning of the late period. From the reign of Sesostris I (1971–1926 B.C.) on, Amun is continually attested with the title "king of the gods" or "king of the Two Lands" (*njswt t'wj*);[52] from the New Kingdom on, "Amon-Re, king of the gods" (in Greek, Amonrasonther) is a normal appellation of the highest god.

But kingly dignity is not restricted to Amun. From an early date a number of other deities also bear the titles "king of the gods" and "king of the Two Lands." As early as the Pyramid Texts Re is described as the king of the next world without

[49]M. A. Korostovtsev, *BIFAO* 45 (1947) 157 l. 3.

[50]Pap. Insinger 24, 6; translation, Lichtheim, *Literature* III, 204, with bibliography p. 186. On the really "small" deities, who have instead of temples only homely shrines, cf. e.g. J. Černý, *Ancient Egyptian Religion* (Hutchinson's University Library, London 1952) 71.

[51]*Pyr.* §1458e, with a parallel from the pyramid of his successor Merenre. On the kingship of gods in general see J. Zandee, "Gott ist König. Königssymbolismus in den antiken Gottesvorstellungen," in C. J. Bleeker et al., eds., *Proceedings of the XIIth International Congress of the International Association of the History of Religions* (SHR 31, 1975) 167–78.

[52]P. Lacau and H. Chevrier, *Une chapelle de Sésostris Ier à Karnak* (Service des Antiquités de l'Egypte, Cairo 1956–69) 168 no. 23 p. 122 §337, pl. 34; 169, pl. 2. The phrase *njswt t'wj* is not the normal title of earthly kings, which is *njswt-bjtj*.

being given the title of king. At the head of his court is the moon god Thoth, who is "vizier,"[53] and from the New Kingdom on often the "representative" (stj) of Re;[54] the deceased wishes to be included as the "scribe" in the sun god's staff of officials. Here the form of kingship on earth is mirrored among the gods in the next world; the Egyptians view many features of the hereafter as continuing the state of things on earth.

By the New Kingdom at the latest, the kingship of the gods is projected onto history. The Palermo Stone, which records the history of the first five dynasties of the double kingdom of Egypt in the form of annual entries, places at the beginning, before the historical period, the rule of kings of the lower, and probably the upper, kingdom. The Turin Canon of the Nineteenth Dynasty, on the other hand, reckons with the rule of gods on earth before the historical period, which begins with Menes, the founder of the state; a millennium later this schema was adopted by the Greek historians of Egypt, most notably Manetho.

At the head of this list of gods who ruled on earth come Ptah, Re, and Shu; then follow Geb, Osiris, Seth, and Horus. At the end are Thoth, Maat, and a second manifestation of Horus, making a total of ten gods, after whom a dynasty of "demi-gods" (akh spirits) forms the transition to the dynasties of the historical period. In the Ramessid period the kingship of the sun god on earth is looked back to as a "perfect time," the return of which is hoped for at the accession of a new king.[55] In the Cairo hymn to Amun, which dates to the Eighteenth Dynasty, the name of the "king of the gods," the sun god, is enclosed in a cartouche,[56] anticipating the highly elaborate royal titulary devised by Akhenaten for his god Aten in the Amarna period.

---

[53]Cf. D. Lowle in J. Ruffle et al., eds., *Glimpses of Ancient Egypt: Studies in Honour of H. W. Fairman* (Warminster 1979) 50–54 pl. 1, where Thoth is shown in the dress of a human vizier.

[54]*Wb.* IV, 8, 4; P. Boylan, *Thoth the Hermes of Egypt* (London etc. 1922) 81–82; *Urk.* IV, 1469, 8; Ahmad Badawi, *ASAE* 44 (1944) 192 (XIII).

[55]Cf. e.g. L. A. Christophe, *BIFAO* 48 (1948) 8 (inscription of Ramesses IV in the Wadi Hammamat).

[56]Grébaut, *Hymne* 6 (2, 2).

In later texts the kingship of the sun god is given a still more earthly cast, and he becomes a king of kings. A hymn to the creator god in Berlin encourages him to protect King Ramesses IX "as you protect the gods who come into being in [this land], for you are their king (*njswt-bjtj*); your rule was in all lands, when you held the kingship of the two lands (that is, Upper and Lower Egypt: *nsjt t'wj*)."[57] Temple texts of the Graeco-Roman period describe in detail god's kingly rule over the "existent"[58] and elaborate upon his kingly title, making him the "king who rules (*nsj*) kings."[59]

Although I have not collected them systematically, examples of the title of king applied to other gods seem to occur usually with those who, according to the Turin Canon of Kings, did in fact rule on earth. This is true of Ptah[60] and Horus,[61] and especially of Osiris, who is worshiped as "king of the gods" from the Middle Kingdom to Ptolemaic times,[62] while as ruler of the dead he sometimes bears the title "king of the living"[63] as well as the common "ruler of the living" (for the Egyptians the blessed dead are "living ones"). He is the first god to have his name enclosed in a royal cartouche; the earliest example of this dates to the end of the Middle Kingdom.[64]

Harsaphes, the ram god who is the principal god of Herakleopolis in northern Middle Egypt, occurs as "king of the Two Lands"[65] but is not one of the ten gods who ruled on earth in the beginning. Here again we encounter the tendency to apply

[57]W. Wolf, *ZÄS* 64 (1928) 42 (xii, 6–7); Assmann, *Liturg. Lieder* 240 n. 65; *id.*, *ÄHG* 333.

[58]E. Drioton, *ASAE* 44 (1944) 122 (Amonrasonther in Karnak). On the kingship of Amun see also G. Posener, *ZÄS* 93 (1966) 119.

[59]Horus of Edfu: M. Alliot, *RdE* 5 (1946) 103 with n. 4; in the same passage Horus is also "ruler of rulers."

[60]M. Sandman Holmberg, *The God Ptah* (Lund 1946) 77, 105, cf. E. Hornung, *Das Grab des Haremhab im Tal der Könige* (Bern 1971) pl. 16b.

[61]Harsiese: Hari, *Horemheb* pl. 59 ll. 19ff.; also called "greatest god" in the same passage.

[62]Selim Hassan, *Hymnes religieux du Moyen Empire* (Service des Antiquités de l'Egypte, Cairo 1928) 106–7; K. A. Kitchen, *Or* 29 (1960) 81–83.

[63]References in Assmann, *Liturg. Lieder* 240 with nn. 61–62.

[64]British Museum, *Hieroglyphic Texts from Egyptian Stelae etc.* III (London 1912) pl. 28 no. 1367 (*Wnn-nfrw*).

[65]H. Kees in Bonnet, *Reallexikon* 249–50; P. Kaplony, *MIO* 11 (1966) 152 n. 80.

titles and epithets of the highest god to comparatively minor deities.[66] The number of these deities becomes still greater if, in addition to the title of king, we take into consideration epithets that characterize the god in some other way as the highest one or the "lord," and thus place him at the top of the social order of deities.

The Eighteenth Dynasty Cairo hymn to Amun, which I have cited frequently, contains an impressive description of the primacy of Amon-Re, the king of the gods: "The gods kowtow at his feet like dogs when they recognize his presence as their lord";[67] yet Amun is by no means the only "lord" and "chief of all the gods."[68] Onuris is also "lord of the gods,"[69] and even the lioness Pakhet, who is worshiped in the vicinity of Beni Hasan as a both dangerous and helpful local deity, is given the title "chief (ḥrjt) of all the gods" on a scarab in the Groppi collection;[70] her elevation may be related to her importance in funerary beliefs from the time of the Coffin Texts, and later at the royal court of the Eighteenth and Nineteenth dynasties.[71]

The most encompassing expression of a deity's rule over all of creation is the title nb-r-ḏr, which is translated "lord of all." This title was devised in the first intermediate period, and in the Coffin Texts it is commonly used to characterize the sun god as the supreme being.[72] In the Instruction of Amenemhat I the title of "lord of all" is also given to the new king Sesostris I,[73] but it is applied to members of the Egyptian pantheon far less frequently than is the title of king.

For Eberhard Otto "the tendency of these appellations . . .

---

[66]Kees in Bonnet, *Reallexikon* 247–51, gave further examples with Onuris, Wepwawet, and Min. He believed that these epithets reflected political rivalries; in the case of Wepwawet he dated these rivalries back to the beginning of Egyptian history.

[67]Grébaut, *Hymne* 7 (2, 5–6).

[68]*Ibid.* 3 (1, 1), 4 (1, 5–6). In *Urk.* IV, 1898, 11 he is "lord of lords."

[69]J. J. Clère, *JEA* 54 (1968) 137, E3.

[70]E. Drioton, *ASAE* 44 (1944) 29–30.

[71]*Amduat* II, 68–69; add *CT* V, 388i, 399a.

[72]J. C. Goyon, *Le papyrus du Louvre N.3279* (IFAO BE 42, 1966) 57 n. 6, cites examples with Atum and Re.

[73]W. Helck, *Der Text der Lehre Amenemhets I. für seinen Sohn* (Kleine Ägyptische Texte, Wiesbaden 1969) §Ic.

[is] without doubt toward monotheistic thought,"[74] and the aim is unquestionably to make one god king of the others and lord of the entire world; but at least since the publications of Raffaele Pettazzoni we know that belief in a supreme being and a king of the gods—whom the Greeks also worshiped in Zeus—does not constitute a stage of development from polytheism to monotheism.[75]

Further, the translation "lord of all" is just as misleading as the rendering of ḏt and nḥḥ as "eternity," and can easily give rise to a falsification of the Egyptian conception of god. "Lord of all" is not what is meant, but quite literally "lord to the end"—to the spatial and temporal end of the created world; as we have seen in Chapter 5, the power of even the highest god ends at that point, so that this title should not be taken as evidence that the god to whom it is applied is genuinely transcendent.

By the end of the Old Kingdom at the latest, the Egyptians had developed their conception of a supreme being[76] who is "king" and "lord" of all that is created, and is also the creator and sustainer of "everything that exists." In Egypt, however, the qualities of this supreme being do not attach to a particular deity, but may be attributed to any deity, even to relatively unimportant local gods. In our sources the qualities of a creator god and ruler are most commonly found attributed to the sun god Re and gods who are combined syncretistically with him, but this group was formed in the course of the historical period and dissolved again in the late period, so that it was truly dominant only during the Middle and New kingdoms.

At any time an Egyptian believer could credit some other deity, who was for him the most important god in the cult in his

[74]*Saeculum* 14 (1963) 274. See also *id.*, "Monotheistische Tendenzen in der ägyptischen Religion," *Die Welt des Orients* 2 (1955) 99–110.

[75]R. Pettazzoni, *L'essere supremo nelle religioni primitive (l'onniscienza di Dio)* (Turin 1957) = *Der allwissende Gott* (Frankfurt a.M. 1960), with appendix, "La formazione del monoteismo" pp. 227–44. This book is a short version of *L'onniscienza di Dio* (Turin 1955) = *The All-Knowing God* (London 1956), but the larger work does not contain a separate section on monotheism.

[76]Cf. J. Assmann, "Primat und Transzendenz. Struktur und Genese der ägyptischen Vorstellung eines 'Höchstes Wesens,'" in W. Westendorf, ed., *Aspekte der spätägyptischen Religion* (GOF 9, 1979) 7–42.

home town, or who incorporated a region of the world which was significant to him at the time, with all the supreme attributes of divine power, even if the deity was not combined syncretistically with Re or Amun. In Hermopolis the author of a royal stela in the temple of Thoth calls Thoth simultaneously the "son of Re," that is, subordinate to Re, and "chief of the gods," superior to all as the supreme being.[77] In New Kingdom Thebes, the stronghold of Amon-Re, and, what is more, in the tomb of a high priest of Amun, Osiris is addressed as the supreme king: "Unique king, whose like there will never be again, king of kings. . . ."[78] Here any explanation in terms of religious politics would be quite absurd; if we are to achieve an understanding of the phenomenon, it is clearly necessary to approach it in a different way.

In the act of worship, whether it be in prayer, hymn of praise, or ethical attachment and obligation, the Egyptians single out one god, who for them at that moment signifies everything; the limited yet colossal might and greatness of god is concentrated in and focused on the deity who is addressed, beside whom all other gods vanish into insignificance and may even be deliberately devalued. "Gods make a king and men make a king, but Amun has made me," says the Kushite King Piye (c. 750–712 B.C.) on a stela from Gebel Barkal.[79] The god who is addressed is superior to the gods, he is more than they are.

This religious phenomenon, whose occurrence in the history of religions is not confined to Egypt, was termed *henotheism* by Schelling, and F. Max Müller studied it in depth, especially its manifestation in Egyptian and Indian religion. In a lecture published in 1859 he said:

Each god is to the mind of the supplicant as good as all the gods. He is felt at the time as a real divinity, as supreme and absolute, in spite of the necessary limitations which, to our mind, a plural-

[77]G. Roeder, *ASAE* 52 (1954) 380 (Thirtieth Dynasty).

[78]J. Zandee, *An Ancient Egyptian Crossword Puzzle* (MVEOL 15, 1966) 3 ll. 2–3.

[79]G. A. Reisner, *ZÄS* 66 (1931) 90 ll. 22–23. Zandee, *Crossword Puzzle* 66, cites a typically henotheistic New Kingdom description of Amun from an unpublished papyrus in Leiden.

ity of gods must entail on every single god. All the rest disappear from the vision . . . , and he only who is to fulfil their desires stands in full light before the eyes of the worshippers.[80]

The term "henotheism," which was coined by Schelling and adopted by Müller, was taken over by le Page Renouf, von Strauss und Torney,[81] Wiedemann,[82] and many others to describe this worship of one god at a time but not of a single god. The term "monolatry," which has been proposed by Erich Winter and Siegfried Morenz[83] and has long been used for Near Eastern conceptions of god,[84] also describes well the nature of this attitude to the divine, which still lives on in Hinduism.

Excursus: The problem of logic

However one describes the emphasizing of the one among the many, the phenomenon itself leads us straight to the problem of logical thought. According to the principles of western logic it would be an impossible contradiction for the divine to appear to the believer as one and almost absolute, and then again as a bewildering multiplicity; we find it surprising that in Egyptian thought these two fundamentally different formulations are evidently not mutually exclusive but complementary. Did the Egyptians think wrongly, imprecisely, or simply in a different way?

This question about Egyptian thought, which we must consider here, has been answered in the most various ways. Egyptian thought has long been said to be "illogical" or at the least "prelogical," and in this way the contradictions that are en-

[80]F. Max Müller, *Lectures on the Origin and Growth of Religion as Illustrated by the Religions of India* (new ed., London 1891) 285, quoting from an earlier work of 1859, for which no reference is cited; quoted by le Page Renouf, *Lectures* 217–18. Le Page Renouf devoted an entire section of his book to Egyptian henotheism (pp. 217–30).

[81]*Götterglaube*, esp. II, 88–91.

[82]*Religion* 8 = 11.

[83]E. Winter in F. König, ed., *Religionswissenschaftliches Wörterbuch* (Freiburg 1956) col. 173 (used of Akhenaten); Morenz, *Religion* 157 = 149.

[84]B. Meissner, *Babylonien und Assyrien* II (Heidelberg 1925) 48; H. Schmökel, ed., *Kulturgeschichte des alten Orient* (Stuttgart 1961) 274, 296–97.

countered have been set aside as imperfections in its structure. Edouard Naville's remarks about Egyptian "soul" concepts, published in 1906, are typical of many judgments:

> All these doctrines are very vague and ill-defined; here, as with all Egyptian ideas, there is an absolute lack of system and logic.[85]

In sharp contrast, Rudolf Anthes points to the "undeniable role that rational thought and action played in public and private life in Egypt."[86] He wishes to find this "rational" (*vernünftig*) thought, which he relates to timeless "common sense" (*gesunder Menschenverstand*), in Egyptian religion and mythology, and he rejects the assumption that there is a different mode of thought which is "mythopoeic," as Henri Frankfort termed it. Hermann Junker had already adopted the same position and made the same criticisms of Frankfort in his last major work,[87] but he was forced to place "antirational magic" in "a separate conceptual world proper to magicians," while explaining other contradictions by reference to the symbolic character of the myths.

This approach cannot produce a viable solution to these well-known difficulties. But in one respect Junker and Anthes are undoubtedly right: in our daily lives we follow, like the ancient Egyptians long before us, impulses in thought and action which are in no way those of formal logic. Often enough we are faithful to the maxim of "doing one thing while not neglecting its opposite," trying to avoid narrowing our decisions to the logical alternatives of yes and no. And where would politics be if it were not the art of compromise, of yes-but decisions that contradict all formal logic?

Ethics, also, can never be accommodated in a rigorously logical system. The maxims of the Egyptian wisdom teachers be-

[85]*Religion* 54–55 = 63–64; retranslated here. See also his similar remarks of 1886 on the contents of the Book of the Dead: *Todtenbuch, Einleitung* 21–22.

[86]*MDOG* 96 (1965) 8; for his views as a whole see this article, "Mythologie und der gesunde Menschenverstand in Ägypten," and earlier *id.*, "Affinity and Difference between Egyptian and Greek Sculpture and Thought in the Seventh and Sixth Centuries B.C.," *Proceedings of the American Philosophical Society* 107 (1963) 60–81.

[87]*Geisteshaltung* 12–25.

tray the "common sense" invoked by Anthes, which solves problems pragmatically, not through application of a system that is free from logical contradictions. This is the reason for the timeless validity and relevance of these maxims—the problems of coexistence and conflict in social life have remained largely the same.

But formal thought in theology, philosophy and science, which is governed by well-defined calculi, is quite another matter. Here problems cannot be solved by "common sense," and this is just as true of ancient Egypt. The highly systematic theology of the New Kingdom is a formal conceptual structure, which must be studied according to strict, formal criteria that cannot be derived from a loose concept of "reason" or "common sense."

Any application of a two-valued logic, which is based on a / not-a distinctions and on the law of the excluded middle, to Egyptian philosophical and theological thought leads at once to insoluble contradictions. We cannot avoid this fact, and "common sense" is no help here. We must choose between two alternatives. Either we equate truly logical thought with two-valued logic, in which case Egyptian thought is undeniably "illogical" or "prelogical"; or we admit the possibility of a different type of logic which is not self-contradictory, which can only be a many-valued logic.

This choice is beyond the competence of an egyptologist. He can do no more than observe in his material that the Egyptians strove earnestly after system, and that they certainly did not proceed carelessly in their thought; he can also sense that their system of thought has a coherence of its own which can often convince the emotions, even though it cannot be analyzed without contradiction according to western criteria, or defined in formal terms. Recent attempts to isolate the characteristics of this thought and find a suitable descriptive term for it have been concerned too much with the general "cast of mind" of the Egyptians and not enough with the formal side of their thought. If Egyptian thought is stated to be "aspective,"[88] that

---

[88]E. Brunner-Traut, "Die Aspektive," epilogue to H. Schäfer, *Von ägyptischer Kunst* (4th ed., Wiesbaden 1963) 395–428 = *Principles of Egyptian Art* (Oxford 1974) 421–28; id., "Aspektive," in W. Helck and E. Otto, eds., *Lexikon der*

statement says nothing about its logical structure. The term "undifferentiated"[89] leads us on the wrong track, for careful differentiation is one of the most distinctive features of Egyptian thought,[90] in comparison with which the concept of "analytic" or "rational" (*rational*) thought, which is intended as its polar opposite, can exhibit a startling lack of differentiation or diversity. Finally, the fact that in Egyptian thought myth is not considered to be contradictory, but is exploited as a legitimate mode of discourse, is not sufficient cause for us to term the thought as a whole "mythical" or "mythopoeic"; myth is one mode of discourse among many, and it is in any case not a form of thought.

One typical Egyptian form of thought—dualistic thought—has long been identified and is often described.[91] As we learned from Egyptian ontology, the order established by the creator god is characterized by "two things" and thus by differentiation or diversity; this idea is incorporated in the teaching that Egypt is the "Two Lands" and in a mass of other pairs that can form a totality only if taken together. The greatest totality conceivable is "the existent and the nonexistent," and in these dualistic terms the divine is evidently both one and many.

Oppositions such as these are real, but the pairs do not cancel each other out; they complement each other. A given *x* can be both *a* and not-*a*: *tertium datur*—the law of the excluded middle does not apply. The Egyptian script, in which individ-

---

Ägyptologie I (Wiesbaden 1975) cols. 474–88. I do not mean to deny that this term is well suited to a number of structures in art, language, and world view, but we should distinguish terminologically between observation and formulation on the one hand, and formal thought on the other.

[89]J. Zandee, *Het ongedifferentieerde denken der oude Egyptenaren* (Leiden 1966); *id.*, *Mens en Kosmos* 21 (1965) 74–79.

[90]Cf. e.g. the remarks on p. 138 about the distinction between god and image, or about the divinity of the king.

[91]The earliest study is probably H. Schneider, *Kultur und Denken der alten Ägypter* (Entwicklungsgeschichte der Menschheit 1, Leipzig 1907); then van der Leeuw, *Godsvoorstellingen* 137–38, who already rejected a political/geographical explanation; E. Otto, "Die Lehre von den beiden Ländern Ägyptens in der ägyptischen Religionsgeschichte," in *Studia Aegyptiaca* I (AnOr 17, 1938) 10–35. For a collection of comparative material see R. Needham, ed., *Right and Left: Essays in Dual Symbolic Classification* (Chicago and London 1973).

ual signs had always been able to be both picture and letter, illustrates how ancient this principle is. I should emphasize that they "were able to be," because we should not exclude the possibility that the Egyptians had special cases in which a particular given *x* was always *a*. For the Egyptians two times two is always four, never anything else. But the sky is a number of things—cow, baldachin, water, woman—it is the goddess Nut and the goddess Hathor, and in syncretism a deity *a* is at the same time another, not-*a*.

In his inaugural lecture in Amsterdam Jan Zandee presented this last structure of Egyptian thought clearly, and pointed out that it contradicts the law of identity in logic.[92] He classified it under his key concept of "undifferentiated" thought, which I do not consider to be adequate; but he also followed John A. Wilson[93] in using the term "complementary." This concept is valuable in two ways: it provides a more precise formulation of the alternative logic alluded to above, and it gives us the insight that if we are to solve our specialized problem we must go beyond the confines of our own discipline.

The concept of complementarity has long played an important part in the debate over the extension of "classical" logic. In 1927 Niels Bohr introduced it in physics in order to describe the ambiguous behavior of energy in quantum mechanics and to explain the simultaneous factors of position and momentum, or of wave and particle, which it seemed impossible to explain in terms of the models of traditional logic. The discussion about the potential and limitations of a "quantum logic" or "logic of complementarity" still continues, and I cannot give a survey of its extent or its problems here.[94]

For us what is important at this stage is to be aware of this debate and to follow its course as it develops—and it can do

[92]Cf. n. 89 above. The term "complementary" is introduced on pp. 14ff. of *Het ongedifferentieerde denken*.

[93]In H. Frankfort et al., *The Intellectual Adventure of Ancient Man* (Chicago 1946) 45 = *id., Before Philosophy* (Harmondsworth 1949) 54.

[94]Of the extensive literature on the subject I have used especially C. F. von Weizsäcker, "Komplementarität und Logik," *Die Naturwissenschaften* 42 (1955) 521–29, 545–55; Aage Petersen, *Quantum Physics and the Philosophical Tradition* (Cambridge, Mass. 1968).

egyptologists no harm to familiarize themselves with the problems and concepts of modern science. As disciplines become ever more specialized, it is comforting to see the unity of research into fundamental problems. And today, when the two-valued logic of yes / no decisions is celebrating triumphs in the field of data processing, the limits of its applicability are becoming clearer in many other areas. To the outside observer it seems as if traditional formal logic, rather like "classical" mechanics, is meaningful and valid only over the center of the field, whereas perspectives are distorted at the largest and smallest extremes, and new conceptual structures become necessary.

So long as the intellectual basis of a many-valued logic remains uncertain, we can indicate only possibilities, not definite solutions. If the basis is not established, Egyptian thought and all "pre-Greek"[95] thought will continue to be open to charges of arbitrariness or confusion. If it is found, we shall be able to comprehend the one and the many as complementary propositions, whose truth values within a many-valued logic are not mutually exclusive, but contribute together to the whole truth: god is a unity in worship and revelation, and multiple in nature and manifestation.[96] A similar case is the mass of complementary substances which in the Egyptian view together make up both a divine and a human person—every person *has* a *ba*, but *is* also a *ba*, and so on; within a many-valued logic this would not be so bewildering and unsystematic as it now seems to us to be.

This journey to the limits of what is at present thinkable leads through an unfamiliar, bizarre landscape in which it is easy to become lost. But it takes us behind the appearance of things and allows us to sense something of how they are related. Our study of Egyptian ontology in Chapter 5 showed that an absolute unity and transcendence of god, indeed any

[95]A term used extensively by Heinrich Schäfer, *Von ägyptischer Kunst* (n. 88 above), to characterize nonperspective art, including Egyptian art.

[96]I use "revelation" (*Offenbarung*) here for cases in which a god makes himself manifest to a single believer (see Chapter 4), and "manifestation" (*Erscheinung*) for the multiplicity of possible forms of a god.

absolute feature of god, is contrary to the Egyptian conception of the existent; only a nonexistent god can have absolute qualities. This excursus on logic now shows that for the Egyptians an exclusive unity or oneness of god was unthinkable, in the full sense of the word, because they thought in terms of complementary propositions. We can also see that monotheism may have been impossible in Egyptian logic, and hence never became a reality, despite all the steps taken toward it.

Quite apart from this last, as yet open question, it has now become clear in logical terms why monotheism does not arise within polytheism by way of a slow accumulation of "monotheistic tendencies," but requires a complete transformation of thought patterns. Tendencies to classify the pantheon should not be equated with an inclination toward monotheism. The only "monotheistic tendency" that can be accepted as such is henotheism, but even there the designation is not very apt. It is true that according to Pettazzoni henotheism is a "relative and rudimentary monotheism,"[97] which for a moment makes the one, omnipotent, exclusive god into a relative reality, that is, a god whose absolute nature is relativized by the complementary conception of the mass of deities in the pantheon. But in logical terms this distinction between relative and absolute reality is decisive; between them lies a transformation. Some tendencies may prepare the way for this transformation, but only a complete revolution in thought allows henotheism—of exactly Pettazzoni's type—or monolatry to change into monotheism. When polytheism is suddenly negated, the complementarity of god and gods is denied, and one of the two propositions—that concerning the multiplicity of gods—is assumed to be null and void.

This last hypothesis, which I have deduced initially from the structure of Egyptian thought, can be confirmed historically. In the fourteenth century B.C. there occurred the earliest attested case of this fundamental transformation of thought, in the person of Akhenaten and his teachings.

---

[97] *L'essere supremo* (n. 75 above) 233 = 112, a description of the views of Schelling.

Excursus: The initiative of Akhenaten

I have referred at several points to peculiarities in King Akhenaten's conception of god, but there are good reasons for placing a consideration of the conception as a whole at this point, immediately after the excursus on the problem of logic.[98]

In the middle of the fourteenth century B.C. Egypt experienced a revolution "from above" which for a brief period affected almost all spheres of life. It has always proved difficult to comprehend the essential features of this revolution, because, as is becoming steadily clearer, it expressed itself for the most part in conventional forms. The phraseology of the hymns of Akhenaten is paralleled more or less word for word in earlier texts; his god Aten was venerated under his two predecessors; and many motifs in Amarna art, such as the disk with rays or the prostrated figures of the subjects, had existed for a long time, at least as literary images. In the social sphere the New Kingdom was always open to novelty—even to revolution—and the change of capital city had been anticipated in the Middle Kingdom. Since there is so much that is familiar, what is truly revolutionary in Akhenaten's actions and ideas?

I believe it to be the implied transformation of thought patterns, in which all the traditional forms were bathed in the glare of a new light which the Egyptians came to find intolerable. Beginning with the change in the king's birth name, from which the name of the god Amun was removed, there was a step-by-step process of elimination. Amun was replaced by Aten, mythical statement by rational statement, many-valued logic by two-valued logic, the gods by God. All this was accomplished according to a well-conceived plan.

Akhenaten was certainly not a "visionary"; he was a methodical rationalist. His reforms were implemented one by one, as soon as the necessary political conditions had been created. This philosopher on the throne of the pharaohs was certainly not unworldly. He manipulated the power of the institutions at

[98]Among recent literature on the reforms of Akhenaten see especially J. Assmann, "Die Häresie des Echnaton: Aspekte der Amarna-Religion," *Saeculum* 23 (1972) 109–26.

his command in virtuoso fashion, and his eventual failure was probably not the result of a loss of political control.

In the fourth year of his reign (1361 B.C.), during the decisive initial phase of the revolution, the high priest of Amun, the god who had hitherto been the most important, was sent on a quarrying expedition, quite literally "into the wilderness," and thus was kept at a remove from events in the capital city. At the same time Amun was replaced by Aten at the head of the pantheon, and a series of temples to the new state god,[99] in which Akhenaten incorporated for the first time his new artistic ideas, was built at the ancient sacred site of Karnak.

On the surface these first steps do not appear to damage the traditional structure of henotheism; and Norman de G. Davies[100] and Hanns Stock,[101] for example, interpreted Akhenaten's conception of god without reservation as henotheism. Akhenaten chose Aten from among all the gods as his preferred god, but for at least another year he bore the name Amun in his birth name Amenophis, and assigned a favored position beside Aten to the ancient solar deities Re, Harakhte, and Shu. On a private stela of this period Harakhte is even said to be "the god like whom there is no other";[102] this epithet does not belittle Aten, but singles out the god who is being addressed, quite in the spirit of earlier henotheistic worship.

Syncretism too was very much alive; Harakhte and Aten were combined in the hawk-headed figure of Re-Harakhte-Aten,[103] and Re-Harakhte was placed at the head of the earlier "royal titulary" that was established for the god Aten as ruler of the world. In the early years of the reign the complementary status of god and gods was not attacked, but the hitherto vast range of the pantheon was restricted in unprecedented fashion to its solar aspect. The dark world of the gods of the dead, Osiris and Sokar, was drawn into the light of the sun god,[104] and finally

[99]Cf. R. W. Smith and D. B. Redford, *The Akhenaten Temple Project* I (Warminster 1976).

[100]*JEA* 9 (1923) 150.

[101]*Saeculum* 1 (1950) 631.

[102]E. Drioton, *ASAE* 43 (1943) 29.

[103]C. Aldred, *JEA* 45 (1959) 19–22 with pl. 3.

[104]On the door jamb of Hatiai (Drioton, *ASAE* 43 [1943] 35–43), especially in the hymn to Osiris.

banished completely from the image of the cosmos. Here too the change was accomplished step by step, not once for all. This well-considered approach seems to be the result of careful planning rather than of the development of the king's ideas. The transformation of Egypt's intellectual landscape was not an uncontrolled outpouring of an individual's ideas put into action without regard for the realities of life.

Sometime between the king's sixth and ninth years of reign this well-planned program reached its provisional goal. These were the first years Akhenaten spent in his new capital city Akhetaten (el-Amarna), far from the ancient religious centers of Thebes and Memphis. The Aten now received a new titulary in which even Harakhte ("Horus of the horizon"), who had hitherto been greatly venerated, no longer appeared; his name was replaced with the newly coined phrase "horizon-ruler." Thus the deity's hawk form, which had been one of the most ancient and favorite manifestations of the sun-god, was removed; but the hawk, like the uraeus snake, remained one of the few divine animals that were tolerated at Amarna.

Now, for the first time in history, the divine has become one, without a complementary multiplicity; henotheism has been transformed into monotheism. The mass of divine forms is reduced to the single manifestation of the Aten with rays (Figure 20), and out of the mass of names of gods all that is left is one double name: Re, who reveals himself ("has come") as Aten. A god "without equal" has become, at an enormous remove, a god "without any other except for himself," and the king too is now the "sole king like Aten; there is no other great one except for him."[105]

For Egyptian ears, as well as ours, such statements constituted as radical a claim to uniqueness as could be imagined. Although Christian Egyptians did not hesitate to apply the ancient word $n\underline{t}r$ to their god, Akhenaten often tried to avoid it;[106] for him there was no "god" in the traditional sense, only the Aten, in whom everything was contained.

---

[105]Sandman, *Texts* 7, 7. For the king see *Urk.* IV, 1999, 13.

[106]For examples see E. Drioton, *ASAE* 43 (1943) 42 n. 2 (the title "perfect god" replaced by "perfect ruler"); H. Kees, *ZÄS* 84 (1959) 61 ("god's offering" re-

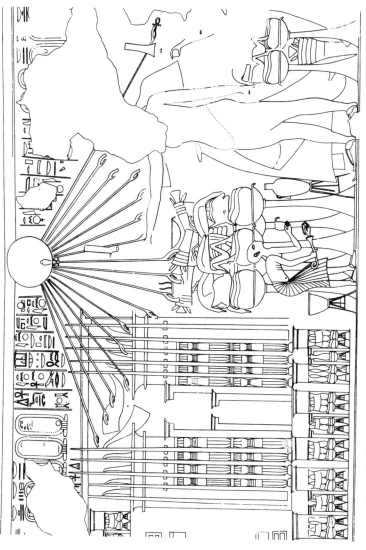

Figure 20. The sun disk with rays shining over Akhenaten (1364–1347 B.C.) and the temple.

Anything that does not fit with the nature of the Aten is no longer divine, and its existence is denied through its not being mentioned. The hymns of Akhenaten, which use familiar phraseology to praise the Aten, differ from earlier hymns principally in what they omit. The relationship between night or death and the Aten is purely negative—they are the negation of the god's presence. Along with the gods, myth must also be abolished. The Aten's nature is not revealed in mythical images, but is accessible only through intellectual effort and insight— and hence is not revealed to everyone, but only to Akhenaten and those whom he teaches. In the great hymn to the Aten the king emphasizes that "there is no one else who knows you," and he is constantly given the epithet Waenre "the unique one of Re."

The Aten, which is so far removed as to be inscrutable, requires an intermediary in order to be accessible to mankind. Intermediaries had become increasingly important in New Kingdom religion before Amarna,[107] and Akhenaten continued this development. But whereas worshipers had hitherto been able to turn to a variety of intermediaries—sacred animals, statues in temples, dead men who had been deified—their only recourse is now the king, the sole prophet of God. As the mass of gods is reduced to one, so is the mass of intermediaries. The faithful of the Amarna period pray at home, in front of an altar that contains a picture of the king and his family, and which Morenz saw as the forerunner of portraits of the Leader of all political complexions; its religious context, however, is the idea that Akhenaten is the sole intermediary, as is stated in Amarna-period hymns. The new creed could, indeed, be summed up in the formula "there is no god but Aten, and Akhenaten is his prophet."

As is hardly surprising, the proclamation of the sole god at Amarna is dogmatic in form. There is a "teaching" about the Aten which the king himself elaborates, and his nature is de-

placed by "Aten's offering"). See also L. V. Žabkar, *JNES* 13 (1954) 93 with n. 95, on the avoidance of the determinative for god. For cases where *nṯr* continues to be used see H. Brunner, *ZÄS* 97 (1971) 14.

[107]Cf. Morenz, *Gott und Mensch* 64–65.

lineated ever more closely and consistently by means of highly complex titularies and definitions. Although his qualities are not absolute, he is a monotheistic God by virtue of his claims to exclusivity—he is a jealous God, who tolerates no other gods beside him.

Nowhere is the transformation to which thought has been subject more clearly visible than in the unparalleled persecution of the traditional gods. Akhenaten's stonemasons swarmed all over Egypt and even abroad in order to remove the name of Amun from all accessible monuments, even on the tips of obelisks, under the gilding on columns, and in the cuneiform letters in the archives; for us today the erasure or later restoration of the name of Amun is an important criterion for dating a monument to the period before Amarna.

Only the name of the god Amun, who had previously been preeminent, was removed with such zeal, but the other gods and sometimes even the plural "gods" were also persecuted, albeit much less consistently. From this evidence we can see that Akhenaten's aim was not just to dethrone Amun, but in principle to deny the existence of all gods except the Aten. This goes against all traditional logic: before Akhenaten the placing of one god in a privileged position never threatened the existence of the rest of the gods. The one and the many had been treated as complementary statements that were not mutually exclusive. Now they were mutually exclusive, and we witness the formulation of a new logic.

In Egypt the shift in thought which can be observed here was a leap away from the central tradition, and it did not survive the reign of Akhenaten. But it renders Akhenaten's proclamation fundamentally different from everything that preceded it, which otherwise appears similar in many ways. The change in logic is surely the intellectual core of his revolution—which for a few years anticipated western modes of thought.

It is significant that the "restoration" after the death of Akhenaten began with the gods. It was some decades before Akhenaten's memory was persecuted, and in art his influence was even longer lasting; for a few years the Aten remained the leading god, and its name never was persecuted. The first step of the restoration was to return the other gods to their rightful positions, and thus to reestablish the complementary status of god and gods. Tutankhamun's temple at Faras has the programatic name "he who sets the gods at rest." While worshiping the one, the Egyptians were not ready to sacrifice the multiple and multivalent nature of the divine.

8 ✎ Conclusion

Everything we have learned in the preceding seven chapters derives from the statements of human beings about the gods of Egypt. In some cases these statements were presented in the form of self-revelations by gods, but these were always recorded in word and image by men, and hence subject to the blindness in which the Egyptians placed the origin of mankind. As are all forms of historical research, the study of the gods is conducted through the medium of words and images; direct contact with the objects of study is impossible. But contact with *these* objects could only be conversion; in that moment of involvement with the deity questioning would cease and observation would be blinded.

Any sort of contact with the world of the Egyptians silences one question, that of the existence and reality of these gods. Egyptian religion lived on the fact that gods exist, and this certainty pervaded all of Egyptian life. If we remove the gods from the Egyptians' world, all that remains is a dark, uninhabited shell that would not repay study. The gods are part of Egyptian reality and hence are for us at the least historical realities that should be taken seriously. The more clearly we comprehend them, the more clearly we see the human beings whom we wish to study. In order to understand the forces that circumscribe the very closed and homogeneous world of the Egyptians, we must inquire after their gods and employ all our conceptual armory in order to seek out the reality of these gods—a reality that was not invented by human beings but *experienced* by them.

The attempt to see in Egyptian conceptions of god precursors of monotheistic belief has the character of an apologia and leads us away from this reality, while the opposition monotheism/polytheism does not seem to provide the key, because it is too narrowly formulated. The concept of pantheism is too far removed from the reality of the cult to be suited to ancient Egypt. The study of our topic is in danger of being bogged down in all these -isms; it needs to be revitalized.

In confronting the topic in this book, I had inevitably to use and test repeatedly the chief concepts that have been current in research up till now. I think that in the future we would do well to abandon the conceptual framework that they provide, for it has proved to be inadequate and does not clarify the realities of the Egyptian pantheon. Above all, it obscures or falsifies the problem of logic which is alluded to in the title of this book—the one and the many—and which in my view opens up a new approach to the reality of god.

Another conceptual schema I have used quite frequently is similarly inadequate, but it does provide a quick, practical indication of the outstanding aspect of a god's nature. This is the classification of deities under headings such as "sun god," "mother goddess," "earth god," "sky goddess," and so forth. Often such a characterization succeeds in providing an initial rough approximation, but equally often, as for example with Osiris or Amun, it leads the search for the nature of a god in a new, unprofitable direction. Terms like these describe only parts of the divine reality which we should not consider to be the sole significant ones. Even new, improved terms will probably never encompass the entire richness of a god's nature. Nonetheless we are not freed from the obligation to try to comprehend a larger part of that nature and to achieve a closer approximation to it. Here the Egyptians themselves set an example for us: for them the nature of a god becomes accessible through a "multiplicity of approaches";[1] only when these are taken together can the whole be comprehended.

[1] H. Frankfort et al., *The Intellectual Adventure of Ancient Man* (Chicago 1946) 16 = *id.*, *Before Philosophy* (Harmondsworth 1949) 25; Frankfort, *Religion*, index s.v.

In the search for new approaches, every apt term and improved formulation of a problem must be welcome. It can do no harm if in addition to the traditional concepts of ethnology, history of religions, and psychology we use those of modern physics or of information theory. In order to describe the characteristic, but at first sight logically contradictory, juxtaposition of the one and the many, we found that the concept of henotheism provided an initial approximation, but only "complementarity" gave us the key that may open up a new logical structure, in which both these propositions about the reality of god can be true without excluding each other.

For the Egyptians the world emerges from the one, because the nonexistent is one. In his work of creation the creator god differentiates not only the world but also himself. From the one emerges the duality of "two things" and the diversity of the "millions" of created forms. God divided, creation is division; only man jumbles everything together again. The divided elements are interdependent, but remain divided so long as they are existent. Only the return of nonexistence fuses what is divided and once more annuls differentiation.

By becoming existent, the divine loses the absolute, exclusive unity of the beginning of things. But wherever one turns to the divine in worship, addresses it and tends it in the cult, it appears as a single, well-defined figure that can for a moment unite all divinity within itself and does not share it with any other god. And the human being who encounters god becomes a single person who has no other beside him and embodies all humanity. This divine and human unity is, however, always relative and never excludes the fundamental plurality that permits all other approaches to the nature of god.

Only Akhenaten attempted to claim absolute and normative value for one of these approaches and sought forcibly to block the others. In this he failed, even though his deeds and his reign had a lasting impact. But he had successors throughout the world; the worship of the one became the worship of the Unique One. The revelation of a sole God who excludes all others came together with a new stage in the development of human consciousness; a mode of thought which seeks to derive all phenomena from a single cause and strives after the absolute; and a two-valued logic based on yes/no distinctions.

This stage of consciousness presented itself as absolute and definitive until our time, when it has become unsure of itself. The "revaluation of all values," which Nietzsche proclaimed, is already coming to pass. As believers and lovers we may be lost in the absolute nature of the moment, but when we observe history we know that nothing existent is definitive. Inexorably history destroys all "eternal" and "absolute" values and demonstrates the relativity of every absolute point of reference which we seek to establish. Hence the fanatical opposition to anything historical—or scorn for it which takes the form of unscrupulous distortion—on the part of those who wish to establish definitive, binding norms.

One church, one state, one order of society for all mankind, the equalizing compulsion of one system for all—these and many other absolutisms have taken to absurd lengths a mode of thought which followed the law of unity and did not tolerate plurality. Although this mode of thought continues to celebrate triumphs, in principle it has reached the end of its development, both because it is not equal to the tasks of the future and because it is no longer in tune with the changed consciousness of mankind. As soon as the dominant mode of thought ceases to fit the structure of the dominant mode of consciousness, it begins to degenerate into something inhuman which cannot, despite its coercive force, change the mode of consciousness.

All the evidence suggests that human society of the near future will be pluralistic and undogmatic—or it will not exist at all. In all spheres of life it will have to allow for the multiplicity of possibilities, without excluding the one as an extreme case. After the shock therapy of this century I believe that society will be thoroughly sick of dogmatic ideologies and "absolute values." It is unlikely that human religious belief will be unaffected by the newly transformed mode of consciousness. Deep faith, in particular, must accept that God has never spoken his last word, even in the revelation of the sole God. A new stage of consciousness is open to a new revelation, the nature of which cannot be predicted at all, except that it will be different.

The world of the many gods is past; no one will ever again

Conclusion

offer a bull to Amun or Zeus. But the present world of the sole God need not be the final one. Both correspond to stages of human consciousness, so that the categories of true and false are not applicable to them. This is not an agnostic attitude, but a relativization of the point of view. Both of these worlds are consistent within their own terms of reference, but neither transcends historical space or can claim absolute validity.

This discussion was necessary in order to place the historical reality of the Egyptian pantheon in a broader context. Now we must return to the characteristics of the gods and differentiate more precisely among them.

These characteristics strive after a universal scope, but do not become immeasurable. Again and again we saw how Egyptian gods can extend their being endlessly, can enter into more and more names, combinations, manifestations, modes of action and response in the cult, and yet remain limited in their nature and their existence. Here too Egyptian religion is the opposite of an "absolute religion." It places in doubt the "eternal values" to which we aspire and wrenches our thinking away from its all too familiar paths.

Even for Walter F. Otto, who made the reality of the gods accessible for us again,[2] there was no question that the gods belonged to the "sphere of the eternal." He showed that in their mode of being the Greek gods of tragedy are so far removed from death that they must not come into contact with the death of mortal human beings. The gods of Egypt are quite different: there is a deep and necessary connection between them and death. Egyptian ontology teaches that the world of the eternal and of immortality is a nonexistent world, the godless world before creation. This limitless *pleroma* regenerates all the existent, including the constantly rejuvenated gods, but it also fuses all the existent into formlessness, into the original undifferentiated state of things. For the Egyptians, departure into the eternal would be departure into nonexistence.

This finite character of the divine, to which omnipresence,

[2]*Die Götter Griechenlands* (3d ed., Frankfurt a.M. 1947) = *The Homeric Gods* (London [1956]); see also *id.*, *Theophania. Der Geist der altgriechischen Religion* (rowohlts deutsche enzyklopädie, Hamburg 1956).

255

omnipotence, and "true" transcendence are alien, presents us with unfamiliar forms of divine revelation, which are not confined to Egypt. It sets a final limit to the propensity to extend and to change, beyond which only the primeval god, who links the nonexistent and the existent, can go; he alone alternates, in a way one might describe as "amphibious," between the two spheres.

In their constantly changing nature and manifestations, the Egyptian gods resemble the country's temples, which were never finished and complete, but always "under construction." The axial form of temples in Egypt is clearly ordered and articulated, and yet never excludes the possibility of continual extension and alteration; every king can add new cult chambers, halls, courtyards, and pylons without affecting the underlying form of the temple. In this Egypt differs markedly from Greece, where both the temples and the gods are relatively finished and complete. However much information we assemble about Egyptian gods, and however receptive we become to their reality, we will never be able to see them as the clear figures that Walter F. Otto perceived in the gods of Greece.

The gods of Egypt cannot be characterized aptly as "the vital essence of a form of existence that recurs in the most diverse circumstances."[3] They are formulas rather than forms, and in their world one is sometimes as if displaced into the world of elementary particles. In his edition of Papyrus Salt 825 Philippe Derchain used similes derived from physics, explicitly disregarding the "moral aspect" of the gods and analyzing them dispassionately.[4] And what striking conceptual parallels there are between the smallest and the greatest! A god is combined with another and becomes a new being with new characteristics, and then at the next moment separates into a number of entities. What he is remains hidden, but his luminous trail can be seen, his reaction with others is clear, and his actions can be felt. He is material and spiritual, a force and a figure, he is manifest in changing forms that should be mutually exclusive,

---

[3]W. F. Otto, *Die Götter Griechenlands* 123 = *The Homeric Gods* 122; retranslated here.
[4]*Le papyrus Salt 825* esp. pp. 11–12.

but we know that within all this something exists and exercises power. The Egyptians were always aware of this formulalike character, as is shown especially by syncretistic combinations of gods, in which names and forms are not the decisive factor, but what they stand for, what they bear witness to. Hence the Egyptians' willingness to adopt new gods, to recognize their own gods in foreign ones who appear in quite different forms, and to "translate" the names of Asiatic or Greek deities into their own language.

For the Greeks as for the Egyptians, every god is a world of his own which is revealed in a specific figure. But the Greeks emphasize more the figure that is revealed, the Egyptians the formula that it communicates, which describes the content of the "world" in question. Normal language is not adequate for this description; a higher, formalized language is needed, which I am inclined to call a "metalanguage," although not in the strict sense of a language in which another language (the object language) is discussed. Here again, my concern is with the formulalike character of deities and with the initially astonishing fact that in Egypt their iconography seems to be so little fixed and varies so very widely. Evidently a single image is not adequate for the metalanguage, which depends on continually changing combinations of many signs.

The outward form of these signs is not decisive. The Egyptians are not concerned to give them as pleasing a form as possible, but to show what they wish to express. The "mixed form," which aroused such antipathy in antiquity and more recently, is only one of many possible combinations; it is not the god, but it makes a statement about him. We may feel that the mixture of the animal and the human is grotesque, but we should recall the saying of Christian Morgenstern: "The material manifestation of God is necessarily grotesque."[5] In this matter the Egyptians were aesthetes enough not to overstep the limit and produce monstrosities.

The image of a god was quite certainly more than a formula

[5]*Stufen. Eine Entwickelung in Aphorismen und Tagebuchnotizen* (Munich: Piper 1927) 256.

to the Egyptians; it had a separate reality and was worthy of respect and worship, for the god's reality was present in it. But the formulalike character which I am speaking of applies also to the many images used in the language to describe the divine. Without discussing in detail myth and its many associated problems, I have made use many times of the images in which the Egyptians speak about their gods. These images cannot be transposed into formulaic definitions in words or into mathematical or physical formulas; they have their own formulalike character and serve to express a content that can perhaps be appropriately expressed only in this way.

I maintain, in opposition to the widespread prejudice against metaphorical and representational images in modern scientific research, that images are among the legitimate systems of signs with which we are provided in order to describe the world. The language in which we speak of the world will never be contained entirely in mathematical formulas, nor will it be contained entirely in words. So long as there is content that cannot be expressed in a univalent form, at every stage of consciousness language will turn to images as an adequate descriptive medium.

The nature and appearance of Egyptian gods are inimical to any closed, final, or univalent definition. We see them develop in history, and we see them leading a constantly changing life of their own. What a god is cannot be *defined*. Whatever statement we make about him, it does not exclude a mass of other statements. Seen in another way, every god contains within himself all the information about a particular content, which took form in him and entered human consciousness in that form. For the Egyptians the gods are powers that explain the world but do not themselves need any elucidation because they convey information in a language which can be understood directly—that of myth. Every myth exhibits and interprets no more than a part of reality, but the totality of the gods and their relationships with one another exhibits and interprets the entire reality of the world.

Whatever the nature of the gods may or may not be, in whatever system of concepts or network of associations we may place them, all attempts to "explain" them have been attempts to express the information they convey in a different, less ambiguous language. We sense that they say something valid about the world and about mankind. But no language has been found whose expressive richness can compare with that of the gods themselves. Again and again they refer us back to themselves, revealing to us the limitations of our conceptual universe. If we are to comprehend the world we still need the gods.

∿ Chronological Table

Early dynastic period (First–Second Dynasty)	c. 2900–2628 B.C.
Old Kingdom (Third–Eighth Dynasty) Instruction texts from 2600 Pyramid Texts from 2350	c. 2628–2134
First intermediate period (Ninth–Eleventh Dynasty) Coffin Texts from 2100	c. 2134–2040
Middle Kingdom (Eleventh–Fourteenth Dynasty)	c. 2040–1650
Second intermediate period (Hyksos)	c. 1650–1551
New Kingdom (Seventeenth–Twentieth Dynasty) Eighteenth Dynasty (Book of the Dead, Amduat, Litany of Re, Book of Gates) Ramessid period (Nineteenth–Twentieth Dynasty)	1551–1070 1527–1306 1306–1070
Third intermediate period (Twenty-first–Twenty-fifth Dynasty)	1070–664
Late period (Twenty-sixth–Thirty-first Dynasty)	664–332
Macedonian period	332–304
Ptolemaic period	304–30 B.C.
Roman period	30 B.C.–A.D. 395

↘ Abbreviations and Bibliography

All series abbreviations and abbreviated titles of books used in the text and in the Glossary of Gods are listed here. Details of primary publications of Egyptian texts are followed, where possible, by brief references to translations into English or German. In addition to the works cited frequently, *ANET*, which is widely available, contains translations of many important Egyptian texts.

AÄA   *Archiv für ägyptische Archäologie* (Vienna 1938)

ADIK   Abhandlungen des Deutschen Archäologischen Instituts, Abteilung Kairo (Glückstadt etc. 1958–)

ÄgAbh   Ägyptologische Abhandlungen (Wiesbaden 1960–)

ÄgFo   Ägyptologische Forschungen (Glückstadt etc. 1936–)

AH   Aegyptiaca Helvetica (Geneva 1974–)

AHAW   Abhandlungen der Heidelberger Akademie der Wissenschaften, Philosophisch-historische Klasse

Allen, *Book of the Dead*   T. G. Allen, *The Book of the Dead or Going Forth by Day* (The Oriental Institute of the University of Chicago, Studies in Ancient Oriental Civilization 37, Chicago 1974)

AMAW   Akademie der Wissenschaften und der Literatur [Mainz], Abhandlungen der Geistes- und Sozialwissenschaftlichen Klasse (Wiesbaden 1950–)

Amduat   E. Hornung, *Das Amduat. Die Schrift des verborgenen Raumes* (3 vols., ÄgAbh 7, 13, 1963–67). Other translations: Hornung, *Unterweltsbücher* 59–194; English: Piankoff, *Ramesses VI* 227–318

Amélineau, *Prolégomènes*   E. Amélineau, *Prolégomènes à l'étude de la religion égyptienne* (2 vols., Bibliothèque de l'Ecole des hautes études, Sciences religieuses 21, 30, Paris 1908–16)

ANET   J. B. Pritchard, ed., *Ancient Near Eastern Texts Relating to the Old Testament* (3d ed., Princeton 1969)

AnOr   Analecta Orientalia (Rome 1931–)

APAW   (Königlich) Preussische Akademie der Wissenschaften, Abhandlungen der Philosophisch-historischen Klasse (Berlin)

262

Abbreviations and Bibliography

ArOr   Archiv Orientální (Prague 1929–)
ASAE   Annales du Service des Antiquités de l'Egypte (Cairo 1900–)
ASAW   Abhandlungen der Sächsischen Akademie der Wissenschaften, Philologisch-historische Klasse (Leipzig)
ASE   Archaeological Survey of Egypt (Egypt Exploration Fund [later Society], London 1893–)
Assmann, ÄHG   J. Assmann, Ägyptische Hymnen und Gebete (BAW, 1975)
Assmann, Liturg. Lieder   J. Assmann, Liturgische Lieder an den Sonnengott. Untersuchungen zur altägyptischen Hymnik I (MÄS 19, 1969)
Baines, Fecundity Figures   J. Baines, Fecundity Figures: Egyptian Personification and the Iconology of a Genre (Warminster, in the press)
BASOR   Bulletin of the American Schools of Oriental Research (New Haven 1920–)
BAW   Die Bibliothek der Alten Welt (Zürich and Stuttgart)
Beiträge Bf   Beiträge zur ägyptischen Bauforschung und Altertumskunde (Cairo 1937–)
Bergman, Ich bin Isis   J. Bergman, Ich bin Isis. Studien zum memphitischen Hintergrund der griechischen Isisaretalogien (Acta Universitatis Upsaliensis, Historia Religionum 3, Uppsala 1968)
BiAe   Bibliotheca Aegyptiaca (Brussels 1932–)
BIE   Bulletin de l'Institut d'Egypte (Cairo 1919–)
BIFAO   Bulletin de l'Institut français d'archéologie orientale (Cairo 1901–)
BiOr   Bibliotheca Orientalis (Leiden 1943–)
Blumenthal, Untersuchungen   E. Blumenthal, Untersuchungen zum ägyptischen Königtum des Mittleren Reiches I (ASAW 61, 1, 1970)
Bonnet, Reallexikon   H. Bonnet, Reallexikon der ägyptischen Religionsgeschichte (Berlin 1952)
Book of the Dead   see Naville, Todtenbuch; Allen, Book of the Dead; Hornung, Totenbuch
Book of Gates   see BPf
BPf   E. Hornung et al., Das Buch von den Pforten des Jenseits I (ÄH 7, 1979). Translations: Hornung, Unterweltsbücher 197–308; English: Piankoff, Ramesses VI 137–224. The divisions of the text used by Hornung and Piankoff are different
Breasted, Development   J. H. Breasted, The Development of Religion and Thought in Ancient Egypt (New York 1912)
BSAE   Egyptian Research Account 1896–1905, British School of Archaeology in Egypt (London 1906–53); cited by "xth year"
BSFE   Bulletin de la Société française d'égyptologie (Paris 1949–)
Budge, Gods   E. A. W. Budge, The Gods of the Egyptians or Studies in Egyptian Mythology (2 vols., London 1904)
CdE   Chronique d'Egypte (Brussels 1926–). The citations give both volume number and issue number
CGC   Service des Antiquités de l'Egypte, Catalogue général des antiquités égyptiennes du Musée du Caire (Cairo and other places 1901–)
CHE   Cahiers d'histoire égyptienne (Cairo 1948–)
Coffin Texts   see CT
CRAIBL   Comptes rendus à l'Académie des inscriptions et belles-lettres (Paris)

263

Abbreviations and Bibliography

CT   A. de Buck, *The Egyptian Coffin Texts* (7 vols., OIP 1935–61). Translation:
R. O. Faulkner, *The Ancient Egyptian Coffin Texts* (3 vols., Warminster 1973–78)

Dendara   E. Chassinat, *Le temple de Dendara* I– (Publications de l'IFAO, Cairo 1934–); from vol. VI: E. Chassinat and F. Daumas

Derchain, *Le papyrus Salt 825*   P. Derchain, *Le papyrus Salt 825 (B.M. 10051), rituel pour la conservation de la vie en Egypte* (Académie royale de Belgique, Classe des lettres, Mémoires, octavo, 2d series 58, Brussels 1965)

DÖAW   Österreichische Akademie der Wissenschaften, Philosophisch-historische Klasse, Denkschriften (Vienna)

DVSM   Det Kgl. Danske Vidernskabernes Selskab, historisk-filologisk Meddelelser (Copenhagen)

Edfou   E. Chassinat, *Le temple d'Edfou* (14 vols., Mémoires de la Mission archéologique française au Caire, Paris 1892–97, Cairo 1918–); vol. I with M. de Rochemonteix

Edwards, *Decrees*   I. E. S. Edwards, *Oracular Amuletic Decrees of the Late New Kingdom* (2 vols., Hieratic Papyri in the British Museum 4th series, London 1960)

Erman, *Religion*   A. Erman, *Die ägyptische Religion* (1st and 2d eds., Handbücher der königlichen Museen zu Berlin, Berlin 1905, 1909; 3d ed.: *Die Religion der Ägypter. Ihr Werden und ihr Vergehen in vier Jahrtausenden*, Berlin and Leipzig 1934)

ERT   Egyptian Religious Texts and Representations (Bollingen Series 40, New York 1954–74)

FIFAO   Fouilles de l'Institut français d'archéologie orientale (Cairo 1924–)

Fragen   J. Assmann et al., eds., *Fragen an die altägyptische Literatur. Studien zum Gedenken an Eberhard Otto* (Wiesbaden 1977)

Frankfort, *Religion*   H. Frankfort, *Ancient Egyptian Religion* (New York 1948)

FuF   *Forschungen und Fortschritte* (Berlin 1925–67)

Gardiner, *Chester Beatty*   A. H. Gardiner, *Chester Beatty Gift* (2 vols., Hieratic Papyri in the British Museum 3d series, London 1935)

Gardiner, *Onomastica*   A. H. Gardiner, *Ancient Egyptian Onomastica* (3 vols., [London] 1947)

GOF   Göttinger Orientforschungen, 4th series, Ägypten (Wiesbaden 1973–)

Grébaut, *Hymne*   E. Grébaut, *Hymne à Ammon-Ra des papyrus égyptiens du Musée de Boulaq* (Bibliothèque de l'Ecole des hautes études, Sciences philologiques et historiques 21, Paris 1874/1875 [title pages carry both dates]). Translations: Assmann, *ÄHG* no. 87; English: *ANET* 365–67

HÄB   Hildesheimer Ägyptologische Beiträge (Hildesheim 1976–)

Hari, *Horemheb*   R. Hari, *Horemheb et la reine Moutnedjemet ou la fin d'une dynastie* (Geneva 1965)

Hornung, *Buch der Anbetung*   E. Hornung, *Das Buch der Anbetung des Re im Western (Sonnenlitanei)* (2 vols., AH 2–3, 1975–76). English translation: Piankoff, *Litany*

Hornung, *Höllenvorstellungen*   E. Hornung, *Altägyptische Höllenvorstellungen* (ASAW 59, 3, 1968)

Hornung, "Mensch als Bild Gottes"   E. Hornung, "Der Mensch als 'Bild Gottes' in Ägypten," in O. Loretz, *Die Gottebenbildlichkeit des Menschen*

Abbreviations and Bibliography

(Schriften des deutschen Instituts für wissenschaftliche Pädagogik, Munich 1967) 123–56

Hornung, *Totenbuch*   E. Hornung, *Das Totenbuch der Ägypter* (BAW, 1979)

Hornung, *Unterweltsbücher*   E. Hornung, *Ägyptische Unterweltsbücher* (BAW, 1972)

IFAO   Institut français d'archéologie orientale, Cairo; monograph series:

BE   Bibliothèque d'étude (1908–)

DF   Documents de fouilles (1934–)

RAPH   Recherches d'archéologie, de philologie et d'histoire (1930–)

JARCE   *Journal of the American Research Center in Egypt* (n.p. 1962–)

JEA   *Journal of Egyptian Archaeology* (London 1914–)

JEOL   *Jaarbericht van het Vooraziatisch-Egyptisch Genootschap Ex Oriente Lux* (Leiden 1933–)

Jéquier, *Considérations*   G. Jéquier, *Considérations sur les religions égyptiennes* (Neuchâtel 1946)

JNES   *Journal of Near Eastern Studies* (Chicago 1942–)

Junker, *Geisteshaltung*   H. Junker, *Die Geisteshaltung der Ägypter in der Frühzeit* (Österreichische Akademie der Wissenschaften, Philosophisch-historische Klasse, Sitzungsberichte 237, 1, Graz etc. 1961)

Junker, *Gîza*   H. Junker, *Gîza* (12 vols., Akademie der Wissenschaften in Wien, Philosophisch-historische Klasse, Denkschriften, Vienna 1929–55)

Junker, *Götterlehre*   H. Junker, *Die Götterlehre von Memphis (Schabaka-Inschrift)* (APAW 1939, 23, 1940)

Junker, *Der grosse Pylon*   H. Junker, *Der grosse Pylon des Tempels der Isis in Philä* (DÖAW, Sonderband 1958)

Junker-Winter, *Geburtshaus*   H. Junker and E. Winter, *Das Geburtshaus des Tempels der Isis in Philä* (Philä-Publikation 2, DÖAW, Sonderband 1965)

Kaplony, *Inschriften*   P. Kaplony, *Die Inschriften der ägyptischen Frühzeit* (3 vols., ÄgAbh 8, 1963; *Supplement* ÄgAbh 9, 1964)

Kees, *Götterglaube*   H. Kees, *Der Götterglaube im alten Ägypten* (Mitteilungen der vorderasiatisch-ägyptischen Gesellschaft 45, Leipzig 1941; 2d ed. Berlin 1956)

KRI   K. A. Kitchen, *Ramesside Inscriptions, Historical and Biographical* (Oxford 1968–)

Lange, *Amenemope*   H. O. Lange, *Das Weisheitsbuch des Amenemope* (DVSM 11, 2, 1925). Translations: Simpson, *Literature* 241–65; Lichtheim, *Literature* II, 146–63

LD   C. R. Lepsius, *Denkmaeler aus Aegypten und Aethiopien* (6 Abtheilungen in 12 vols., cited by Abtheilung, Berlin n.d. [1849–59])

Le Page Renouf, *Lectures*   P. le Page Renouf, *Lectures on the Origin and Growth of Religion as Illustrated by the Religion of Ancient Egypt* (The Hibbert Lectures 1879, London 1880, 4th ed. 1897)

Lepsius, *Götterkreis*   R. Lepsius, *Über den ersten ägyptischen Götterkreis und seine geschichtlich-mythologische Entstehung* (APAW 1851, 4 [1852]). Page references to academy volume and to separate printing are given

Lichtheim, *Literature*   M. Lichtheim, *Ancient Egyptian Literature: A Book of Readings* (3 vols., Berkeley etc. 1973–80)

Litany of Re   see Hornung, *Buch der Anbetung*; Piankoff, *Litany*

Abbreviations and Bibliography

MÄS   Münchner ägyptologische Studien (Berlin 1962–)

MDAIK   Mitteilungen des Deutschen Archäologischen Instituts, Abteilung Kairo (until 1944: *Mitteilungen des Deutschen Instituts für Ägyptische Altertumskunde in Kairo*) (Augsburg 1930–35, Berlin 1936–44, Wiesbaden 1956–69, Mainz 1970–)

MDOG   Mitteilungen der Deutschen Orient-Gesellschaft (Berlin 1899–)

Medinet Habu   The Epigraphic Survey, *Medinet Habu* (8 vols., OIP, 1930–70)

MEEF/S   Memoirs of the Egypt Exploration Fund (later Society) (London 1884–)

MES   A. M. Blackman, *Middle-Egyptian Stories* (BiAe 2, 1932). Contains Sinuhe and the Shipwrecked Sailor; translations: Simpson, *Literature* 50–74; Lichtheim, *Literature* I, 222–35, 211–15

MIFAO   Mémoires de l'Institut français d'archéologie orientale (Cairo 1902–)

MIO   Mitteilungen des Instituts für Orientforschung (Berlin 1953–72)

Morenz, *Gott und Mensch*   S. Morenz, *Gott und Mensch im alten Ägypten* (Leipzig 1964, Heidelberg 1965)

Morenz, *Heraufkunft*   S. Morenz, *Die Heraufkunft des transzendenten Gottes im alten Ägypten* (SBSAW 109, 2, 1964); reprinted in Morenz, *Religion und Geschichte* 77–119. Page references are to the two editions, in the order given here

Morenz, *Religion*   S. Morenz, *Ägyptische Religion* (Die Religionen der Menschheit 8, Stuttgart 1960) = *Egyptian Religion* (London and Ithaca, N.Y. 1973). Page references are to German and English editions, in that order

Morenz, *Religion und Geschichte*   S. Morenz, *Religion und Geschichte des alten Ägypten. Gesammelte Aufsätze*, ed. E. Blumenthal et al. (Weimar 1975)

Moret, *Rituel*   A. Moret, *Le rituel du culte divin journalier en Egypte* (Annales du Musée Guimet, Bibliothèque d'Etudes 14, Paris 1902)

Münster, *Isis*   M. Münster, *Untersuchungen zur Göttin Isis* (MÄS 11, 1968)

MVEOL   Mededeelingen en Verhandelingen van het Vooraziatisch Egyptisch Gezelschap "Ex Oriente Lux" (Leiden 1934–)

Naville, *Religion*   E. Naville, *La religion des anciens Egyptiens* (Annales du Musée Guimet, Bibliothèque de vulgarisation 23, Paris 1906) = *The Old Egyptian Faith* (Crown's Theological Library 30, London and New York 1909). Page references are to French and English editions, in that order

Naville, *Todtenbuch*   E. Naville, *Das aegyptische Todtenbuch der XVIII. bis XX. Dynastie* (3 vols., I–II and *Einleitung*, Berlin 1886). Translations: Allen, *Book of the Dead*; Hornung, *Totenbuch*

NAWG   Nachrichten (von) der Akademie der Wissenschaften in Göttingen, 1, Philologisch-historische Klasse (earlier: Nachrichten von der Gesellschaft der Wissenschaften zu Göttingen, Philologisch-Historische Klasse)

Neugebauer-Parker, *EAT*   O. Neugebauer and R. A. Parker, *Egyptian Astronomical Texts* (3 vols. in 4, Brown Egyptological Studies 3, 5–6, London and Providence, R.I. 1960–69)

OIP   The University of Chicago, Oriental Institute Publications (Chicago 1924–)

OLZ   Orientalistische Literaturzeitung (Berlin 1898–1908, Leipzig 1909–44, Berlin 1953–)

266

Abbreviations and Bibliography

OMRO   *Oudheidkundige Medede(e)lingen uit's* (later: *het*) *Rijksmuseum van Oudheden te Leiden* n.s. (Leiden 1920–)

Or   *Orientalia* n.s. (Rome 1932–)

OrAnt   *Oriens Antiquus* (Rome 1962–)

Otto, *Gott und Mensch*   E. Otto, *Gott und Mensch nach den ägyptischen Tempelinschriften der griechisch-römischen Zeit* (AHAW 1964, 1)

Otto, *Osiris und Amun*   E. Otto, *Osiris und Amun. Kult und heilige Stätten* (Munich 1966) = *Egyptian Art and the Cults of Osiris and Amon* (London 1968). Page references are to German and English editions, in that order

PÄ   Probleme der Ägyptologie (Leiden 1953–77)

Piankoff, *Litany*   A. Piankoff, *The Litany of Re* (ERT 4, 1964)

Piankoff, *Ramesses VI*   A. Piankoff, *The Tomb of Ramesses VI* (2 vols., ERT 1, 1954)

PSBA   *Proceedings of the Society of Biblical Archaeology* (London 1879–1918)

Pyr.   K. Sethe, *Die altägyptischen Pyramidentexte* (4 vols., Leipzig 1908–22); cited by §. Translations: *id.*, *Übersetzung und Kommentar zu den altägyptischen Pyramidentexten* (incomplete, 6 vols., Glückstadt n.d.); R. O. Faulkner, *The Ancient Egyptian Pyramid Texts* (Oxford 1969)

Pyramid Texts   see *Pyr.*

RdE   *Revue d'égyptologie* (Paris 1933, Cairo 1936–51, Paris 1950–)

Rec. trav.   *Recueil de travaux rélatifs à la philologie et à l'archéologie égyptiennes et assyriennes* (Paris 1870–1923)

RHR   *Revue de l'histoire des religions* (Paris 1880–)

Les sagesses   *Les sagesses du Proche-Orient ancien, Colloque de Strasbourg 17–19 mai 1962* (Bibliothèque des Centres d'études supérieures spécialisés, Travaux du Centre . . . histoire des religions de Strasbourg, Paris 1963)

SAK   *Studien zur altägyptischen Kultur* (Hamburg 1974–)

Sandman, *Texts*   M. Sandman, *Texts from the Time of Akhenaten* (BiAe 8, 1938)

SBBAW   Sitzungsberichte der Bayerischen Akademie der Wissenschaften, Philosophisch-historische Klasse (Munich)

SBSAW   Sitzungsberichte (until 1962: Berichte über die Verhandlungen) der Sächsischen Akademie der Wissenschaften zu Leipzig, Philologisch-historische Klasse

Sethe, *Amun*   K. Sethe, *Amun und die acht Urgötter von Hermopolis* (APAW 1929, 4)

Sethe, *Urgeschichte*   K. Sethe, *Urgeschichte und älteste Religion der Ägypter* (Abhandlungen für die Kunde des Morgenlandes 18, 4, Leipzig 1930)

Shipwrecked Sailor   see *MES*

SHR   Studies in the History of Religions (Supplements to *Numen*) (Leiden 1954–)

Simpson, *Literature*   W. K. Simpson, ed., *The Literature of Ancient Egypt* (New Haven and London 1972; 2d ed. 1973; later reprints with alterations)

Sinuhe   see *MES*

StG   *Studium Generale* (Berlin etc. 1948–)

Te Velde, *Seth*   H. te Velde, *Seth, God of Confusion* (PÄ 6, 1967; 2d ed. 1977)

ThLZ   *Theologische Literaturzeitung* (Leipzig 1876–)

Abbreviations and Bibliography

UGAÄ   Untersuchungen zur Geschichte und Altertumskunde Ägyptens (Leipzig 1896–1945, Berlin 1952–56)

Urk.   *Urkunden des ägyptischen Altertums* (Leipzig 1903–39, Berlin 1955–61)

Van der Leeuw, *Godsvoorstellingen*   G. van der Leeuw, *Godsvoorstellingen in de oud-aegyptische pyramidetexten* (Leiden 1916)

Vandier, *Manuel*   J. Vandier, *Manuel d'archéologie égyptienne* (6 vols. in 9, Paris 1952–78)

Vergote, "La notion de Dieu"   J. Vergote, "La notion de Dieu dans les livres de sagesse égyptiens," in *Les sagesses* 153–90

Volten, *Anii*   A. Volten, *Studien zum Weisheitsbuch des Anii* (DVSM 23, 3, 1937). Translation: Lichtheim, *Literature* II, 135–46

Volten, *Politische Schriften*   A. Volten, *Zwei altägyptische politische Schriften* (Analecta Aegyptiaca 4, Copenhagen 1945). Translations of the Instruction for Merikare: Lichtheim, *Literature* I, 97–109; Simpson, *Literature* 180–92

Von Strauss und Torney, *Götterglaube*   V. von Strauss und Torney, *Der altägyptische Götterglaube* (2 vols., Heidelberg 1889–91)

Wb.   A. Erman and H. Grapow, *Wörterbuch der ägyptischen Sprache* (7 vols. in 12, Leipzig 1926–40, Berlin 1950–63)

WdO   *Die Welt des Orients* (Göttingen 1947–)

Wiedemann, *Religion*   A. Wiedemann, *Die Religion der alten Ägypter* (Darstellungen aus dem Gebiete der nichtchristlichen Religionsgeschichte 3, Münster 1890) = *Religion of the Ancient Egyptians* (London 1897). Page references are to German and English editions, in that order

Winter, *Untersuchungen*   E. Winter, *Untersuchungen zu den ägyptischen Tempelinschriften der griechisch-römischen Zeit* (DÖAW 98, 1968)

WZKM   *Wiener Zeitschrift für die Kunde des Morgenlands* (Vienna 1886–)

Žabkar, *Ba Concept*   L. V. Žabkar, *A Study of the Ba Concept in Ancient Egyptian Texts* (The Oriental Institute of the University of Chicago, Studies in Ancient Oriental Civilization 34, Chicago 1968)

Zandee, *De hymnen aan Amon*   J. Zandee, *De hymnen aan Amon van Papyrus Leiden I 350* = OMRO 28 (1947). Translation of parts: Assmann, *ÄHG* nos. 132–42, 194

ZÄS   *Zeitschrift für ägyptische Sprache und Altert(h)umskunde* (Leipzig 1863–1943, Berlin and Leipzig 1956–)

ZAW   *Zeitschrift für die alttestamentliche Wissenschaft* (Giessen 1881–1933, Berlin 1933–)

ZDMG   *Zeitschrift der Deutschen Morgenländischen Gesellschaft* (Leipzig 1846–1944, Wiesbaden 1950–)

∿ Sources for Figures

1. The hieroglyph for "god," "staff bound with cloth."
Original sources: (a) P. E. Newberry (see citation below) states the source to be M. A. Murray, *Saqqara Mastabas* I (Egyptian Research Account, tenth year 1904, London 1905) pl. 1 (Third Dyn.), but this precise form does not occur there. The source may be pl. 8 or pl. 20 (both Fifth Dyn., the date Newberry gives), where very similar but not identical forms occur; (b) Ivory label from the tomb of King Aha at Abydos (First Dyn.), W. M. F. Petrie, *The Royal Tombs of the Earliest Dynasties, 1901* II (MEEF 21, 1901) pl. 3A no. 5; (c) Pottery mark of the First Dynasty, Petrie, *Royal Tombs* pl. 55A no. 151.
Drawing by A. Brodbeck after P. E. Newberry, *JEA* 33 (1947) 90 fig. 3d (a here); fig. 4 (b here); fig. 2 (c here).

2. Other hieroglyphs for "god."
Mastaba of Ptahhotpe at Saqqara (Fifth Dyn.).
Drawing by A. Brodbeck after N. de G. Davies, *The Mastaba of Ptahhetep and Akhethetep at Saqqarah* I (ASE ˙8, 1900) pl. 7 no. 87 (a here [part only]); pl. 4 no. 11 (b here).

3. Gardiner hieroglyphic sign list, category C.
Reproduced from A. H. Gardiner, *Egyptian Grammar* (3d ed., London 1957) 544 (after models of various periods).

4. Shu separates the sky and the earth (shown in the form of Geb and Nut).
"Mythological" mortuary papyrus of Tentamun, Paris, Bibliothèque Nationale no. 172 (Twenty-first Dyn.).
Reproduced from S. Morenz, *Gott und Mensch im alten Ägypten* (Heidelberg 1965) 131 fig. 40, who reproduces from H. Schäfer, *Ägyptische und heutige Kunst und Weltgebäude der alten Ägypter* (Berlin and Leipzig 1928) 105 fig. 29, who redraws from R. V. Lanzone, *Dizionario di mitologia egizia* (Turin 1881–86) pl. 155 upper = vol. I p. 401, who gives a wrong source reference. The scene is published in a photograph by A. Piankoff, *Egyptian Religion* 4, 1 (1936) 63 fig. 4.

Sources for Figures

5. The goddess Maat.
Drawing by A. Brodbeck after a hieroglyph, N. de G. Davies, *Mastaba of Ptahhetep I* (fig. 2 above) pl. 4 no. 13 (Fifth Dyn.).

6. Fecundity figures.
North side of subsidiary entrance to mortuary temple of King Sahure, now Cairo Museum JE 39534 (Fifth Dyn.).
Reproduced from W. S. Smith, *A History of Egyptian Sculpture and Painting in the Old Kingdom* (London 1946) 183 fig. 71. Original source: L. Borchardt et al., *Das Grabdenkmal des Königs Saȝḥu-Reʿ* II (Ausgrabungen der Deutschen Orient-Gesellschaft in Abusir 1902–1908 7, Leipzig 1913) pl. 30. The figures are the first, third, and fifth in a set of six.

7. Isis and Osiris.
Mortuary papyrus of Nestanebetishru (Pap. Greenfield), British Museum 10554 (Twenty-first Dyn.).
Reproduced from G. Roeder, *Die ägyptische Götterwelt* (Die ägyptische Religion in Texten und Bildern I, BAW 1959) 130 fig. 16. Published in photograph by E. A. W. Budge, *The Greenfield Papyrus in the British Museum* (London 1912) pl. 89.

8. The "Battlefield" palette, recto.
British Museum 20791 (lower); Oxford, Ashmolean Museum 1171–1892 (upper) (late predynastic).
Reproduced from W. S. Smith, *History of Egyptian Sculpture* (fig. 6 above) 112 fig. 27.

9. The Narmer palette, verso.
Cairo Museum CG 14716 (late predynastic).
Reproduced from J. E. Quibell, "Slate Palette from Hieraconpolis," *ZÄS* 36 (1898) pl. 13.

10. Figures of gods on early dynastic objects.
Late Second Dynasty jar sealings and a figure incised on an early dynastic jar (no. 6).
Reproduced from W. S. Smith, *History of Egyptian Sculpture* (fig. 6 above) 122 fig. 40. Smith reproduces from (figures numbered from left to right) Petrie, *Royal Tombs II* (fig. 1 above): (1) pl. 22 no. 178–79, (2, 3) pl. 21 no. 176, (4) pl. 23 no. 192, (5) pl. 23 no. 199; W. M. F. Petrie et al., *Tarkhan I and Memphis V* (BSAE nineteenth year, 1913) pl. 3, 1.

11. Hathor pillar.
Small temple at Abu Simbel, pillared hall (reign of Ramesses II, 1290–1224 B.C.).
Reproduced from G. Jéquier, *Manuel d'archéologie égyptienne. Les éléments de l'architecture* (Paris 1924) 189 fig. 114, who reproduces from LD 3, 192c. Full

270

publication C. Desroches Noblecourt and C. Kuentz, *Le petit temple d'Abou Simbel* (Cairo 1968) pls. 28–29, 59–65.

12. Figures of gods in the Litany of Re.
Painting in the tomb of Tuthmosis III (1490–1436 B.C.) in the Valley of the Kings.
Reproduced from Piankoff, *Litany* 15 fig. B (bottom three registers, reconstructed order). Piankoff reproduces and rearranges from P. Bucher, *Les textes des tombes de Thoutmosis III et Aménophis II* I (MIFAO 60, 1932) pl. 26, 25. Now also reproduced in Hornung, *Buch der Anbetung* II, 57.

13. "Soul" birds.
Figures in the Book of Gates in the tomb of Ramesses VI (1142–1135 B.C.) in the Valley of the Kings.
Reproduced from Piankoff, *Ramesses VI* 192 fig. 55.

14. The cult statue of a god in procession.
Bark of Amun, relief on the shrine of Philip Arrhidaeus (323–316 B.C.) at Karnak, south exterior wall, middle register, second scene from left.
Reproduced from A. Piankoff and N. Rambova, *Mythological Papyri* (ERT 3, 1957) 18 fig. 1.

15. Horus in a marsh thicket.
Relief of the reign of Ptolemy VIII Euergetes II (145–116 B.C.) in the birth house of the temple of Isis at Philae, sanctuary, north wall.
Reproduced from G. Roeder, *Mythen und Legenden um ägyptische Gottheiten und Pharaonen* (Die ägyptische Religion in Texten und Bildern II, BAW 1960) 158 fig. 32, which is probably reproduced from LD 4, 36b. Now published in Junker-Winter, *Geburtshaus* 18.

16. The sun god as a child on the primeval lotus.
Relief in the birth house of the temple of Mont and Raettawy at Armant, inner hall, architrave in west hall (now destroyed; reign of Ptolemy XV Caesarion, 44–30 B.C.).
Reproduced from H. Bonnet in H. Haas, ed., *Bilderatlas zur Religionsgeschichte* fasc. 2–4 "Ägyptische Religion" (Leipzig and Erlangen 1924) fig. 8, who reproduces from LD 4, 61g.

17. Apopis, bound.
Figure in the Book of Gates in the tomb of Ramesses VI (1142–1135 B.C.) in the Valley of the Kings.
Reproduced from Piankoff, *Ramesses VI* 218 fig. 71.

18. The sun god as a child within the Ouroboros.
"Mythological" mortuary papyrus of Hirweben A, Cairo Museum "no. 133" (Twenty-first Dyn.).

Reproduced from Piankoff and Rambova, *Mythological Papyri* (fig. 14 above), 22 fig. 3. Photograph *ibid.* no. 1.

19. King Ramesses II (1290–1224 B.C.) offers Maat to Ptah.
Relief on the south enclosure wall of the central area of the temple of Karnak. Reproduced from Bonnet, in *Bilderatlas* (fig. 16 above), fig. 90, who reproduces from LD 3, 147b. Photograph: W. Helck, *Die Ritualszenen auf der Umfassungsmauer Ramses' II. in Karnak* plate vol. (ÄgAbh 18, 1968) 27 Bild 36.

20. The sun disk with rays shining over Akhenaten (1364–1347 B.C.) and the temple.
Relief in the tomb of Meryre I at el-Amarna.
Reproduced from N. de. G. Davies, *The Rock Tombs of El Amarna* I (ASE 13, 1903) pl. 27.

✎ Sources for Plates

I. Re and Osiris united, between Isis and Nephthys.
Tomb of Nofretiri in the Valley of the Queens (reign of Ramesses II, 1290–1224). Photo A. Brack. Reproduced in color in G. Thausing and H. Goedicke, *Nofretari* (Monumenta Scriptorum, Graz 1971) pl. 41.

II. The king before Hathor.
Tomb of Tuthmosis IV (1412–1402 B.C.) in the Valley of the Kings. Photo A. Brack.

III. Mehetweret with the head of a cow.
Pillar in the tomb of Tawosret (1188–1186 B.C.) in the Valley of the Kings. Photo A. Brack.

IV. The god Khepry.
Tomb of Nofretiri in the Valley of the Queens (reign of Ramesses II, 1290–1224 B.C.). Photo U. Schweitzer. Reproduced in color in Thausing-Goedicke, *Nofretari* (Pl. I above) pls. 24, 31, 131.

V. Figure of a god in the Amduat.
Tomb of Sethos I (1304–1290 B.C.) in the Valley of the Kings. Photo A. Brack.

∿ Glossary of Gods

In order to give nonspecialist readers some orientation among the mass of names of Egyptian gods, I have added a brief description after each name. These descriptions can only indicate a few salient aspects of the deity; they cannot supply an adequate characterization. For more detailed and more precise information the reader is referred to H. Bonnet, *Reallexikon der ägyptischen Religionsgeschichte* (Berlin 1952); W. Helck et al. eds., *Lexikon der Ägyptologie* (Wiesbaden 1972–); and to the bibliography given at the ends of entries. Only the most important syncretistic combinations are included.

All names of gods are in *italics*.

Aker, ancient personification of the earth and hence also of the underworld. Depicted as a strip of land with a human head; a form with a human head on either side is elaborated into a double lion or double sphinx. Acts as guard at the entrance to and exit from the underworld, and may be threatening or helpful to the deceased. Bibliography: C. de Wit, *Le rôle et le sens du lion dans l'Egypte ancienne* (Leiden 1951) 91–106.

Akhti, "He of the horizon," appellation of the sun god when he is manifest on the horizon (see also *Harakhte*).

Amaunet, "The hidden one" (fem.), female counterpart of *Amun*, with a cult of her own. Bibliography: see *Amun*.

Amon-Re

Amun, "The hidden one." Shown with a tall crown of feathers; often also in the form of Min, as well as ram and goose forms. His cult is attested first in the Theban nome, but he is mentioned earlier as a primeval deity, and in later times he belongs to the system of the Hermopolitan ogdoad. From 2000 to 1360 B.C. he is preeminent among deities, and combines in a single figure all the characteristics of the creator and sustainer of the world. Bibliography: K. Sethe, *Amun und die acht Urgötter von Hermopolis* (APAW 1929, 4). E. Otto, *Osiris und Amun. Kult und heilige Stätten* (Munich 1966) = *Egyptian Art and the Cults of Osiris and Amon* (London 1968).

Anedjti, "He of Andjet" (in the ninth Lower Egyptian nome), was absorbed at an early date by Osiris, who may have taken over from him the ruler's attributes of crook and flail.

Anubis, "Puppy" (?), the god responsible for embalming, who is also lord of the necropolis. Depicted as a black canine ("jackal"), or in the mixed form, with a "dog's" head and human body.

Anukis, anthropomorphic goddess who wears a crown of feathers. From the New Kingdom on she is grouped with *Khnum* and *Satis* to form the divine triad of Elephantine. Her sacred animal is the gazelle. Bibliography: D. Valbelle, *Satis et Anoukis* (Mainz 1980).

Apis, bull worshiped in Memphis from the early dynastic period on, guarantor of the fertility of the land; later becomes a form or a "herald" of the god *Ptah*. The Apis bull has special markings on its hide and wears the sun disk between its horns (later reinterpreted as a lunar disk); occasionally depicted as a human being with a bull's head. Bibliography: E. Otto, *Beiträge zur Geschichte der Stierkulte in Ägypten* (UGAÄ 13, 1938). G. J. F. Kater-Sibbes and M. J. Vermaseren, *Apis* I (Etudes préliminaires aux religions orientales dans l'Empire romain 48, Leiden 1975).

Apopis, the snake enemy of the sun god, who must constantly be repulsed from the solar bark, and thus embodies the continual threat of disorder to the ordered world.

Ash, god of the western desert who is often called "lord of Libya." He can be shown in human form or with a hawk's head, and occasionally with the head of the *Seth* animal.

Aten, "Sun disk," not worshiped as a deity until the New Kingdom; raised by Akhenaten to the status of the unique, exclusive God. Depicted at first with a hawk's head, and then as a sun disk with rays that terminate in human hands.

Atum, "The undifferentiated one," at once primeval being and creator of the world. In mythology he is placed at the head of the ennead of Heliopolis; in later periods he is worshiped as the evening manifestation of the universal sun god. Usually represented in purely human form. Bibliography: K. Myśliwiec, *Studien zum Gott Atum* I–II (III forthcoming) (HÄB 5, 8, 1978–79).

Glossary of Gods

Bat, goddess of the seventh Upper Egyptian nome; her form with a cow's head relates her closely to *Hathor*. Bibliography: H. G. Fischer, "The Cult and Nome of the Goddess Bat," *JARCE* 1 (1962) 7–23; 2 (1963) 50–51.

Bes, general term for various dwarf gods with monstrous faces who often have a crown of feathers and a lion's mane. They are helping deities who repel evil, especially at the birth of a child. Bibliography: F. Ballod, *Prolegomena zur Geschichte der zwerghaften Götter in Ägypten* (Dissertation, Munich; Moscow 1913).

Creator god. The most varied deities can be the creator god, but the most important is the sun god; often the creator is anonymous.

Dedwen, Nubian god attested sporadically in Egyptian texts from the Pyramid Texts on.

Djebauti, "He of Djebaut," god worshiped at Buto in the form of a heron.

Geb, earth god of a more universal character than *Aker*; Geb is both judge and "hereditary prince" or "father" of the gods, especially of *Osiris*. Depicted in purely human form (see also *Nut*).

Grain god, in Egyptian *Nepri*, shown in human form, often as a child suckled by *Renenutet*.

Grḥ (*Gereh*), "Night" or perhaps "Cessation," forms a pair of primeval gods with his female doublet *Gerhet*; attested on a single monument of the late period.

Hapy, "Inundation" of the Nile, personification of the fecundity inherent in the Nile and hence depicted as an obese human figure. Bibliography: A. de Buck, "On the meaning of the name Ḥ'PJ," in *Orientalia Neerlandica* (Leiden 1948) 1–22. J. Baines, *Fecundity Figures* (Warminster, in the press).

Harakhte, "Horus of the horizon," the daytime form of the sun god, depicted as a hawk, or in human form with a hawk's head surmounted by a sun disk.

Harmachis, "Horus in the horizon," the name for the deified Great Sphinx of Giza.

Harpokrates, "Horus the child," manifestation of *Horus* as a threatened child who is saved from every danger; particularly popular in the late period.

Harpre, "Horus the sun (god)," name of the young *sun god* attested primarily in the Theban area in the late and Graeco-Roman periods; forms a triad with *Mont* and *Raettawy*.

Harsaphes, "He who is on his lake," creator god in ram form, whose chief place of worship is Herakleopolis. Bibliography: T. G. H. James, *The Ḥekanakhte*

276

Papers and Other Early Middle Kingdom Documents (Metropolitan Museum of Art, Egyptian Expedition, New York 1962) 122–24.

Harsiese, "Horus son of Isis," aspect of Horus as a son, sometimes contrasted with *Haroeris* "the elder Horus."

Hathor, "House of Horus," probably the most universal Egyptian goddess, who has marked characteristics of a mother, but, as the "eye of Re," also brings ruin to all enemies, and in addition is worshiped as a goddess of the dead, especially in Thebes. Usually shown as a woman with cow's horns and sun disk or as a cow, but also as a lioness, snake, tree nymph, and so forth. Bibliography: S. Allam, *Beiträge zum Hathorkult* (MÄS 4, 1963). C. J. Bleeker, *Hathor and Thoth* (SHR 26, Leiden 1973).

Hatmehit, "She who is before the fishes," goddess of the nome of Mendes in the delta, depicted as a fish or as a woman with the fish symbol on her head. Bibliography: I. Gamer-Wallert, *Fische und Fischkulte im alten Ägypten* (ÄgAbh 21, 1970) 98–101.

Heqet, goddess in frog form who has a helping function in childbirth and more generally; as a primeval deity she is often the consort of *Khnum*. Her most important cult places are in Middle Egypt.

Hike, "'Magic,'" anthropomorphic personification of this creative force, also revered in the cult from an early date, especially in the delta and at Esna; frequently accompanies the sun god. Bibliography: H. te Velde, "The God Heka in Egyptian Theology," *JEOL* 21 (1970) 175–86.

Horus, "The distant one" (?), ancient god of the sky and of the kingship who absorbed a whole set of gods with hawk form. His close links with the sun god and later with *Osiris* and *Isis* lead to many new associations, and his martial and youthful aspects become especially prominent.

Hu, personification of the "Utterance" with which the creator god calls things into being. With *Hike* and *Sia* he is one of the three creative forces that constantly accompany the sun god; not worshiped in the cult.

Huh, "Endlessness," forms, with his female doublet *Hauhet*, one of the four pairs of primeval gods of Hermopolis. Bibliography: K. Sethe, *Amun und die acht Urgötter von Hermopolis* (APAW 1929, 4).

Input, "Bitch" (?), female doublet of *Anubis*, the god of embalming, with a cult of her own in the seventeenth Upper Egyptian nome.

Ishtar of Niniveh

Isis, whose name is written with the sign for "throne," the sister and wife of *Osiris* and mother of *Horus*, whom she protects from many dangers in her

Glossary of Gods

role as the magician goddess. Usually shown as a woman with the sign for "throne" on her head, but also depicted, because of her multiple connections with other goddesses, in countless other forms, so that she becomes the "multiform one" par excellence. Bibliography: M. Münster, *Untersuchungen zur Göttin Isis* (MÄS 11, 1968). J. Bergman, *Ich bin Isis* (Acta Universitatis Upsaliensis, Historia Religionum 3, Uppsala 1968).

Iusaas, "She comes, being great," worshiped as a consort of *Atum* and represented as a woman with a scarab on her head. Bibliography: J. Vandier, "Iusâas et (Hathor)-Nébet-Hétépet," *RdE* 16 (1964) 55–146; 17 (1965) 89–176; 18 (1966) 67–142; 20 (1968) 135–48; also published as a volume.

Jrj (Iri) "Sight," worshiped from the New Kingdom on as one of the forces that help the creator god. Bibliography: E. Brunner-Traut, "Der Sehgott und der Hörgott in Literatur und Theologie," in *Fragen* 125–45.

Khatery, "Ichneumon," manifestation of *Horus* as a sun god. Bibliography: E. Brunner-Traut, *Spitzmaus und Ichneumon als Tiere des Sonnengottes* (NAWG 1965, 7).

Khededu, the god of fishing, attested from the Old Kingdom on.

Khefthernebes, "She who is opposite her lord (that is, Amun)," personification of the Theban necropolis, attested from the Eighteenth to the Twenty-first Dynasty. See also *Thebes*.

Khentamenti, "Foremost before the Westerners," ancient god of the dead (the "Westerners"), and lord of the necropolis of Abydos, in dog form. After the end of the Old Kingdom Khentamenti is no more than an epithet of *Osiris*, the universal god of the dead. Bibliography: E. Meyer, *ZÄS* 41 (1904) 97–107. J. Spiegel, *Die Götter von Abydos* (GOF 1, 1973).

Khepry, "He who is coming into being," the morning manifestation of the sun god; usually shown as a scarab, more rarely in human form with a scarab for a head.

Khnum, ram-headed god who was worshiped from the early dynastic period on, active chiefly in the cataract area around Elephantine. In the New Kingdom and later he was worshiped there in a triad with the goddesses *Satis* and *Anukis*. Bibliography: Ahmad Mohamad Badawi, *Der Gott Chnum* (Glückstadt etc. 1937).

Khons, "The wanderer," moon god shown in human form with the sign for the moon on his head. As the "child" of *Amun* and *Mut*, with whom he is grouped to form a triad, he also wears the sidelock symbolic of youth.

Kuk, "Darkness," forms with his female doublet *Kauket* one of the four pairs of primeval deities of Hermopolis. Bibliography: see *Huh*.

278

Maat, personification of the "Order" of the world which was established at creation; shown as a woman with a feather in her hair. She was considered to be the daughter of the creator god (*Re*), had a widespread cult, and is also found doubled as the "two *Maats*" from an early period. Bibliography: C. J. Bleeker, *De beteekenis van de egyptische godin Ma-a-t* (Leiden [1929]).

Mafdet, the "Runner" (fem.), violent goddess in panther form who is one of the protective powers in the king's suite. Bibliography: W. Westendorf, "Die Pantherkatze Mafdet," *ZDMG* 118 (1968) 248–56.

Mahes, "Raging lion," god in lion form who was worshiped chiefly in the delta. Bibliography: C. de Wit, *Le rôle et le sens du lion dans l'Egypte ancienne* (Leiden 1951) 230–34.

Mehetweret, Greek *Methyer*, perhaps "The great flood;" goddess of the primeval flood who is closely related to *Hathor*; depicted in cow form, or in the mixed form with a cow's head.

Meresger, "She loves silence," protective goddess of the Theban necropolis, depicted in the form of a snake; worshiped especially in the form of the mountain peak that dominates the necropolis. Bibliography: B. Bruyère, *Mert Seger à Deir el Médineh* (MIFAO 58, 1930).

Mestasytmis, personification of "The hearing ear," attested primarily in the Graeco-Roman period. Bibliography: G. Wagner and J. Quaegebeur, "Une dédicace grecque au dieu égyptien Mestasytmis de la part de son synode," *BIFAO* 73 (1973) 41–60.

Min, god worshiped in fetish form in predynastic times, and in the historical period as a man with erect penis. He is the lord of procreation and protector of tracks in the desert, while at the festival of Min the fertility of the land is renewed. His most important cult places are Akhmim and Koptos. Bibliography: C. J. Bleeker, *Die Geburt eines Gottes* (SHR 3, Leiden 1956).

Mnevis, attested from the New Kingdom on as the sacred bull of Heliopolis, who is a manifestation or "herald" of the sun god; he is occasionally shown red like the sun. Bibliography: E. Otto, *Beiträge zur Geschichte der Stierkulte in Ägypten* (UGÄA 13, 1938) 34–40. S. Morenz, "Rote Stiere, Unbeachtetes zu Buchis und Mnevis," in *Religion und Geschichte* 360–65.

Mont, "The wild one" (?), ancient principal god of the Theban area; in the New Kingdom worshiped primarily as a war god whose role the fighting king adopts. Mostly shown with a hawk's head, which is surmounted by the sun disk with uraeus, or double uraeus, and feathers.

Mut, "Mother," shown as a vulture or as a woman with the double crown; worshiped in Thebes as the consort of *Amun*. Through her close links with other goddesses Mut, who was at first an insignificant figure, acquired rather more universal characteristics.

279

Glossary of Gods

Nebethetepet, "Mistress of offering" (or possibly "Mistress of the vulva"), manifestation of *Hathor* who was worshiped chiefly at Heliopolis. Bibliography: see *Iusaas*.

Nefertem, god of the primeval lotus, shown as a human figure with a lotus on the head, or as a child sun god on the lotus. In Memphis he forms a triad with *Ptah* and *Sakhmet*.

Neith, "The terrifying one" (?, fem.), goddess whose attributes are weapons (arrows and shield) held in the hand or shown above the head. Primeval goddess (often androgynous) and protector of the king; chief cult centers are Sais and Esna. Bibliography: S. Schott, "Ein Kult der Göttin Neith," in E. Edel et al., *Das Sonnenheiligtum des Königs Userkaf* (Beitrage Bf 8, 1969) 123–38. Ramadan el-Sayed, *Documents relatifs à Sais et ses divinités* (IFAO BE 69, 1975).

Nekhbet, "She of Nekheb (el-Kab)," upper Egyptian goddess in vulture form who protects the king. Her most important cult place is el-Kab. Bibliography: M. Werbrouck, in *Fouilles de El Kab. Documents* II (Fondation égyptologique Reine Elisabeth, Brussels 1940) 46–60.

Nemty, "The wanderer" (formerly read Anty), hawk-form god of the twelfth Upper Egyptian nome. Bibliography: O. D. Berlev, "'Sokol, plyvušij v lad'e,' ieroglif i bog," *Vestnik drevnej istorii* 1 (107) (1969) 3–30. ["'Falcon in boat,' a hieroglyph and a god," with English summary.]

Nephthys, "Mistress of the house," anthropomorphic goddess who is seldom worshiped except in connection with her sister *Isis*.

Nepri, see Grain god.

Nun, personification of the primeval waters from which everything arose, and hence "father of the gods," out of which the sun comes daily anew. With his female doublet *Naunet* he forms the most important of the four pairs of primeval deities of Hermopolis. Bibliography: see *Huh*.

Nut, the ancient goddess of the sky, who is shown as a woman arching over the earth god *Geb*. She gives birth to and then swallows all the heavenly bodies, but also takes the deceased into her protection.

Onuris, "He who brings the distant (goddess)," an ancient god of hunting, worshiped as an anthropomorphic god with four feathers on his head. His domain is the desert at the edge of the world, and from this "distant" region he brings back the eye of the sun. Bibliography: H. Junker, *Die Onurislegende* (Kaiserliche Akademie der Wissenschaften, Phil.-hist. Klasse, Denkschriften 59, 1–2, Vienna 1917).

Glossary of Gods

Osiris, the god who suffered a violent death; depicted in human form without indication of limbs. His attributes of crook and flail allude to ancient links with the kingship and with pastoralism; other features provide analogies with the death and resurgence of nature. But the most important aspect of this most complex of gods is his role as ruler of the dead. At an early period Abydos becomes his most important cult center. Bibliography: E. Otto, *Osiris und Amun. Kult und heilige Stätten* (Munich 1966) = *Egyptian Art and the Cults of Osiris and Amun* (London 1968). J. G. Griffiths, *The Origins of Osiris and His Cult* (SHR 40, 1980).

Pakhet, "Tearer apart" (fem.), goddess in the form of a lioness who was worshiped at the mouth of a wadi in Middle Egypt, and also acquired some importance at the royal court and in beliefs about the afterlife.

Primeval gods. The gods or divine couples who embody the categories of the world before creation. In Hermopolis they were grouped to form the "ogdoad" (four couples), of which *Nun* and *Kuk* are the most important members; they were later joined by *Amun.* Bibliography: see *Huh.*

Ptah, depicted in human form without indication of the limbs; in Memphis he is combined from an early period with *Apis* and *Sokar,* and later with Tatenen. Worshiped mainly as a creator god and as the patron of every type of craftsmanship. Bibliography: M. Sandman Holmberg, *The God Ptah* (Lund 1946).

Raet, often called *Raettawy* "Raet of the Two Lands," female doublet of the sun god *Re;* depicted as a female figure with cow's horns and sun disk. She had a cult of her own.

Re, the most important and most widespread name of the sun god, who is combined syncretistically with many other gods; usually depicted in human form, and worshiped primarily as the creator and sustainer of the world. He travels in a bark through the sky by day and the underworld by night. From an early date Heliopolis was his chief cult center.

Re-Atum

Renenet, "She who nourishes," goddess of destiny who is named primarily in conjunction with *Shay.* Bibliography: S. Morenz and D. Müller, *Untersuchungen zur Rolle des Schicksals in der ägyptischen Religion* (ASAW 52, 1, 1960). G. Fecht, "Schicksalsgöttin und König in der 'Lehre eines Mannes für seinen Sohn,'" *ZÄS* 105 (1978) 14–42.

Renenutet, "Snake who nourishes" (fem.), goddess of the harvest and mother of the grain god *Nepri,* worshiped especially in the Faiyum (Greek name *Thermuthis*). Shown as a snake or a woman with a snake's head. Bibliography: J. Leibovitch, "Gods of Agriculture and Welfare in Ancient Egypt," *JNES* 12 (1953) 73–113. J. Broekhuis, *De godin Renenwetet* (Assen 1971).

Glossary of Gods

Sakhmet, "The most powerful one" (fem.), goddess with the ambivalent nature of a lioness, usually shown as a woman with the head of a lioness; worshiped primarily in Memphis, where she forms a triad with *Ptah* and *Nefertem.* Sakhmet disseminates and cures disease, and, in her role as the sun's destructive eye, attacks hostile powers. Bibliography: S.-E. Hoenes, *Untersuchungen zu Wesen und Kult der Göttin Sachmet* (Habelts Dissertationsdrucke, Ägyptologie 1, Bonn 1976).

Satis, "She of (the island) Sehel," goddess worshiped on Elephantine and its neighboring islands and at the royal court; shown in human form with the Upper Egyptian crown and a pair of antelope's horns. Together with *Khnum* and *Anukis* she forms the triad of Elephantine, which dispenses the "cool water" of the sources of the inundation. Bibliography: D. Valbelle, *Satis et Anoukis* (Mainz 1980).

Sḏm (Sedjem), "Hearing," revered from the New Kingdom on as one of the forces that aid the creator god. Bibliography: see *Jrj.*

Selkis, "She who causes (the throat) to breathe," deity who protects the deceased, shown in human form with a scorpion on her head. *Isis* can also appear in the form of *Selkis.*

Sepa, "Millipede," helping deity who protects against malicious animals, worshiped especially in Heliopolis; as a god of the dead he is combined with Osiris from an early date. Bibliography: H. Kees, *ZÄS* 58 (1923) 82–90.

Seshat, the goddess of writing and of learning, often the companion of *Thoth.* She plays an important part in foundation ceremonies. Shown in human form with her symbol, which has not as yet been elucidated, on her head.

Seth, violent and ambivalent god who is shown as a fabulous animal (the "Seth animal"), or as a human being with the head of the same animal; connected with foreign countries, the desert, and marginal regions of the ordered world. His fratricidal conflict with *Osiris* and *Horus* clothes the constant struggle of the world in a comprehensible form; he also, however, helps the sun god against *Apopis.* Bibliography: H. te Velde, *Seth, God of Confusion* (PÄ 6, 1967; 2d ed. 1977). E. Hornung, "Seth. Geschichte und Bedeutung eines ägyptischen Gottes," *Symbolon* n.s. 2 (1974) 49–63.

Shay, personification of "Destiny," the *Agathodaimon* of the Greeks. Depicted in human form, and at a late date as a snake. Bibliography: S. Morenz and D. Müller, *Untersuchungen zur Rolle des Schicksals in der ägyptischen Religion* (ASAW 52, 1, 1960). J. Quaegebeur, *Le dieu égyptien Shai dans la religion et l'onomastique* (Orientalia Lovaniensia Analecta 2, Louvain 1975).

Shed, "The savior," helper of mankind in times of need; as a youthful god he is close to Horus in character. Bibliography: H. Brunner, *MDAIK* 16 (1958)

13–19. E. Otto, "Gott als Retter in Ägypten," in G. Jeremias et al., eds., *Tradition und Glaube. Das frühe Christentum in seiner Umwelt. Festgabe für K.G. Kuhn zum 65. Geburtstag* (Göttingen 1972) 9–22.

Shezmu, the god of the wine press, who threatens the dead. Bibliography: S. Schott, "Das blutrünstige Keltergerät," *ZÄS* 74 (1938) 88–93. B. J. Peterson, *Orientalia Suecana* 12 (1963) 83–88. M. Ciccarrello, "Shesmu the Letopolite," in *Studies in Honor of George R. Hughes* (The Oriental Institute of the University of Chicago, Studies in Ancient Oriental Civilization 39, Chicago 1977) 43–54.

Shu, god of the space between earth and sky and of the light that fills that space. Through his separation of earth and sky Shu takes part in the creation of the world. Depicted in human form or with a lion's head. Bibliography: A. de Buck, *Plaats en betekenis van Sjoe in de egyptische theologie* (Mededeelingen der Kon. Nederlandsche Ak. van Wetenschapen, Afd. Letterkunde, n.s. 10, 9, Amsterdam 1947).

Sia, personification of the planning "Percipience" which, together with *Hu* and *Hike*, renders the work of creation possible.

Sobek, Greek *Suchos*, lord of stretches of water, worshiped in crocodile form or as a human being with crocodile head, especially in the lakeside area of the Faiyum. Bibliography: C. Dolzani, *Il dio Sobk* (Atti dell' Accademia nazionale dei Lincei, Memorie, Scienze morali, 8th series, 10, 4, pp. 163–269, Rome 1961).

Sokar, god of craftsmanship and of the dead, worshiped in Memphis; closely connected with *Ptah* from the Old Kingdom on, and later also with *Osiris*. Shown as a hawk or with a hawk's head and a human body whose limbs are not indicated.

Sokaret, female doublet of *Sokar*, attested in the ritual of burial.

Sons of Horus, the four gods who protect the deceased and his internal organs.

Sothis, the star Sirius, worshiped from an early date as the harbinger of the inundation. Depicted in human form or as a cow; often a manifestation of *Isis*.

Sun god. Many Egyptian gods can be the sun god, especially *Re, Atum, Amun*, and manifestations of *Horus*. Even *Osiris* appears as the night form of the sun god in the New Kingdom. It is often not defined which particular sun god is meant in a given instance.

Tatenen, interpreted as meaning "risen land." Embodiment of the depths of the earth, combined with *Ptah* in Memphis from the New Kingdom on, also in

Glossary of Gods

the form *Ptah-Tenen*. Depicted in human form with ram's horns and a crown of feathers. Bibliography: H. A. Schlögl, *Der Gott Tatenen* (Orbis Biblicus et Orientalis 29, Fribourg and Göttingen 1980).

Tefnut, goddess who forms, with *Shu*, the first divine couple, engendered by *Atum* without a female partner. *Shu* and *Tefnut* are envisaged as a pair of lions, and *Tefnut* also appears as the eye of the sun.

Thebes, often called "Victorious Thebes" (*w'st-nḫtt*, fem.), personification of Thebes with martial associations, depicted as a woman with the hieroglyph for the Theban nome on her head, holding mace, bow and arrows in her hands. Bibliography: W. Helck, *MDAIK* 23 (1968) 119–26.

Thoeris, "The great one" (fem.), popular protective goddess attested by countless amulets; together with *Bes* she protects mothers in childbirth and during the initial period of suckling. Depicted as a fat hippopotamus with pendulous human breasts, lion's paws, and crocodile's tail, or, more rarely, with a human head.

Thoth, moon god, messenger of the gods and patron of the art of writing, as well as mediator in the conflict of *Horus* and *Seth*. His chief cult places are two towns, called Hermopolis in Greek, in Middle Egypt and in the delta; commonest manifestations are as ibis and baboon. Bibliography: P. Boylan, *Thoth the Hermes of Egypt* (London etc. 1922). C. J. Bleeker, *Hathor and Thoth* (SHR 26, Leiden 1973).

Wadjet, "The papyrus-colored one" (fem.), protective goddess in snake form from lower Egypt, also shown with the head of a lioness; worshiped primarily at Buto. Bibliography: J. Vandier, "Ouadjet et l'Horus léontocéphale de Bouto," Fondation Eugène Piot, *Monuments et Mémoires* 55 (1967) 7–75.

Wenut, "The swift one" (fem.), goddess in Middle Egypt (Hermopolis) who originally had snake form but was later interpreted as a hare.

Wepwawet, "Opener of ways," god in jackal form who was worshiped primarily at Asyut; at Abydos he is linked with the cult of *Osiris*.

Werethekau, "She who is rich in magic," epithet of various goddesses, especially *Sakhmet*; also known as a goddess in her own right, who is shown as a snake or with the head of a lioness.

West, goddess of the (*Amentet*), goddess of the dead who is shown with the hieroglyph for "west" on her head, mostly a manifestation of *Isis* or of *Hathor*.

Yamm, semitic personification of the sea.

↘ Index

Italic numbers refer to pages on which illustrations occur. The words "monotheism" and "polytheism," which recur constantly throughout the text, are not indexed. For identification and descriptions of deities, see also the Glossary of Gods.

285

Index

animals: burial of, 100–101; sacred, 64, 82, 100–101, 137–138, 229, 274–284 (*see also* birds; bulls; cows; lions/lionesses; mixed form of gods)
Ankhnesneferibre, 132
Ankhsheshonq, 53n62, 55
Ankhtifi, 211
annihilation, 181
Anthes, Rudolf, 66, 238, 239
anthropomorphism, 83, 101–103, 109; defined, 39
anthropomorphization of powers, 105–107, 123, 124
Antoninus Pius, 85
Anubis, 31, 45, 46, 67, 85, 115, 124, 125, 187, 218
Anukis, 69, 70, 218
Apis, 53n62, 109, 136
Apopis, 158, *159*, 164, 169, 178, 208, 209
army, 220, 279, 284 (*see also* Qadesh)
aroma, gods', 64, 133–134, 149–150, 197
art, 244, 245 (*see also* iconography)
articles, definite/indefinite, 48
Ash, 109
Asia, 147, 167, 226, 257
Aten, 43, 56, 148, 162, 167, 171, 186, 200, 201, 202, 220, 230, 232, 244, 245, 246, 248, 249 (*see also* Akhenaten)
Atum, 66, 67, 77, 79, 86, 88, 92, 97, 146, 147, 148, 150, 151n26, 153n31, 160, 163, 187, 188, 189, 221n17, 222
attributes, divine, signs of, 121, 122–123 (*see also* nature, gods')
ax in *nṯr*, 34

bꞌw, use of term, 60–62
ba, *bꞌ*, 45, 62, 242; iconography of, 123; linking gods by, 93; location of, 228; as manifestations of powers, 138
Badari, 101, 102
Barth, Karl, 30
Bat, 103
"Battlefield" palette, 103–105, *104*
behavior in instruction texts, 56–57

belief in gods, 100–101
Beni Hasan, 234
Bes, 118
Beth, Karl, 26–27
birds (*see* hawks; soul birds)
birth, 171; gods', 143–151; kings' divine, 142; Seth's, 158 (*see also* genesis; rebirth)
Bonnet, Hans, 66, 91, 127, 157
Book of Caverns, 114, 115, 162
Book of Gates, 77, 123–124, 157, 167, 168
Book of the Dead, 95, 156–157, 172, 177–178
Book of the Divine Cow, 153–154
Book of the Two Ways, 155, 163
boundaries, 168–169, 177, 181
Breasted, James Henry, 24
breath of life, 199
Brugsch, Heinrich, 21–22
Bubastis, 225
Budge, E. A. Wallis, 24–25
bulls, 136–137, 138, 275
burials, animals', 100–101
Buto, 60, 144n3, 276, 284
Byblos, 166

Cairo hymn to Amun, 200–201, 208, 228, 232, 234
cataract, first, 69–70, 79, 278
Celsus, 138
chalcolithic period, 100–101
chaos, 66, 163, 164, 165, 195, 209
charm, love, 210
Cheops, 50
chick in the egg, 200, 201
children, 164; naming of, 48
Christians, 124–125, 177, 246 (*see also* Copts)
Church fathers, 16
classification of gods, 217–226, 230–236, 252, 258–259
clothes, 121–122
cloth on cult objects, 34–40
Coffin texts, 58–59, 151; conceptual personifications, 76; creator, 149, 150, 169, 171, 198–199; deities, 146–

286

Index

Index

Library of Congress Cataloging in Publication Data

Hornung, Erik.
  Conceptions of God in ancient Egypt.

  Translation, with revisions, of: Der Eine und
die Vielen.
  Includes bibliographical references and indexes.
  1. Gods, Egyptian.   I. Title.
BL2450.G6H6713 1982   299'.31   82-71602
  ISBN 0-8014-1223-4

296